WOMEN-CHURCH

WOMEN-CHURCH

Theology and Practice of Feminist Liturgical Communities

Rosemary Radford Ruether

1817

Harper & Row, Publishers, San Francisco

Cambridge, New York, Philadelphia
London, Mexico City, São Paulo, Singapore, Sydney

FIRST HARPER & ROW PAPERBACK EDITION PUBLISHED IN 1988.

Library of Congress Cataloging-in-Publication Data

Ruether, Rosemary Radford.
    Women-church: theology and practice of feminist
liturgical communities.

    Bibliography: p.
        1. Women—Religious life. 2. Church. 3. Patriarchy—
Religious aspects—Christianity. 4. Feminism—Religious
aspects—Christianity. 5. Liturgics. 6. Liturgies.
I. Title.
BV4527.R83 1985   262'.0088042   85-45724
ISBN 0-06-066834-2-cloth
ISBN 0-06-066835-0-paperback

---

88 89 90 91 92 HC 10 9 8 7 6 5 4 3 2 1

This book is dedicated to Martha Ullerstam, Ulla Carin Holm, and Anna Karin Hammer, and to the Forum för Kvinnliga Forskare och Kvinnoforskning of Lund University, Lund, Sweden, who made possible the Fulbright grant to lecture in feminist theology in Scandanavia, during which most of this book was written.

Acknowledgments and Permissions

This book is a collective creation that reflects the contributions of many people in the emerging movement of women-church and feminist liturgics. Several people contributed liturgies that they developed for themselves for particular occasions, and others wrote liturgies specifically for this volume. I wish to acknowledge particularly Florence Perrella Hayes's "Ritual of Divorce," Kate Pravera's "Naming Rite," Rebecca Parker and Joanne Brown's "Coming-Out Rite for a Lesbian," Marilyn Gherashe's "Naming Celebration," Adele Arlett's "Coming of Age Ritual," Phyllis Athey and Mary Jo Ostermann's "Covenant Celebration," Janet Kalven's "Croning Liturgy," Chris Carol's "Hallowmas Rite," The Eighth Day Center for Justice for the "Good Friday March for Justice," and Nancy Ore, for her account of the Summer Solstice liturgy. I also wish to thank Mary Whittaker for her architectural rendering of the plans for the Women-Church celebration center.

In addition I wish to acknowledge the use of the following previously published material:

Holy Near, "Sister Woman Sister," © 1978, permission to reprint from Hereford Music Company.

Carole Etzler, "Hey Sister Come Live at the Edge of the World," © 1975, permission to reprint from Carole Etzler.

Julia Esquivel, "I am not longer Afraid of Death," permission to reprint from The Brethern Press.

Gregory Norbet, "New Life, New Creation," © 1973, permission to reprint from The Benedictine Foundation of the State of Vermont, Inc. Weston, Vermont.

Ernesto Cardenal, "Apocalypse," permission to reprint from New Directions Publishing Corporation.

Robert Jay Lifton, testimonies of Survivors of Hiroshima, permission to reprint from Robert Jay Lifton and Basic Books, Inc.

Woodie Guthrie, "This land is your land," permission to reprint from Ludlow Music Inc.

Del Martin, *Battered Wives*, pp. 1–5, permission to reprint from Volcano Press, Inc, formerly Glide Publications.

James Rado, Gerome Ragni and Galt MacDermot, "Air," from the musical comedy *Hair*, permission to reprint from CBS Songs.

Contents

Outline of Liturgies

Women-Church

INTRODUCTION

This book is written at a moment of profound crisis and trans-
mutation in the religion of Western Europe and North America,
a crisis that is beginning to be felt in other parts of the world as
well. This crisis is taking place particularly in Christianity, but it
is also found in American Judaism. Islam and other major religious
traditions are also beginning to be challenged. For more than a
century, Western thinkers have heralded the demise of religion as
teacher and shaper of the symbolic universe of meaning in Western society. They have interpreted this as a process of secularization by which religion, as a medium and interpretation of experience, would disappear, to be replaced by forms of knowledge
drawn from science. This was seen as the coming of age of modern
"man," "his" liberation from cultural childhood under the tutelege
of religious authority.

The process of secularization has failed to unfold in the manner
predicted by its prophets. Although Western societies, especially
those in Western Europe, were gradually secularized in the nineteenth and twentieth centuries, science has failed to provide a
sufficiently satisfying substitute for religion as a vehicle of meaning. The social orders created by liberalism and socialism have
generated fears of a future impoverished of meaning, if not indeed
devastated by pollution, poverty, depletion of basic resources, and
war. Religion, whose demise as a vehicle of meaning and truth has
been so long announced, has reemerged as a vehicle of protest and
a tool for envisioning new possibilities. This has taken opposite
forms. Traditional or conservative Christianity has reemerged as
a reactionary force against the perceived excesses of modernity or
the dangers of totalitarianism. Sometimes it serves as a base for a

mass counterculture to the government, as in Poland, and sometimes it takes the form of a small but potent minority, as in revived evangelical Christianity in the United States or Sweden.

On the other hand, in Latin America and other Third World areas, liberation theology and basic Christian communities have become new religious forms for reenvisioning a socialist future. Religious groups protest the crushing burdens of poverty and repression built by national security states on the foundation of international capitalism. Protest groups in Western industrialized countries also embrace this kind of left-wing Christianity in support of Third World liberation struggles.

However, a third force in the revival of religion consists of women, specifically feminist women, who ask critical questions about the role of religion in the sanctification of patriarchal societies. These women have begun to take the shaping of the symbolic universe of meaning into their own hands. The question of women is not absent from the other two movements as well. For antimodernist evangelicals, feminism is a creature of modern apostasy from God and traditional social order. Thus their crusade to restore traditional Christian society often focuses on negating women's liberation and restoring women to their traditional place in the patriarchal family. Male liberation theologians have tended to see feminism as a distraction from the real business of liberating oppressed classes and nations, or, at best, a subtheme in that struggle. For them, liberation theology is simply the recovery of true biblical faith.

The emerging feminist religion has a much more ambivalent relationship to biblical origins than male liberation theology, although it too rejects the secularist view that religious symbol and ritual are no longer needed. Some feminist religious thinkers would reclaim aspects of the biblical tradition. They see its fundamental protest against oppression and its vision of peace and justice as part of feminist hopes, and they expand it by an explicit critique of patriarchy. Other feminists see biblical religion as hopelessly tainted by patriarchy, and they instead call for a revival of ancient Goddess religions. However, both groups tend to recognize that what they are striving for both reaches behind traditional patriarchal religion, as represented by the New Testament and the Hebrew Scriptures, and also reaches beyond the hopes of modern male liberalism and socialism. The feminist religious revolution thus promises to be more radical and far-reaching than liberation theologies. It goes behind the symbolic universe that has been constructed by patriarchal civilization, both in its religious and in its modern secular forms. It reaches forward to an alternative that can heal the splits between "masculine" and "feminine," between mind and body, between males and females as gender groups, between society and nature, and between races and classes.

One important aspect of this emerging feminist religion or spirituality is its recognition of the need for intentional communities of faith and worship. It is not enough to hold an ideology of criticism and social analysis as an interpretive base, nor to participate in protest and action groups and organizations as vehicles of change. One needs communities of nurture to guide one through death to the old symbolic order of patriarchy to rebirth into a new community of being and living. One needs not only to engage in rational theoretical discourse about this journey; one also needs deep symbols and symbolic actions to guide and interpret the actual experience of the journey from sexism to liberated humanity.

The recognition of our need for prayer, ritual, and communities of faith and nurture is shared not only by Christian feminists, but also by those who seek to revive the old religions of the Goddess. Feminist witches such as Starhawk have typically written books that intend not only to describe the history and theory of their movement, but also to provide handbooks for community formation, prayer, and ritual.[1] Jewish feminists also are seeking to reshape the community of prayer and study into vehicles for liberation from patriarchy.[2]

This book on women-church is written from the perspective of religious feminists who seek to reclaim aspects of the biblical tradition, Jewish and Christian, but who also recognize the need both to go back behind biblical religion and to transcend it. Women-church embraces a liminal religiosity. It does not claim to have an original "true" faith that can be revived in the style of the Reformation. Nor does it claim to know the shape of the future. It stands on two thresholds, looking backward to options in biblical and prebiblical faiths that were hinted at but probably never developed, and looking forward to new possibilities whose shape is unclear. It does not repudiate all that has gone on in between, but it seeks to appropriate its best insights as material for a new future.

This book is also written out of a recognition that Christian feminists cannot wait for the institutional churches to reform themselves enough to provide the vehicles of faith and worship that women need in this time. Some Protestant churches have ordained women, but, for the most part, women pastors in these churches find themselves confined to traditional institutional maintenance or, at best, able to take tiny steps toward new symbols and rituals against the determined opposition of most church members.

Roman Catholic women watch their church organizing for a long fight against the ordination of women. The church has launched a drive to repress efforts to incorporate feminist consciousness into the church that have taken place in renewed religious orders, seminaries, departments of theology at Catholic schools, and in peace and justice centers.[3] Thus, while not necessarily repudiating all concern for renewal of existing church institutions or continued membership in such churches (this topic will be discussed in greater depth later), Catholic women especially, but also a growing number of Protestant women, are beginning to recognize the need for autonomous bases for women's theologizing and worship.

Women in contemporary churches are suffering from linguistic deprivation and eucharistic famine. They can no longer nurture their souls in alienating words that ignore or systematically deny their existence. They are starved for the words of life, for symbolic forms that fully and wholeheartedly affirm their personhood and speak truth about the evils of sexism and the possibilities of a future beyond patriarchy. They desperately need primary communities that nurture their journey into wholeness, rather than constantly negating and thwarting it. This book takes steps to end that famine of the words of life and to begin to bake the new bread of life now. We must do more than protest against the old. We must begin to live the new humanity now. We must begin to incarnate the community of faith in the liberation of humanity from patriarchy in words and deed, in new words, new prayers, new symbols, and new praxis. This means that we need to form gathered communities to support us as we set out on our exodus from patriarchy.

The call for new communities of faith and ritual assumes that existing institutional churches do not have a monopoly on the words of truth or the power of salvation, indeed that their words for women are so ambivalent, their power so negative, that attendance at their fonts poisons our souls. They have become all too often occasions of sin rather than redemption, places where we leave angry and frustrated rather than enlightened and healed. We do not form new communities lightly, but only because the crisis has grown so acute and the efforts to effect change so unpromising that we often cannot even continue to communicate within these traditional church institutions unless we have an alternative community of reference that nurtures and supports our being.

This book begins by laying some historical and theological foundations for understanding the church as a community of liberation from patriarchy. It reviews the history of the tension between historical institution and community of faith in the history of Christianity and in contemporary Christian basic communities. Then it discusses the biblical model of the *ecclesia* or assembly of faith as an exodus community and shows why that model has not provided a means for including women in its vision of liberation. This leads to discussing the theology of church as a feminist community or a community of liberation from patriarchy. To what extent can such a community authentically claim to be church, while at the same time rejecting so much of what has been historical Christianity? How can it avoid becoming sectarian, unable to correct its own myopias by reference to the larger wisdom of the tradition and of the other human communities around it? How can it affirm a specifically women's journey of liberation without becoming separatist and negating the humanity of males and their need also to be incorporated into such a journey of liberation from patriarchy?

The book then moves on to revisioning church as a community of liberation from patriarchy. How will women-church[4] understand the primary sacramental symbols of baptism and Eucharist? How will it relate faith and praxis? The final section of the book crystallizes theory into liturgical forms. It presents both new versions of traditional sacramental and liturgical forms and also imagines new forms of ritual that will sacramentalize women's rites of passage that have been either ignored or relegated to the profane: the onset of menstruation, the break from parent's home to autonomous life, marriage, divorce, coming out as a lesbian, embarking on new stages of life, menopause, sickness, and death.

It also discusses special liturgies for moments of crisis and of healing, such as rituals of healing for a raped women, for a woman who is seeking to break or has broken from a battering marriage, for a woman seeking to heal psychic wounds from earlier sexual abuse or physical abuse in the family. These are moments where women cry out wordlessly for words of understanding, for hands laid on in healing, but find nothing but silence and closed doors in most churches. I provide examples of new liturgies that have been developed, as well as resource books for songs and prayers.

This is not a prayer book with words and forms to be repeated. It is an invitation to enter into a process. Every idea here can be reshaped and improved upon by communities who undertake to begin this journey of liberation from patriarchy. Each ritual needs to be contextualized in the particular group that uses it, since groups have their own process and their own history. Rituals of healing and rites of passage need to take on the specificity of this or that person, time, and place. New ideas and occasions not imagined here can be added. Recipes are provided so that each community of cooks can experiment with their own unique ingredients to make the bread fitted to nourish their own lives.

This assumes that the creation of liturgy is properly a function of local communities who are engaged in a collective project woven from the fabric of many concrete stories that make up the lives of each member of that body. Thus the function of a book such as this is not to write packaged scenarios of worship for local communities, but to provide resources for the liturgical work of communities, with which they can mourn and weep, repent and heal, rejoice, and celebrate their life together.

I. HISTORICAL AND THEOLOGICAL REFLECTIONS ON WOMEN-CHURCH

1. Spirit-filled Community and Historical Institution: Tension and Relation

The history of Christianity is a history of continual tension and conflict between two models of church: church as spirit-filled community and church as historical institution. This conflict goes back to the very origins of the religion. Christianity began as a spirit-filled messianic sect within historical Judaism. Jesus and the earliest disciples did not envision a break with Judaism but saw themselves as a renewal movement within Judaism, restoring prophetic Judaism and revealing the Israel of messianic times. Therefore they did not attempt to create a separate historical institution, much less a separate historical religion. Rather, they originally conceived of their mission as preaching "good news" to Israel.[1]

The models of early Christian ministry were charismatic. They were based on the belief that the spirit of prophecy restored in messianic times was present in their midst, manifest through powers of ecstatic revelation, exorcism, and healing. These early charismatic concepts of ministry tended to include women, first, because a ministry of charismatic gifts by definition affirms spiritual talents directly, rather than mediating them through appropriate leadership dictated by gender or other established social hierarchies. Second, early Christians apparently believed that the subordination of women was related to a procreative familial order in history that was being transcended in the messianic age. Family relations would no longer be necessary, since death, and hence birth, would be no more. Their view of church as anticipating a messianic order suggested that traditional hierarchies of the family could be dissolved, and women could enter into the new covenant as equals with men.[2]

The antihistorical concept of the early church gradually fell into crisis as time went on and the decisive return of Christ as the Human One,[3] ushering in the millennium, did not take place. The Christian church had to adapt to historical existence. By the late first century, a post-Pauline Christianity had begun to develop that drew on the traditional leadership pattern of the synagogue. It constructed a congregational ministry based on a hierarchy of presider (bishop), elders, deacons, and deaconesses. This nascent episcopal Christianity consciously affirmed the patriarchal family order as its model of the church and accounted those men worthy to serve as ministers who had proved themselves responsible as a *pater familias*. This type of patriarchal Paulinism set out to repress earlier inclusion of women in ministry, which it associated with antifamilialism.

By the late second century, the episcopal model of leadership had developed into an urban hierarchy in which the bishop became the presiding pastor at the major congregation of the city and also supervised daughter congregations led by presbyters or elders. This pattern of episcopal hierarchy would expand in the next two centuries into provincial and then imperial forms by which presiding bishops at major sees would supervise bishops and elders under him. Gradually, the church began to duplicate the political structures of the late Roman Empire and to evolve an ecclesiastical counterpart to the Roman systems of urban and provincial governors, with the presiding bishop of Rome claiming to be the spiritual counterpart of the emperor.[4]

In the second and third centuries, this evolving episcopal Christianity engaged in hostile conflict and suppression of the remaining expressions of charismatic, prophetic, and millennialist Christianity. In the second century, the Montanists came under fire. This movement attempted to revive the earlier type of ecstatic Christianity and the earlier belief that the ministry of prophecy was given equally to women. Instead, episcopal Christianity developed a theory of historical legitimacy based ·on the myth that the twelve apostles of Jesus were the first bishops and the founders of the leading episcopal sees. Bishops, in turn, owed their legitimacy to continuous historical succession from the founding apostle-bishops.[5] This historical myth of legitimacy justified the right of episcopal Christianity to claim to be the heir of the original or "apostolic" Christianity. It allowed episcopal Christianity to drive out the representatives of charismatic Christianity represented by Montanists and also, to some extent, by Gnostics, although Gnostics had developed a philosophically dualistic interpretation of redemption foreign to earlier Christianity.

In the third century, further struggles took place between episcopal and charismatic concepts of ministry in the conflict between Cyprian of Carthage and the "confessors" or "martyrs." Martyrdom, or suffering for Christ in conflict with the theocratic claims of the Roman state, was highly prized by prophetic and millennialist Christians. Those who had suffered for the faith were regarded as possessing the Spirit in a unique way and endowed with gifts of exorcism, healing, and forgiveness. (The word "martyr" means witness and thus included living persons who had been tortured and not just the dead.)

The crisis came to a head during the period of Decian persecution in the middle of the third century. Many Christians faltered under the rod of persecution and offered homage to imperial images, later seeking reconciliation with the church. Who had the right to forgive their sin and readmit them to communion with Christ and the church: bishops or confessors? By claiming that bishops alone had this power and that confessors had no power to forgive, Cyprian sought to break the power of charismatic ministry. He substituted the sole authority of bishops for the power of the "keys"; that is, the right to decide who was in communion with Christ and would enter the New Age, and who would not.[6]

In the late third and fourth centuries, Christianity became ever more closely integrated into the social structure of Roman imperial society and was finally taken over by the Roman Emperor Constantine as the imperial religion. Those seeking a Christianity of radical conversion and commitment then turned to monasticism. Monasticism expressed the ascetic element in prophetic Christianity that had been practiced by some since the beginning. What was new in the movements of this period was the development of ascetic communities separated from the local churches. By withdrawing from society and from a Christianity integrated into society, and by joining a community that renounced the body and dedicated itself to communion with God in prayer, the ascetic was able to continue the early Christian idea of the church as a community that radically renounces the "world." This entailed forsaking the family as well as sex and procreation. And so monasticism continued early Christian millennialist antifamilialism.

For women and some male monastics, this renunciation of the familial procreative order also meant transcending the patriarchal subordination of women and entering the new humanity where men and women are equal. However, asceticism also suggested to male ascetics that women represented the threat of a lower sinful world of sexuality. Thus monasticism contained an ambivalent theology toward women. One line of asceticism moved toward spiritualist equivalence of men and women in a community of the redeemed beyond the fallen historical order, while another line led to deepened misogyny and a pathological hatred of women as the embodiments of evil. As asceticism merged with ordained priesthood in the fourth to the ninth centuries, culminating in the Gregorian reforms in the eleventh century that forbade all priests in Western Christianity to marry, this misogynist tradition also won out against the earlier egalitarian tradition.

However, monasticism remained throughout the Middle Ages the primary vehicle for attempts to reconstitute the spirit-filled community of radical commitment *vis à vis* historical institutions that had become routinized. In monasticism the institutional church found a means of both legitimizing this urge and at the same time containing, channeling, and controlling it. Again and again throughout the Middle Ages the impulse for a more radically committed Christian community arose, expressing dissatisfaction with the institutionalization not only of local churches, but also of earlier monastic movements. New groups of zealous Christians arose and sought out the desert, the woods, or the mountains as places of retreat from "the world," renewing the original spirit of a community dedicated to rigorous asceticism, intense prayer, and discipline. Often these groups dissolved the class hierarchies that had arisen in monasticism when it abandoned earlier patterns of shared manual labor. Over time, monks and nuns had ceased to do their own work, since it was done for them by lay monks and nuns or by servants. The return to an egalitarian community of poverty or simple living was a key part of such monastic renewal movements.[7]

In the twelfth century, as the revival of urban life took place, the older form of monasticism based on agricultural manorialism changed to urban preaching and service orders. The elevation of the standards of lay understanding of the gospel through preaching and teaching and service to the poor became important missions of these orders. But the new urban orders, such as the Franciscans and Dominicans, were reluctant to allow the same freedom to female monastic counterparts.

The reforms of the church in the eleventh century had made it increasingly difficult for women to start independent orders or even to enter existing orders. Rules were laid down that sharply curtailed female autonomy in ruling their own convents and particularly in supervising their own spiritual life. Male monks or priests were necessary to govern the external financial and internal spiritual affairs of the nuns. Moreover, nuns were required to have large doweries to join convents, so only the nobility or upper bourgeoisie could afford to enter traditional female monasticism.

Yet the religious renewals of the period generated large numbers of women who longed for religious community. Thus there arose in the later Middle Ages the Beguine movement. Beguines were urban religious women who took no permanent vows and who lived under simple rules of prayer and work within ordinary houses in the town. The founders of many of these communities were from the upper bourgeoisie or even the nobility who sought a more dedicated life than that afforded by traditional monasticism. But these communities soon became vehicles for urban working-class women who could not enter the older convents. Most of these female communities were perfectly orthodox, yet they fell under constant suspicion and persecution by the hierarchical church precisely because they were largely autonomous of ecclesiastical control. Sometimes they received their charter as a corporation from towns rather than from church officials, and they supported themselves as workers within the guild system of urban crafts. Many Beguines put themselves under the supervision of the Dominicans and so gained legitimacy in this way.[8]

The urge to reconstitute spirit-filled community in the Middle Ages did not always succeed in being contained within the official system of monasteries and orders approved by the hierarchical church. Sometimes the new movement arose with too radical a critique of the existing church and too strong a demand for alternative ways of living to be contained within the existing framework. The hierarchical church, if unable to accommodate itself to the new movement, then forbade and persecuted it as heretical. This experience, in turn, drove the movement to more negative evaluations of the existing institutional church. In the twelfth century, the Waldensians were such a preaching order calling for radical poverty. Unlike the Franciscans, they were rejected by the pope and so became a sectarian movement that survived persecution underground rather than being turned into a religious order. Some of the Beguines and the spiritualist wing of the Franciscans and other such radical movements of "brethren" in the later Middle Ages fell into this status of persecuted sects. This experience of persecution spurred them to revive more radical visions of the church as a millennial community of spiritual Christians who would replace the present historical church. The dominant church they regarded as the anti-Christ, the whore of Babylon of the book of Revelation, rather than the true successor of the church of the apostles.

In the sixteenth century, the traditional Catholic strategy of containing renewal of spiritual community through religious orders collapsed, particularly as Europe was also becoming divided by the new sense of nationalism that was rending the earlier fabric of pan-European Christianity. National or regional churches arose in Germany, the Scandinavian countries, Scotland and England,

and Switzerland. The French and Spanish churches remained Roman Catholic largely because there the monarchs had already gained effective control of the national church in the fifteenth century without breaking with the papacy. But even the Reformation strategy of new territorial churches based on towns, principalities, and nations could not contain the urge for spirit-filled community. Spiritualist and Anabaptist movements arose on the left wing of the Reformation, seeking covenantal churches based on personal conversion and rejecting state churches.

These free or convenantal churches were severely persecuted by magisterial Protestants as well as Roman Catholics, and they often survived by fleeing eastward to the margins of Europe or migrating to new lands in America. In England, in the mid-seventeenth century, civil war broke out between Anglican and Puritan concepts of state church, which included a secondary struggle with more left-wing free church concepts. After the return of the English monarchy, the reestablishment of the Anglican state church, and an unsuccessful attempt to force both Puritans and free-church Christians into conformity, England became the first Christian country to allow a limited toleration to free churches.

In Puritanism we see played out once again the conflict between charismatic and institutional concepts of church and ministry and its implications for excluding or including women in leadership. Puritan theology distinguished between the covenant of grace and the covenant of works. In the covenant of grace all humans were equal before God. All equally had sinned and deserved hell, but some were elected to grace, apart from any gender or class status in worldly society. In the covenant of works, however, God had ordained a fixed social order of men over women, masters over servants, parents over children. For magisterial Puritanism, this hierarchical social order was the context in which all experienced salvation. Although the lowest serving girl might be one of the elect while the king was one of the damned, the serving girl was not thereby released from her servive but must fulfill the "offices" of her social station all the better.[9]

However, for radical Puritans, the covenant of grace superseded that of works. A grace-filled person could teach and preach to others even if she were a woman or an unlearned servant. This was the view taken by the antinomians, led by Anne Hutchinson, in Massachusetts in the mid-seventeenth century.[10] Recognizing the seriousness of this threat to their social order from such an interpretation of their own theology, the Puritan ministers and magistrates put Anne Hutchinson and her followers on trial. Convicted of heresy, they were expelled into the wilderness. Other radical Puritans, such as the Levellers and the Fifth Monarchy Men in the English Civil War, took the distinction of the two covenants even further and suggested that all class distinctions could be overcome and that a lower-class community of saints could rebel against all hierarchical authority of church or state.[11]

The Quakers in the seventeenth century gave the fullest and most lasting development to these egalitarian tendencies of radical Puritanism. This was, in part, due to the work of Margaret Fell, collaborator and eventually the wife of George Fox. In early Quaker theology, the covenant of grace restores the original equality of all persons in the image of God. Grace abolishes all class and gender distinctions, particularly in religious functions. A servant girl can be called to preach. Indeed, early Quakerism was renowned for its women evangelists who took the message not only throughout England, but into the colonies as well, where they were duly persecuted by the Puritan authorities of Massachusetts.[12] Early Quakers suffered severe repression in England also, particularly because of their direct challenge to established clerical and class hierarchy. Quakers distinguished themselves by crying out against "hireling priests" in the established church and by refusing to do "hat service" to the upper classes.[13] Quakers also developed a parallel system of men's and women's meetings, giving to women a large role in church administration.[14]

These egalitarian tendencies in charismatic leadership were also found in early Methodism in eighteenth-century England. Although Wesley, an Anglican, held traditional notions about women's place in society and the church, he became convinced through experiencing women's effectiveness as evangelists and teachers that this should be allowed. Although women were not ordained, they abounded as lay preachers and leaders of class meetings. Methodism, like Pietism in Germany, developed the tradition of the *ecclesiola in ecclesia,* the committed small gathering for prayer, religious instruction, and mutual exhortation that met alongside the regular liturgies of the historical church.

The founders of these covenantal communities intended that their followers would continue to attend the regular services in the established churches as well. However, Methodists eventually broke with the established church and became a separate denomination. This took place, in part, because the American Revolution deprived Methodists of adequate ordained ministers from the Anglican tradition, so they felt obliged to ordain their own ministers to provide the sacraments. Thus the break of Methodism with Anglicanism was based less on sectarian concepts of the church than on traditional catholic beliefs in the necessity of an ordained clergy to provide the sacraments to the faithful. Wesley concluded from his study of the Pastoral Epistles that a presiding elder was the equivalent of a bishop in New Testament times, and so elders could be ordained by other elders. This break with episcopal polity and the episcopal theory of apostolic succession was decisive for the Anglican rejection of Methodist clergy.[15]

The conflict between charismatic leadership and the historic church was a continuing characteristic of American Christianity in the eighteenth and nineteenth centuries. Both revivalist and utopian movements of church renewal flourished in the Second Great Awakening of the early nineteenth century. Revivalism tended to break down the gap between clergy and laity, the ordained and the unordained. Both as revival subjects who predominated among the converted, and as revival organizers, women played prominent roles in revivalism. Charismatic preachers, endowed with the gifts of dynamic speaking, prophecy, and healing, were validated directly by the response to them from the believing community, without benefit of university education or hierarchical ordination. Such a concept of the spirit-endowed preacher allowed many women—including some notable black women, such as Jarena Lee,

Amanda Berry Smith, Sojourner Truth, and Rebecca Jackson—to flourish in the American revival circuit and even to carry their message abroad to England and Africa.[16]

Nineteenth-century American Evangelicals generally believed that conversion had social consequences. Those who renounced the reign of sin over their personal lives should also withdraw from participation in its social expressions. The more radical wing of revivalism thus flowed into abolitionism and pacifism in the decades before the Civil War. Renouncing participation in war and slavery was the logical consequence of rejecting the power of evil in one's life. In the wing of abolitionism and pacifism led by William Lloyd Garrison, feminism also received its receptive audience. The feminist abolitionist lecturers Sarah and Angelina Grimké—the latter married to the famous abolitionist revival preacher Theodore Weld—interpreted the decision against slavery as a decision against all unjust patterns of social relations that subjugated one social group to another, whether it was the servitude of blacks to whites or the servitude of women to men.[17]

Visions of the social consequences of mass conversion suggested to American Protestants that revivals prepared the earth for a millennial redemption that was about to dawn. Christian revivalism was seen as part of a vast final effort to renovate not only hearts but also social structures in accordance with the Golden Rule, in preparation for the millennial reign of Christ on earth. Such millennialism went hand-in-hand with a perfectionist doctrine of salvation typical of Methodism. That the converted would not only win justification or acceptance by God, but could become sanctified, renouncing the power of all sin over their lives, was preached with new fervor by the Holiness movement. Translated into social terms, perfectionism suggested a vision of the future in which all evils of injustice, intemperance, and war would speedily be abolished by a rising revolution of the saints.

Millennialist currents from revivalism met and merged with renewed utopianism in nineteenth-century America. Some utopian movements stemmed from the sixteenth- and seventeenth-century radical Protestant sectarianism of Mennonites and Moravian Brethren. Others were rooted in the eighteenth-century Dunkers (German Baptists) or the English Shakers, while still others flowed from English and French secular socialist utopianism, such as the Owenites, the Fourierites, the Icarians, and the Saint Simonians. Together, utopian movements spurred the foundation of many utopian colonies on American soil in the nineteenth century. Most religious utopians saw their colonies as the beginning of the millennial church, anticipating the reign of the saints with Christ in the kingdom of God upon a renewed earth. Even secular socialists betrayed religious leaning in their tendencies to think of their movement as a new or true Christianity.[18]

Most of these utopian movements saw implications in their project of redemption for a new relationship between men and women. Some believed that God was androgynous and that the redeemed humanity would overcome the alienation between the masculine and the feminine in human nature and create a new wholistic "man." For some groups, such as the Shakers, this meant both a second dispensation of Christ in female form to complete the revelation of God's Wisdom or female aspect, and the parity of men and women in leadership in the Millennial Society of Christ's Second Appearing, as the Shakers were officially called.[19]

Other utopians believed that the communal society would abolish the division between productive and domestic labor and thus allow women to participate in society as the new equals of men. The collectivization of productive labor, land ownership, and the means of production, and also the collectivization of domestic labor and child raising, were seen as essential parts of a coming age of human emancipation that would remove from women their particular servitude to men in familial and public hierarchies. Thus, in nineteenth-century utopianism, visions of a redeemed society mingled with visions of the church as the historical agent of human emancipation and the avant-garde of a redeemed humanity. Both visions contained some notion of emancipation of women and a new parity of masculine and feminine principles and spheres of life.

As we look back over the nineteen hundred years of church

history between early Christianity and the end of the nineteenth century, we can discern certain patterns of tension between historical institution and spirit-filled community. The tension appears again and again, whether we are speaking of early Christianity itself over against the historical institutions of Judaism and Greco-Roman society that surrounded it, or whether we speak of countercultural, prophetic, and mystical Christianity in the patristic period. Tension crops up between monasticism and popular ascetic communitarian movements in the Middle Ages, between magisterial and Anabaptist reform in the sixteenth century, and in revivalist and utopian movements in American Christianity.

Throughout this history we find a tension and contradiction between two fundamentally different concepts of church. The church as historical institution tends to sacralize the established social order—its political as well as its familial hierarchies. The polity of the church tends to reflect the social and political hierarchy of the established society, whether that be the political hierarchy of the Roman imperial ruling class over the plebeians, or the feudal nobility over the peasantry, or the managerial class over the consumers in modern times. The gender hierarchy of male over female, father over children, and lord over servant is reduplicated in both the imagery and the organization of clergy vis-à-vis the laity.

By contrast, the concept of the church as spirit-filled community tends to break down these social hierarchies. It suggests that all Christians are endowed with the spirit and should minister to one another. All have gifts that are needed to build up the whole body. This egalitarianism can, at times, be set in an iconoclastic relation to the hierarchies of established religious and civil institutions. In the redeemed humanity, the spirit of prophecy will be poured out on the despised of the present world, and they will teach and prophesy. Women will be emancipated and given an equal place as leaders in the community of the new humanity.

The church as spirit-filled community thus believes itself called into an exodus from the established social order and its religious agents of sacralization. It is engaged in witnessing to an alternative social order demanded by obedience to God. This new social order is characterized by certain departures from the existing social order. Instead of individual private property, the millennial community holds all things in common. Instead of a hierarchy of rich and poor, this shared economy not only allows all members to have adequate means of life, but it also fosters a new social ethic of mutuality rather than competition. Many radical Christians have also repudiated all forms of war and violence and refused to participate in the armies of their states. Pacifism is a key part of their witness to the new age of God's shalom or peace on earth.

Radical Christianity thus sets itself in tension with established society and tends to see the traditional religion of those societies, including established Christian churches, as false or fallen religions. These religions or churches worship the idols of oppressive power rather than the living God. Radical Christianity anticipates the New Age, expecting it soon to dawn upon the earth and seeking to pattern itself after what it believes to be the social order of redemption.

Yet such experiments with spirit-filled community, anticipating a new order beyond history, are unstable within history. They have always been either repressed by existing historical institutions of religion and state, or they separate and become new historical institutions, or are coopted into existing religious and social institutions in a way that may leaven and enrich the whole, but stifles, within a generation or two, the more radical countercultural vision.

The vision of the church as a spirit-filled community that anticipates and serves the coming of the New Age kingdom must come to terms with ongoing unredeemed human history. How does the church transmit itself historically, both in teaching and in organization, in a way that allows room for the continual rebirth of the Spirit and the recreation of spirit-filled community in its midst? To explore this question further, I turn to the contemporary expressions of spirit-filled community and their renewed tension with historical institutions of church and state.

2. Community and Institution Today: Experience and Theological Reflection

The conflict between community and institution has arisen again in contemporary Christianity, particularly in Roman Catholicism, as a result of the movements for renewal initiated by the Second Vatican Council. This conflict takes several forms. For instance, the charismatic movement revives ancient ideas of the direct experience of the gifts of the Spirit in prayer meetings. Healing, speaking in tongues, and ecstatic experiences characterize these assemblies. Many of these groups maintain a conservative view toward the social order. They see salvation as pertaining only to the individual soul, not to changes in social relations. Some have even become fundamentalist and have adopted a strict doctrine of male headship as the order of society and the family. They demand all-male leadership and strict acquiescence from female members.[1] Yet even these groups evoke nervousness from the ecclesiastical hierarchy, which see rival leadership arising that is not under its control. So strict laws have come from the episcopacy demanding that no leadership be exercised that is not approved by the hierarchy.[2] Many charismatic groups conform to these demands by accepting an appointed chaplain.

However, many charismatic groups break the bounds of institutional limits. They cross denominational boundaries. They cultivate spiritual gifts directly in a way that does not depend on control or interpretation from an appointed priestly chaplain. They accept female leadership on the basis of talent, not official credentials. Some see themselves as harbingers of a renewed ministry that would include women and more democratic participation by the laity. Some also extend these hopes to social issues and look for a more just society.

A second movement, fed by liberation theology, sees the transformation of society as the essential context for its understanding of church. Redemption is not confined to the individual soul, to interpersonal relations, or to the ecclesial sphere. It is fundamentally the redemption of humanity, the redemption of creation, the overcoming of systemic injustice in history. Liberation theology thus revives the messianic perspective of the biblical prophetic tradition. It sees the church not as a separate sacred sphere that points away from society toward heaven, but as a harbinger of these hopes for redeemed humanity in history. The church is where the Word of God is preached as the denunciation of social evil and the annunciation of an alternative possibility of justice, and where people are motivated and empowered to enter this struggle in solidarity with the most victimized sectors of the society.

Basic Christian communities are thus the ecclesial expression of liberation theology. It is here that liberation theology is to be done and lived out in practice. Basic Christian communities are gatherings of Christians who have already declared an option for the poor of the society and who seek to reflect on the gospel in the light of this commitment to create a just society. The community is presumed to be engaged on some level in community work, whether that be efforts to create better conditions in their neighborhood or struggles to prevent nuclear missiles from being placed on their national soil. This social engagement becomes a concrete context for theological reflection. Social engagement brings out in the open the contradiction of the established society and its bias toward the rich and powerful. In the light of their social engagement, communities read the Scripture and discern there a model of God's option for the poor and the annunciation of new possibilities.

Basic Christian communities hold prophetic tradition as the

normative tradition of Scripture. Christians who read the Scripture from the perspective of option for the poor are seen as having a "hermeneutical privilege"; that is, they read Scripture rightly because they read it from the same perspective from which Scripture itself is written.[3] On the other hand, those who interpret Scripture from the side of the status quo will not read it correctly, since they will split social and personal, sacred and secular, in order to confine the message of salvation to an abstract realm where it does not really impinge on daily life. Thus by reading and interpreting Scripture in communities of commitment to justice, the people of the church also reappropriate the Word of God from its clerical and scholarly alienation where it has been distorted into a vehicle of sacralizing unjust power and pacifying the victims.

Most Catholic basic Christian communities do not take over sacramental functions from the priesthood. Either they have priestly leadership who performs the sacraments, or they continue to receive the sacraments at the local church. The meetings, however, will include prayer, songs, and mutual help. The main focus, however, is a liberation Bible reading and discussion that is done in the context of social praxis and that motivates and empowers the connection between Christian faith and social commitment. Yet the hierarchy has considered these movements very threatening. It has continually reinforced the message that they are to be allowed only as extensions of the evangelizing mission of the hierarchy and are to be under the local priest, who is, in turn, under the bishop. However, in Latin America and Africa, the hierarchy has been forced in many places to encourage these structures because of the lack of ordained priests and the inability of the institutional church to catechize the laity without such forms of lay ministry.

At the third meeting of the Latin American Bishops' Conference in Puebla, Mexico, in 1979, this conflict between catechetical needs and hierarchical control came out in the open. The more conservative hierarchy, reinforced by representatives from Rome, sought to suppress basic Christian communities, along with liberation theology. However, the more pastoral bishops that formed the liberal majority felt that they could not dispense with this vehicle of lay evangelism if they were to reach the millions of people in their dioceses. Liberation theologians and more radical bishops, who thought of basic Christian communities as a basis for social change and not just evangelism, worked with these pastoral bishops to outvote the conservatives and to support the legitimacy of basic communities. The final document of the council reaffirmed basic Christian communities, although from a conservative perspective that interpreted these communities as the bottom rung of a hierarchical church carrying on the evangelical mission of the clergy and under their direction.[4]

Liberation theologians could accept this conservative legitimizing interpretation since they knew that, in practice, basic Christian communities would transcend these limits and act as a vehicle for critical social consciousness and action. This is because only bishops that are open to this perspective really encourage them.[5] Such communities are developed and led by radical nuns and priests who have a liberation perspective. By and large, it is the conscious sectors of the peasant and working class or engaged intellectuals who participate in such communities, and they are already committed to making the links between evangelism and social transformation.

Nicaragua is perhaps the first country where a social revolution has been created with input from basic Christian communities inspired by liberation theology. Many Christians who participated in the revolution began in the late sixties by joining basic Christian communities, usually led by a radical priest who had consciously chosen to work in the parish of a poor barrio. The Bible study and discussion in these groups created the formation of conscience that then led these people to become active revolutionaries. After joining the revolution, many of these Christians felt they no longer had time to continue to meet in these communities. Reflection had been translated into all-absorbing action.

After the revolution, many new community groups arose that were engaged in creating the new society: militia and national guards to defend the revolution against counterrevolutionaries, neighborhood groups involved in creating new housing, day care centers, and medical clinics. The basic Christian community continued to meet in the barrio, but only a small group attended. They often faced conflicts between attending this meeting or other community meetings that absorbed their time and commitment in creating new social structures.[6]

Yet this small participation in the gathering for Bible study should not be interpreted as a split between the explicitly religious activity and the other secular revolutionary activities. For engaged Christians, all these activities are of a piece. All express the real meaning of the gospel. Whether one sits down to reflect on Bible passages in the light of social struggle or goes to the town meeting to discuss the next steps in social reconstruction, one is equally living the gospel. Reflection on the gospel indeed should lead one precisely to such an engaged life. Where the church becomes the motivating center of this social struggle, the church provides a focus for dealing with crises. When a conservative hierarchy tries to remove a popular priest, or when members of the village are killed by contras, the processions and liturgy of the church become the vehicle for symbolizing and expressing this crisis. The funeral mass and procession turn into a village assembly, gathered to protest injustice and express its commitment to its own identity.

Because basic Christian communities in Nicaragua have shown the revolutionary potential of such an understanding of church in action, they have also become the focus of the greatest repression from conservative church hierarchy, both within the country and internationally. The Vatican has continually tried to force radical priests in the revolutionary government to resign and to denounce the "popular church," as it has come to be called. The bishop of Managua, Bishop Obando y Bravo, has become the spokesperson both for hierarchical control over the priests, nuns, and laity, and also for support of the wealthy property holders against the revolution. Thus it becomes clear that the struggle between conservative hierarchy and the popular church also reflects the class struggle in society and, in fact, both are aspects of the same struggle.[7]

This split between conservative hierarchy and popular church reflects also the level of international intervention. Not only does the Vatican attempt to reinforce the hierarchy against the engaged Christians at the base, but the American government tries to establish this conservative position as the legitimate Catholic church in Nicaragua. Not only through enormous monetary support to the contras, but also through media and diplomatic means, government officials portray the Nicaraguan church as one "persecuted" by an anti-Christian Marxist government and try to make Christians committed to the revolution appear marginal and unrepresentative. Much of this American governmental campaign against the Nicaraguan popular church is aimed at American Catholics, attempting to convince them that the Nicaraguan hierarchy is the expression of Catholicism they should support and to dissuade them from sympathizing with the popular church. American Catholics are seen as a dangerous potential counterforce to American intervention in popular revolutions in Latin America.[8]

Since American Catholic bishops have taken stands against military funding in Central America and also against nuclear arms, there are efforts by government sympathizers to neutralize their authority as well. However, priests and nuns on the side of the popular church in Central America often belong to orders with ties to the United States, so that alternative information and interpretation continually flows back to American Catholics, including bishops, feeding an alternative viewpoint. Thus, in a surprising way, the rather conservative American hierarchy, traditionally bent on proving the patriotism of American Catholics, today finds itself a significant dissident force against American foreign policy. The roots of this lie in the participation of missionaries in a popular Christianity that has opted for the poor.

Basic Christian communities have also developed in European Catholicism, although without the same dramatic results as in Nicaragua, since these countries are not in the same revolutionary situation. In Holland a strong basic Christian community movement was generated as a result of the Dutch appropriation of the reforms of the Second Vatican Council.[9] For a while it looked like the Dutch church would be dramatically reformed to include married priests, women pastoral workers, and a democratic government in which laity and religious participated with priests and bishops in making church policy. However, the Vatican intervened to split this liberal Dutch hierarchy by creating new dioceses to which they appointed reactionary prelates. The Dutch hierarchy was enjoined to repudiate married priests who continued to work in parishes and to repress expressions of the popular church.

Thus, although a network of basic Christian communities continue to exist, some of them Roman Catholic and some ecumenical in membership, the positive working relations with the Dutch hierarchy that might have prevailed have been cut off. These groups function in a more alienated way from the official church and see themselves as committed to various social ministries, such as work with migrant laborers and against nuclear weapons. It is taken for granted in these groups that the promotion of equality for women is part of their social perspective. But young Dutch Catholic feminists feel increasingly hostile to the institutional church in any form and tend to assume that Christianity is inherently misogynist and cannot be reformed.

In Italy also a strong basic Christian community movement formed in the wake of the liturgical and church reforms of the council. But, unlike Holland, the Italian hierarchy never really supported these reforms in practice. So popular parish groups that tried to implement them, both in new catechetical and liturgical expressions and also in new social commitment to the poorer classes, soon fell into conflict with the hierarchy. They were expelled from local parishes, and their priestly leaders were deprived of clerical status. These groups have had to adjust to living outside the official institution. One such group, the basic community of the historic Church of St. Paul's Outside the Walls in Rome, regrouped in a warehouse near the old basilica, where they have continued to worship since the late sixties. Another parish community in Florence, expelled from their church building, took up headquarters in some old school buildings across from the church and have continued to celebrate mass in the piazza in front of the parish church.[10]

Moreover, basic Christian communities in Italy have formed networks of communication with each other and also with movements in other European and Latin American countries.[11] Most of their members belong to leftist political parties and are engaged in social action, such as antinuclear movements. Since the Italian hierarchy is highly politicized and has traditionally supported the Christian Democrats—in past decades even forbidding Catholics to vote socialist or communist—simply belonging to a leftist political party is itself an act of dissent against the hierarchy. Italian Catholics have been long accustomed to seeing themselves as Catholic while dissenting from the hierarchy on social policy— seldom attending church except for baptisms, marriage, and burial —so that basic Christian communities who have met for decades outside of hierarchical control do not find it hard to continue to define themselves as Catholics.

In the United States the situation of new communities is more diffuse. Popular liturgical groups that met in living rooms or schools arose in the sixties as the expression of liturgical reforms, but this underground church gradually disappeared or was absorbed into popular masses within parishes. Basic Christian communities evangelize in Hispanic communities, but they take a conservative form led by priests who for the most part promote approved forms of catechetics (although many priests and lay workers in Hispanic ministries hope for more engaged styles of Christian life). Thus probably the most dramatic expression of new liturgical communities in the United States is the development of feminist liturgies. Since these groups arise out of frustration with male leadership and male-dominated theology and the hierarchy's refusal to integrate women and feminist theology into worship, they necessarily take forms outside institutional control. These groups are the subject of this book, so I will turn to more particular discussion of them later on.

In the rest of this chapter I wish to discuss the theological problems involved in defining the church that is created by this historical and contemporary conflict between spirit-filled community and historical institution. The basic assumption of this book is that the church cannot be defined only as historical institution or only as spirit-filled community. Rather, the church exists as a dialectical interaction between the two elements. But the relationship between the two has been constantly misdefined, usually by the historical institution, but at times by the renewal community as well. And so the relationship breaks down into repression and separation. Seldom does the interplay between the two take place with optimal creativity.

The error of historical institutions lies in their attempt to make false claims of spiritual efficacy for purely institutional forms of mediation of words, symbols, and rituals. The institutional church tries to make itself the cause of grace and the means of dispensing the Spirit, rather than simply being the occasion and context where these may take place. It institutionalizes forms of communicating religious meaning, and it pretends that these are the only valid channels of grace. It claims that only the words preached by preachers whom it has designated and whose theology it controls preach a true Word of God, and that only the rituals it validates mediate salvation. The church creates a sacramental materialism when it teaches people that only the actions of the validly ordained can cause the power of God to be present, and they do this by simply performing the ritual acts without either the minister or the people appropriating their meaning. The communication of grace, in other words, can happen magically; that is, without real experience of meaning or conviction on either side.

The church has created a false faith in the spiritual efficacy of material acts. It has claimed that spiritual power is available only because the church stands in a legitimate succession of institutional transmission back to the apostles. Therefore apostolic succession is the first lie to be cleared away. The myth of material mediation of the Spirit through sacramental acts that transmit power from head to hand through the centuries is the basic legitimizing myth by which the historic church claims to control the mediation of the Spirit. It thus renders actual experience of the Spirit unnecessary or secondary to its own institutional structures. It defines itself as spirit-filled community and then dismisses all need for further spiritual experience. We must be clear that all of this is a falsification or at least a serious confusion of functions. Material acts of word or deed do not and cannot mediate the Spirit *ex opere operato,* without the receiver personally appropriating their meaning.

It is a historical falsehood that Jesus founded such an institutional church and established the structures of priesthood and sacraments and hierarchical government that have been transmitted in unbroken continuity through the ages. As we have seen, it is unlikely that Jesus intended to found a separate religion outside Judaism, much less an institutional church with a Roman juridical structure. The apostolic church itself was primarily a voluntaristic community with charismatic forms of ministry and little recognition of the need to create historical institutions, since they expected history to come to an end in their generation. Thus, the institutional church of episcopacy and apostolic succession arose precisely by suppressing the actual apostolic church.

However, this does not mean that institutionalization as such as illegitimate. The spirit-filled community deludes itself by imagining that it can live without any historical structure at all. As we have seen, early millennialist Christianity could not have survived in its literal form. It needed a theological translation; that is, it needed a reinterpretation of the meaning of the "coming of the kingdom" that could be understood as something continuously available in each generation, a view of the New Age that would not be refuted if it failed to literally appear and the end of the world did not come. Early millenialist Christianity needed to translate the gospel into historical forms of church organization, canonical texts, rituals, and ministries, in order to catechize the next generation, to historically transmit its culture, and to gather a people together to enter into the experiences of Christian life.

Thus what must be rejected is not institutionalization as such, but the myth that some particular form of historical institution is the only legitimate one and has been dominically and/or apostolically founded. The church, in all its historical expressions, must accept its historical relativity. There is no right church structure, which was intended by Christ and which alone transmits redemptive grace. It is futile to pretend that Christ founded bishops, much less the papacy, and it is equally futile to try to go back behind episcopal forms to resurrect some earlier church polity—presbyterian or congregational—and claim that this was founded by Christ and alone mediates the Spirit. All forms of church polity are equally nondominical. All are historical creations in the context of particular social and political configurations: the cities and provinces of the late Roman Empire, the nation state of Reformation Europe, the town life of Switzerland or Colonial America, or the affinity groups of religious movements of renewal.

The only legitimate discussion of church polity concerns not apostolic polity, but whether polity is capable both of assuring responsible transmission of the tradition and, at the same time, of being open to new movements of the Spirit by which the meaning of the tradition can come alive. The optimal polity is the polity that can be most responsible in transmitting and communicating Christian culture while erecting fewest barriers to the workings of the Spirit. So far, no historical polity has proven to do this infallibly, nor has any polity proven an insurmountable barrier to the workings of the Spirit. Each has its strengths and deficiencies. A congregational polity may become coterminous with spirit-filled community, or it may simply become a Christian rotary club in which wealthy members censure new ideas and prevent creative pastoral leadership. On the other hand, a polity designed for maximum hierarchical control, such as counter-Reformation Roman Catholicism, may not be capable of preventing the birth of spirit-filled community in its midst, as we have seen in this chapter.

Thus historical institutions must accept both their historical relativity as institutions and also their limits as vehicles of transmission and communication. What they transmit is not the Spirit or the living presence of God as such, but rather forms of interpretation of the presence of God that have been shaped by past historical experiences of encounter with God and reflection upon them. At their best, institutions carry with them some collective wisdom about what has worked and what has not, how ecstatic experience can be abused by charlatans and power mongers, or how to draw people of different age groups into learning and participation. All of this cultural heritage is very important. But all of this is dead without living persons who, in each particular moment, engage in transforming both their experience and the traditional forms into the spark of lived meaning. This is the Spirit actually alive in our midst.

At their best, historical institutions create the occasion for the experience of the Spirit. But they cannot cause the presence of the Spirit, which always breaks in from a direct encounter of living persons and the divine. Historic institutions also transmit a culture of interpretation around such spiritual encounters, but this culture of interpretation cannot be closed and finalized. It is, at best, an open system of symbolism that gives guidelines to interpret the experience and translate it into daily life. But the living encounter with the Spirit is also an occasion for new appropriation of meaning by which the given culture of interpretation is itself renewed and reshaped. Tradition, to remain alive, must be open to this continual reshaping of interpretive culture by new spiritual experience.

The agents of tradition have a valid task of "testing the spirits," for not everything that claims to be of God is so. This becomes all too evident in incidents such as Jonestown, where a charismatic preacher gathered what claimed to be a Christian community of mutual help and justice and led them into exploitation and finally mass suicide.[12] But the ability to validly test the spirits cannot happen by simply employing institutional or legal norms. It must itself depend on the spiritual gifts of the testers who exercise pastoral oversight. Unless they too are open to the Spirit, they will be threatened by and will repress the real movements of spirit-filled community, while overlooking and neglecting the Jonestowns until it is too late.

Schism has taken place in historical Christianity again and again because existing historical institutions have not been able to recognize and accommodate themselves to new movements of spirit-filled community. They have seen communities fostering direct religious experience as threats to their institutional authority and have sought to repress them by declaring them heretical or invalid. Usually, the committed community itself intended to reform the existing historical church and spent a longer or shorter time trying to do so. Sometimes such movements and their leaders bend to hierarchical sanctions to avoid a split and silence themselves, perhaps surviving underground until a more favorable time. Many of the Roman Catholic reform movements that came out in the open and were able to shape the changes of the Second Vatican Council had survived such an underground gestation period of one or two generations.

Other movements of reform have grown frustrated and angry with repression and vilification and have elected to break with their parent historical church. In the Reformation, this generated violent wars of religion at a time when church and state were linked and it was believed that there could be only one church institution. Today, when secular states allow a plurality of churches, it is possible to start a new church at any time, provided it does not violate general cultural and legal standards. However, the decision to split with a parent church has its price. It means that one gives up any effort to change the parent institution or effectively communicate with people in it, for this can be done only by those who continue to claim a shared identity with the parent community.

Schism also means that the new community itself must inevitably become a historical institution if it is to perpetuate its own options and development and pass them down to a new generation. It, too, cannot expect to transmit spiritual community by spiritual and unhistorical means, but it must enter into the dialectic of spirit and institution. Its experiences, however lively to its founders, may be dead to its children who inherit only the embodied forms and must learn for themselves how to translate them into living faith. As long as a community can remain, even marginally, within a parent institution and claim some part of its structures, it does not have to duplicate all the functions of historical institutions itself. It can be carried along by existing institutions, use their facilities to communicate, and disband when its energy has dissipated.

Moreover, the decision to create a final institutional break with a parent community generally entails excessive bitterness and misrepresentation on both sides. Not only does the parent institution vilify the new movement, but the new movement has often moved toward an angry demonization of the parent community, denying its own source and claiming that the parent church is incapable of producing any true spiritual fruit. This decisively blocks creative communication and shuts each side up in mutual rigidity. Neither group can admit any good in the other lest its own legitimacy be called into question.

The future of feminist basic communities in this dialectic of spiritual community and parent historical institution is uncertain. The model for relating the two depends very much on how one sees the radicality of the change demanded by religious feminism. Is it a "reformation"; that is, is it a return to a true original Christianity that existed in the beginning in some pristine moment and is now being reclaimed to reform a historical Christianity that fell away from this original truth? This has been the model of change proposed by the Reformation and by most renewal movements in Christian history.

However, today we must recognize that this concept of reformation as return to origins is itself a historical myth. No reformation ever literally returns to the origins. It may recover insights buried in past tradition, but it is also engaged in making new adaptations that correspond to the needs of the present time. Thus a Christian feminism particularly cannot use the reformation model literally. It can legitimately claim that there are insights in the biblical tradition and in some lines of historical tradition that point in a direction of feminism, but they have never been developed explicitly. So Christian feminism does not revive any literal past form of Christianity, but it uses material from the tradition to make a significantly new interpretation and development.

Many feminists will find even this model of development of tradition inadequate. They see feminism as a revival of an option for humanity that was lost, not only biblical times, but even earlier. All of biblical religion arises as an expression of a patriarchal revolution that had suppressed an earlier cultural option for women's equality. Some of these feminists believe that there was really a matriarchal era before the rise of patriarchy and a feminist religion that expressed this earlier idyllic time. Feminism is the most radical "reformation"; that is, a return to the original religion of humanity before patriarchy.[13] Others disclaim any full-blown feminist religion in some aboriginal time, but they believe that feminists are making such a radical break with all established religions that feminism must be seen as totally discontinuous with patriarchal culture. It is a new revelation or a new dispensation which reconnects us with our original but undeveloped possibilities.[14]

I believe that there is truth to this sense of the radicality of feminist claims. Culturally speaking, feminism does not simply go back to earliest Christianity or Judaism, but it reaches back to lost options behind them. It seeks to recapitulate the whole development of human culture and reenvision it. Yet, in doing so, it does not really have an alternative culture or tradition from the "beginning" upon which to stand. It is dependent upon patterns of thought transmitted through Judaism and Christianity as well as Western culture. Even its idea of a radical return to original human possibilities lost at the dawn of history is a thoroughly Christian myth, reformulated in feminist terms. This does not mean that some feminists cannot legitimately seek new religions generated from hints of ancient times and their own experience. But it also means that it is not illegitimate to continue to make claims on the parent cultures we have inherited, to invite them to respond and to make creative leaps of interpretation of their historical identity.

It is not likely that all of historical Christianity will be able to make this kind of reinterpretation. The reaction against and stifling of feminism is all too evident in contemporary churches. Yet feminists cannot claim that every door is closed against them. The institutions are porous, and, in a variety of nooks and crannies, the new spirit is at work. As long as feminist thinkers themselves do not become total separatists, there remain Christian groups who continue to invite them and seek to hear them. Thus it is by no means appropriate to claim that all possibility of creative dialectic is futile.

It is my view that the feminist option will be able to develop much more powerfully at the present time if it secures footholds in existing Christian churches and uses them to communicate its option to far larger groups of people than it could possibly do if it had to manufacture these institutional resources on its own. Feminists who claim to have rejected all "male" institutions fail to appreciate how much their ability to function is based on a constant use of institutions that they have neither created nor maintained. One must learn to make creative use of existing institutions without being stifled or controlled by them. In the process these institutions become more flexible and become vehicles for further creativity. This is precisely what is meant by the positive working of the dialectic of spiritual community and historical institution.

Feminists who have opted to remain in dialogue with the historic traditions of Judaism and Christianity, although not necessarily accepting their limits, thus engage in a double dialogue. On the one hand, they are in dialogue with the historic culture of parent institutions and are able to appropriate its best insights into their new option. But they are not limited to this dialogue. They also engage in dialogue outside this tradition and never before allowed by it, dialogue with heresies and rejected options of earlier Christianity that can now be read with new eyes, dialogue with pre-Christian and prebiblical religion. They also engage in a contemporary dialogue with other religious feminists who opt to work in other traditions, Jewish feminists and Goddess feminists who themselves interpret their roots in the past in a variety of ways. Perhaps feminists of other religions, such as Islam, will also join the dialogue.

Jewish and Christian feminists are also in dialogue with secular feminism, which has given up on or become ignorant of religion, but which provides valuable work on history or sociology or psychology. Thus the feminism we envision is one that is able constantly to build an integral vision of a new humanizing culture beyond patriarchy without becoming closed or sectarian toward any living cultural option or human community. It remains open to authentic spirit wherever it is found, and it extends to all the invitation to join a new dance of life without which life itself may not survive.

3. The *Ecclesia* of Patriarchy and Male Exodus Communities

I have suggested that women can find some positive roots in the biblical tradition in prophetic patterns of thought, the tradition that has also been claimed as normative by liberation theology. Yet, the prophetic tradition in the Bible is never applied explicitly to the critique of the bondage of women under patriarchy, although there are some hints of it in the New Testament. Feminist theology has to make this application of the prophetic critique of patriarchy as a new development. What is the prophetic tradition, and why has it never before been applied clearly and explicitly to the critique of patriarchy?

Most human religions, including Christianity in most of its historical practice, has functioned to sacralize the social status quo. They have taken the existing social hierarchies of gender, class, and ethnicity to be divinely given. They have pictured the heavenly world as a divine mirror image of this human social world, and they have then imagined that the Gods created the world as it is and gave it its laws. To obey God is to accept one's social station. The ruling classes are seen as agents of God or the Gods to rule the earth and the "lower orders" of society.

Biblical religion is unique in having a theological world view that breaks with this function of religion as sacralization of the status quo. Its foundational myth in the Exodus is that of a slave people liberated from the most powerful ruler on earth, the pharaoh, who is defeated by God. The former slaves are led by God out of the land of bondage into a journey toward a new land of freedom. Here God is not the divine sanctifier of the rulers, but one who takes the side of those who have been oppressed and forced into servitude and liberates them.

This perspective is continued in prophetic renewal movements reflected in Hebrew Scripture, as well as in the teaching of Jesus. The Word of God comes to the prophet or prophetess, who speaks words of judgment against the rich and powerful, castigating them for their unjust practices in oppressing the poor. The prophet not only criticizes social oppression as contrary to God's will, but also exposes the corruption of religion as a justification of oppression and as a means of ignoring the issues of justice. The religious leadership is denounced as "hypocrites and blind guides."

But prophetic faith does not end with denunciation. It also calls for repentance. It calls the people, especially the leadership, to return to the true perspective of the God of justice. Sometimes disasters upon the people—famines, droughts, defeats in war, and exile under surrounding enemies—are imagined as means by which God is purging the people of their corruption so they can return with a truer faith. God is seen as active in historical processes by which the present rulers will be overthrown and the poor will be raised up. A new age is imagined after this purgation and repentance, in which life as God wants it will be established. This is typically imagined as a simple society of economic equality of small landholders: "Each will sit under their own vine and fig tree and none will be afraid" (Mic. 4:4). War and oppression will be abolished. Peace will reign on earth, not only between human and human, but also with the nonhuman world as well: "The lion will lay down with the lamb and the little child will lead them" (Isa. 11:6).

Yet this pattern of denunciation and annunciation is never explicitly applied to the bondage of women under patriarchy and to hopes of gender equality. The obvious reason for this is that women did not control the definition of prophetic tradition. It came from male prophets whose consciousness was shaped by the sociology of an oppressed class and ethnic group over against the mighty empires of antiquity and the wealthy landholders of Canaan. Although women prophets appear in the Hebrew Scripture and New Testament, their identity has been transmitted by a male-defined tradition. Thus Hulda, the prophetess of Josiah's time, is lauded as one who validated a king's revolution against Goddess worship in the temple (2 Kings 22:11–20). Miriam, the great priestess and prophet of the Exodus, is remembered as one who was turned into a leper and spat upon because of her assertion of autonomy against Moses (Num. 12:12–16).

In Christian tradition, Mary Magdalene, the key female apostle of Jesus, is debased into a prostitute who weeps at Jesus' feet,[1] while the prophetess who teaches churches in Asia Minor is called a "Jezebel."[2] Thus, although the power of women to prophesy is never denied, it is controlled and defined by a male religious perspective. The key to the erasure of women in religious history, as in all of patriarchal history, is not that women were inactive, but that they have not been able to shape the tradition by which the story of what they have done is remembered and carried on.

Although the Exodus and prophetic traditions define key elements of the identity of Israel as God's chosen (in Hebrew Scripture) and of the church (in the New Testament), the memory of women's participation in these liberating moments is continually erased or reinterpreted according to male interests. The revolt of subjugated males against one system of oppression is gradually redefined as a new religious and social system in which women are again put in their place as subordinates in a divine plan of social order. We can see this translation of male exodus communities back into the *ecclesia* of patriarchy not only in Hebrew Scripture and the New Testament, but repeatedly in renewal movements in the Christian church and even in modern movements of social liberation. In this chapter we will briefly review this history and analyze its patterns of thought.

The key paradigm for God's liberation of Israel and "his" formation of Israel as "his" people is the Exodus and the giving of the law at Sinai. In the story of the Exodus we find that the first acts of rebellion against Pharaoh are those of women. The mother of Moses refuses to obey the decree to kill her newborn son and hides him in the bulrushes. The sister of Moses (who later tradition identified with Miriam)[3] seizes the opportunity to save him by presenting him to the daughter of Pharaoh who comes to the river to bathe. Pharaoh's daughter also disobeys by accepting the Hebrew child and bringing him up as her own. Thus a conspiracy of women takes place across class and ethnic lines to save the child who will be the liberator of Israel (Exod. 2).

In the Exodus narratives, Moses, Aaron, and Miriam are described as the three who together led the people of Israel out of bondage,[4] yet, as we have mentioned, later tradition displaced Miriam from her equal status by blasting her with leprosy for criticizing Moses for marrying a foreign woman. Aaron also criticizes Moses, but is not so punished. Clearly, it is Miriam's authority which the writer of the tradition wished to marginalize, although it is also said that the people of Israel refuse to continue their march through the desert until Miriam is restored.

In the story of the giving of the law at Sinai, the people are told to assemble and prepare themselves for the great revelation that will be the charter of their life as a nation of God. Yet, we are startled to read that the "people" are told to keep strictly away from women for three days in order to be ready for the revelation.[5] Suddenly, we realize that the author simply assumes that the "people" means males. The "assembly" (ecclesia in the Septuagint translation, from which the New Testament takes its word for the church) of male, free adults is presumed to be "Israel." Women are not only invisible, but they are also seen as sources of pollution inimical to the receiving of divine revelation. Male sacrality is defined by negation of the female sexual body.

In the Levitical laws, a patriarchal definition of Israel prevails. The laws are presumed to be given to male heads of family who alone are the direct correspondents with God. Females, servants, and other dependents in the patriarchal family do not receive the Law directly but are defined by it through their relations with males as fathers and husbands.[6] They are systematically regarded as of lesser status than males. One pays a lesser price for killing or injuring women than men. Women's bodily functions are sources of pollution that distance one from the holy. Moreover, a woman is polluted for twice as long if she bears a female child than if she bears a male child. By contrast, the holding of Hebrew slaves is regarded as unjust and provisions are made for their release, particularly during the Jubilee year. The Hebrews are to remember that they were once slaves of Pharaoh in Egypt by limiting the holding of fellow Hebrews in servitude (Lev. 25). But the servitude of women is never mentioned as something either to be criticized or to be rectified in the light of the Exodus.

The New Testament church also defined itself as an exodus community, although its exodus is not simply from one historical occasion of servitude, but is the ultimate exodus of the people of God from all historical conditions of servitude, demonic possession, sin, and death. New Testament traditions vary on the meaning of this. Some traditions keep the strong note of social transformation of the prophetic tradition: the last shall be first. Those despised by the present social hierarchy will be first in the Age to Come. The poor will be vindicated, while the rich will be sent empty away. The Lord's Prayer sees the future age as a new era of humanity in this world, where all will receive their daily bread and debts will be cancelled.[7]

Other more apocalyptic interpretations see redemption as a transcendent new world that will come upon the earth after the present ruling empire and its demonic world rulers have been decisively overthrown by God and God's agent, Christ, returns on clouds of glory as a warrior Messiah (Rev. 19–20). Others, such as Paul and particularly John, tone down the element of social transformation and think of the New Age as something that can be experienced here and now as an inner new being that links one up with a heavenly world that will become all in all in a transformed future or to which one will go after death.

Women participated decisively in the spreading of early Christianity and continued for centuries to be the first converts through which Christianization spread to their male relatives. They played important leadership roles as local ministers, traveling evangelists, and patrons who lent their houses for the Christian assembly.[8] Some strata of early Christianity extended the prophetic vision of an egalitarian messianic age to mean that the hierarchies of gender, servitude, and ethnicity would also be overcome. Through baptism these distinctions are banished: "There is no more slave or free, Jew or Greek, male or female, but all are one in Christ" (Gal. 3:28). They saw the participation of women, slaves, and freedmen in ministry and the breaking down of the ethnic-religious line between Jew and Gentile to be the sign of this new, unified humanity.[9]

The Gospel stories often apply this vision of prophetic revolution to women by making women of despised groups—Samaritans, Canaanites, widows, women with a flow of blood, sinners—be the ones who are able to recognize and believe in Christ, while males of the ruling classes, and especially of the religious elite, reject him.[10] All the Gospels culminate in a story line in which the religious leaders, the crowds, and finally the male disciples betray Jesus, while the women disciples remain faithful to him at the cross and are the first witnesses of the resurrection.[11]

Yet, the tradition is shaped to erase or deny the implications of this early participation of women for gender equality in the church. Paul understands the line of witnesses to the resurrection, of which he accounts himself the last, to be decisive for the apostolic commission. Yet his account of the resurrection lacks the tradition of the first appearances to Mary Magdalene and the women disciples and begins instead with Peter (1 Cor. 15:4–8). Mary Magdalene is displaced as the central figure among Jesus' female disciples, and she is translated into a sinner forgiven by Christ.

We now know that the ministry of women was the source of strong conflict between developing episcopal or Petrine Christianity, and the more charismatic and spiritualist traditions represented by Montanism and Gnosticism. In the Gnostic Gospels Mary Magdalene (who is never described as a former sinner) is seen as the disciple closest to Jesus. In a conflict with Peter, who tries to deny her apostolic authority, the Gnostic Gospels vindicate her role[12] and, in doing so, also vindicate the equal participation of women in leadership in their communities. For example, in the

Gospel of Mary (Magdalene), Mary is begged by the apostles to provide them with an interpretation of the meaning of the gospel. After she has done so her authority is challenged by Andrew and Peter, but she is vindicated in the following words:

When Mary said this, she fell silent, since it was to this point that the Savior had spoken with her. But Andrew answered and said to the brethren, "Say what you [wish to] say about what she has said. I at least do not believe that the Savior said this. For certainly these teachings are strange ideas." Peter answered and spoke concerning these same things. He questioned them about the Savior: "Did he really speak privately with a woman [and] not openly to us? Are we to turn about and all listen to her? Did he prefer her to us?"

Then Mary wept and said to Peter, "My brother Peter, what do you think? Do you think that I thought this up myself in my heart, or that I am lying about the Savior?" Levi answered and said to Peter, "Peter, you have always been hot-tempered. Now I see you contending against the woman like the adversaries. But if the Savior made her worthy, who are you indeed to reject her? Surely the Savior knows her very well. That is why he loved her more than us. Rather let us be ashamed and put on the perfect man, and separate as he commanded us and preach the gospel, not laying down any other rule or other law beyond what the Savior said." . . . and they began to go forth to proclaim and to preach.[13]

Gnostics, however, were denounced as heretics by the mainline tradition. The fact that they were often the earliest Christians in many Eastern cities is covered up by the myth of apostolic succession, and Gnostic tradition is remembered only as an aberrant movement of fanciful dualistic cosmology. Only the discovery of a major Gnostic library at Nag Hammadi in Upper Egypt, which was buried in the Theodosian era of the late fourth century when the burning of all nonorthodox texts had been ordered, has enabled us to form a more just estimate of Gnosticism and to realize that it did preserve elements of a simpler, less hierarchical Christianity. Thus the reevaluation of the role of women in Christianity necessarily involves criticizing the formation of canon and tradition in its marginalization of types of Christianity that included women.[14]

Although the New Testament preserves remnants of this earlier role of women, the authority of these stories as the basis for gender equality has been erased or marginalized. Instead, the canon is shaped to direct us to read the understanding of the church from texts such as Ephesians 5 and 1 Timothy. Here the patriarchal hierarchy of men over women is set forth as the model for interpreting the relationship of Christ and the church. The female *persona* of the church in these passages does not mean, as it does in the Magnificat of Luke, that women symbolize the poor of the world who are to be liberated by the messianic advent. Instead, the female image of the church is used to reinforce the hierarchy of men over women by seeing it as the image of the subjugation of creatures to God and the church to Christ. The woman should look at her husband as head and lord, as the church looks to Christ as her head and Lord.[15]

In the legends of the *Acts of Paul and Thecla,* one group of Pauline Christians vindicated the ministry of women by telling how Thecla was commissioned to preach by the Apostle Paul. However, the pastoral Epistles denounce this tradition as "old wives' tales" and instead establish a patriarchal Paul as normative.[16] This is a Paul who tells women to keep silence and declares that their only redemptive role is in the bearing of children (1 Tim. 2:11–15). Genesis 2 and 3 are used to establish the theological model for defining women as second in creation but first in sin. The inclusion of 1 Timothy in the Christian canon and the exclusion of other texts, such as the *Acts of Paul and Thecla* (which perhaps goes back, in oral form, to before 1 Timothy), means that all subsequent Christian theology will be directed to read its view of women in biblical teaching through the lens of 1 Timothy. Alternative possibilities will be forgotten, such as Mary Magdalene, the first witness of the resurrection, early Christian prophetesses, apostles, and local leaders, such as Prisca, Eudokia, Phoebe, and Thecla, or the vision of a new humanity that emerges from the waters of baptism in which "there is neither Jew nor Greek, slave nor free, male nor female." The church in 1 Timothy is modeled after the patriarchal family in which males who have successfully ruled their wives, servants, and children as *pater familias* are those best qualified as bishops, elders, and deacons (I Tim. 3). The normative Christian community is one where wives obey their husbands, children their parents, and slaves their masters (Col. 3:22–23; I Tim. 6:1–2, I Pet. 2:18–21). Christian tradition reads these household codes as descriptions of an original consensus, rather than evidence of an alternative Christianity against which emerging patriarchal Christianity was contending.[17]

This story of the promise of liberation and the betrayal of women is repeated again and again in renewal movements throughout Christian history. In the first chapter we described this pattern in Christian monasticism and also in the English Reformation in the conflict between radical and magisterial Puritanism. Renewal groups that had initially included women on the basis of a ministry of prophecy often later excluded them as they became established and accepted the patriarchal norm of church organization. Thus Waldensians in the twelfth century included women among its preachers, but in the sixteenth century, when they accepted the Calvinist theology of Switzerland, they suppressed this early tradition of women preachers.[18] English Baptists in the Puritan Revolution had many women preachers,[19] but this tradition faded away as Baptists accepted a clerical definition of ministry. The eighteenth-century English Methodist tradition of women preachers and class leaders was suppressed by the more established Methodist churches in the nineteenth century, although it continued on the local level among some Methodists.[20] American Evangelicals also turned fundamentalist in the 1930s and made the doctrine of male headship the key to their definition of the Christian family and church, denying earlier traditions that taught the recognition of ministry among those women, as well as men, to whom the gifts of the Spirit have been given.[21]

A similar pattern of promise and betrayal of women also appears in modern secular reform and revolutionary movements, such as liberalism, socialism, and Third World liberation. Liberalism has been decisive in shaping the world view that gave rise to feminism. Throughout Christian history, beginning with Paul (the Paul of the original epistles, and not just the Paul of I Timothy), it has been assumed that patriarchy was the order of creation and hence the necessary order of familial and political society. Patriarchal Christians assumed that this order of creation also defined the social order of the church in history, even though women were equally redeemed and would be saved in heaven without reference to gender hierarchy. Radical Christians also assumed that patriarchy was the order of creation and hence of the procreative family and the political order. But they believed the social order of the church should reflect that of redemption, rather than creation, so they vindicated the rights of women to exercise charismatic gifts of church leadership.

It was in the philosophy of the Enlightenment that this identification of patriarchal social order and the order of creation was broken. Liberalism began with a belief in "original nature" in which all human share the same human nature and hence have equal rights in society. This new starting point in equality as original nature allowed liberalism to evaluate various social hierarchies, not as expressions of nature, but rather as an unjust distortion of nature that has arisen through privilege and has been imposed on society as a departure from natural law. They could then imagine their own social reform or revolution, which overthrew the *ancien régime* of European clericalism and feudalism, as the "restoration of nature," the creation of a new society where the possession of a common human nature dictates equal civil rights.

However, this universalist egalitarian theory was not, in fact, applied to women, nor to the servant and nonpropertied classes, in the liberal revolutions of the late eighteenth and nineteenth centuries. The emerging bourgeois wished to claim civil equality for themselves over against the older ruling classes, not to apply it to groups that they regarded as their "natural" dependents.

Olympe de Gouges, leading feminist of the French Revolution, who wrote a treatise claiming equality for women in the new definition of the citizen, was guillotined by her Jacobin male confreres.[22] The Napoleonic code, written to consolidate the bourgeois revolution, imposed rigid legal subordination on women in the family and the state.

The conflict between universalist rhetoric and limited application of the theory of natural rights emerges clearly in the well-known exchange of letters between Abigail and John Adams. During the Constitutional Convention, the American Constitution was being written by the victorious males of the planter and merchant classes of the former colonies. Abigail Adams utilized the rhetoric of the Revolution itself when she petitioned her husband to "remember the ladies" and to incorporate civil rights for women into the new laws they were writing, declaring that if women were not given such rights, they would be justified in fomenting a rebellion, just as the colonists had done against the English crown. Women would not be bound by any laws under which they lacked representation.

However, her husband refused to take this threat seriously. He replied, in a jocular tone, that already it had been feared that their revolution had loosed the bonds of legitimate social authority, that slaves, servants, and Indians had become insolent to their masters and were slighting their guardians. But, he said, her letter was the first indication that another yet more numerous group had grown discontent.[23] Thus, Adams inadvertently revealed not only the exclusion of women from equal rights, but also the other classes of dependents which the Constitution had no intention of enfranchising. Yet this contradiction did not sit easily with Adams and other writers of the Constitution, and they were at pains to justify this discrimination against groups over which they ruled, particularly the continuance of slavery under the Constitution.[24]

The universalism of liberal ideology allowed both women and blacks, as well as disenfranchised white males, to mount struggles in the nineteenth and twentieth centuries for inclusion in the civil liberties of democratic governments. But this was granted only after long struggles, including the Civil War. The enfranchisement of black males after the American Civil War was followed by their disenfranchisement in the Jim Crow laws of the 1880s, and so another struggle for civil rights for blacks had to be mounted in the 1960s. Americans still have few blacks or women in top government positions, and only in the 1984 presidential campaign were there serious efforts to consider them as presidential or vicepresidential candidates. Thus liberalism in practice has devised a variety of ways of keeping gender, class, and racial hierarchy intact, despite its claims of establishing universal human rights.

Socialism is the tradition that has specifically focused on the analysis of class hierarchy in modern industrial capitalism. But it has been much more ambivalent about race and gender hierarchy, generally refusing to consider the possibility that these structures of oppression might have additional and distinct social sources other than capitalist class relations. Socialists have preferred to think that these discriminations can be included as subcategories of class and will automatically fade away when class hierarchy is overcome.

The earliest socialist theory of the 1830s, expressed in Owenism in England and Fourierism in France, focused on a collective that would include women's domestic work of cooking, housekeeping, and child raising. They saw the socialist revolution not only as returning to the base community of workers' ownership of the means of production, but also doing it in a way that would socialize the work of the home as well. This early socialism included strong participation by women and saw the emancipation of women as a key element in its future vision.[25] In 1825, the Owenite socialists William Thompson and Anna Wheeler wrote and published the treatise *Appeal to One Half of the Human Race, Women, Against the Pretensions of the Other Half, Men, to Retain Them in Civil and Domestic Slavery*, (London), probably the strongest feminist tract written in any period up until contemporary feminism.

However, in the second half of the nineteenth century, these earlier socialist traditions were decried by Marxists as mere "utopianism" against which Marxists claimed to bring truly "scientific" socialism. Marxism meant, in practice, ignoring the subjugation of women by domestic servitude. The socialist revolution was defined solely by the revolution of the industrial proletariat against the capitalist owning class to be carried out by political (and military) means, resulting in a state system of collective ownership that would overcome the class hierarchy of workers and owners. In reality it functioned largely to create a new ruling class in party bureaucrats who now unite economic, legal, and police powers in one total system of control.

Moreover, Marxism established an official position of hostility to any feminism that focuses specifically on the oppression of women as women. This was labeled mere "bourgeois" feminism. Working-class and socialist women were called upon to renounce such feminism and to work in solidarity with men of the working class for the liberation of "all" workers.[26] Although official Communist states have typically granted equal civil rights to women and have made efforts to facilitate their entrance into the work place on equal terms by providing collective day care, they remain hostile to any elaboration of feminism that goes outside the questions of paid work and discusses the effects of unpaid domestic work on women.

In practice, this has meant that Marxist states have only modified, but not made radical changes in, gender hierarchy. Because of the difficulties of obtaining consumer goods, women's work in the home has become all the more time-consuming. Women's role as the exclusive provider of domestic labor also decisively biases women's equality on the job and keeps most women in low-paying and low-status jobs at the bottom of the economic ladder in socialist societies. The private relation of male consumer and female provider of unpaid domestic service also keeps intact the basic cultural model of male domination in society as a whole.[27]

Promise and betrayal have also appeared in black and Third World liberation movements in the 1960s to 1980s. Third World liberation movements based on cultural nationalism, in fact, have been pathologically chauvinist against women. Feminism is seen as a decadent Western colonialist ideology that weakens the fiber of the traditional family and society. The revolution is seen as reestablishing a traditional patriarchal culture over against modernism and secularism that have opened up new roles for women outside the family. The Iranian revolution has shown the most extreme reactionary chauvinism of anticolonial revolutions based on cultural nationalism.

Much of American black theology and ideology in the 1960s and 1970s was also shaped by cultural nationalism. Class analysis was rejected in favor of an exclusive focus on race prejudice, no doubt to prevent the conflict between middle-class and poor blacks from coming out in the open. Black women particularly were told to step back and let the black male take power. It was suggested that the strong role played by black women in the survival of the black community was somehow a fault and that black "matriarchy" was responsible for the weakness of black males. Black ideology often included a fierce compensatory male chauvinism, which implicitly or explicitly told black women to accept their subordinate place in a reconstituted black patriarchy. Black Muslims are the most extreme case of this compensatory black patriarchalism in American black cultural nationalism.[28]

The source of this explicit chauvinism in male liberation groups lies, it appears, in the ego conflicts between dominant and subordinate males in class and race relations. Subordinate males are humiliated by dominant males and not only as subjugated classes and races. Subordinate males experience their inferiority explicitly as an assault on their masculinity. Dominant males refer to subordinate males as "boys" and make sexual use of subordinate women in ways that send the message to minority males that they are unable to "protect" their women. This means that a revolt of subordinate males carries with it a strong psychological need to vindicate their injured masculinity. This is acted out both by efforts to subordinate women of their own group, but also by demonstrating masculine prowess against former ruling males by raping, dating, or marrying "their" women.[29]

The ego conflict between subordinate and dominant males,

acted out on the territory of patriarchal models of male domination, possibly gives the clue to why male exodus groups seldom wish to include women in their vision of liberation. Lessening of class or race hierarchy among males in a society, therefore, does not necessarily promise to include greater equality for women. In fact, a lessening of hierarchy among males is often compensated for by a more rigid marginalization of women as women. When class differences between males are lessened, women often lose spheres of power that they had exercised on the basis of class membership. For example, feudalism gave women who inherited property independently some limited right to exercise the political rights that went with property ownership. Modern bourgeois revolutions, which overthrew feudal classes and replaced them with a male-defined citizenship, removed these remnants of political power exercised by propertied women. All women as women were declared unable to exercise public political power as citizens.[30]

Third World liberation movements, based on socialist theory, have also shown their ambivalence toward women. This ambivalence combines the feelings of injured masculinity of colonized males, taking out their resentment on women, with the traditional Marxist hostility to any feminism that does not subordinate itself to the class revolution. Feminism is decried as merely a white, Western, middle-class movement having no relevance to Third World women. There is an effort to drive a wedge between white Western and Third World women and to prevent them from communicating with each other. Although undoubtedly Third World women have to contextualize feminism in terms of their own situation, greater communication between women of the two worlds would undoubtedly reveal they have many issues in common.

Many Third World women have been intimidated by this male revolutionary rhetoric and have been prevented from doing their own analysis of sexism, both the sexism shaped by traditional patriarchal society and that brought by colonialist and Christian culture. Although they are praised for unselfish dedication to the revolutionary struggle, the lack of analysis of sexism gives little hope that the new society that is to be built will give explicit attention to this issue aside from the traditional Marxist solutions of day care, civil rights, education, and inclusion of women in the work force. These are indeed often dramatic changes for many Third World women, but they mask the extent to which a new hierarchy of gender, created by the double female work role, is being put in place.[31]

This hostility to feminism has also been reflected in the liberation theology produced by blacks and Third World males. Recently, significant participation of black and Third World women has appeared in both American black theology and in the theological gatherings of the Ecumenical Association of Third World Theologians (EATWOT). These women refuse to accept the marginalization of women or women's issues. Mercy Oduyoye has spoken of this protest of Third World women as the "explosion within the explosion," referring to the earlier male description of the voice of the poor as the explosion of consciousness within theology. Black feminists in America also are staking their claims to a feminist application of black theology.[32]

Male black and Third World liberation theologians listen respectfully to these women, especially since this position is being taken by women of their own group and can no longer be claimed to be merely a white women's viewpoint. But it is not clear whether they are really convinced in their hearts that feminism is essential to their definition of liberation. One notes a marked tendency for this issue to be addressed only when large numbers of women are present and making themselves heard and to forget about it again when this is not the case. It is clear from the history of promise and betrayal in male liberation movements that women cannot trust their liberation to male liberators. The issue of women's liberation will be addressed only when women themselves define the terms from their own perspective and shape the movements of liberation to include the liberation of women from patriarchy.

4. Women-Church: A Feminist Exodus Community

Israel and the Church, as communities of exodus from oppression and journey toward liberation, have been defined historically by males. Women have typically participated enthusiastically in the early stages of exodus movements and have believed themselves included in this liberation *as women* and not simply as adjuncts to a male project. The language of the exodus and prophetic traditions which spoke of "Israel"; the language of the early Church which spoke of "brethren" as including all in a new humanity in Christ without regard to gender, ethnic group, or social station; the language of the Reformation and of modern liberation ideologies all have led women to believe that they were included. But, in fact, women have been betrayed by these male-defined projects of liberation. The male leaders of the exodus have set themselves up as a new ruling class of priests, ministers, and magistrates, politicians or party apparachiks. In the laws of the new community of redemption, women have again been defined as subordinate or, at best, auxiliary to a male-defined social order.

Women-Church represents the first time that women collectively have claimed to be church and have claimed the tradition of the exodus community as a community of liberation from patriarchy. This means that patriarchy is rejected as God's will. It is rejected as the order of creation or as a reflection of biological nature. Patriarchy is named as a historically contrived social system by which the "fathers"—that is, ruling-class males—have used power to establish themselves in a position of domination over women and also over dependent classes in the family and society. Ruling-class males have built social structures and systems of cultural justification to assure that they would monopolize the cultural, economic, and political power of the society. Others are forbidden access to this power and are confined to auxiliary status as physical laborers in production and reproduction, while the ruling males own and command the fruits of this labor.

Women-Church means not only that women have rejected this system and are engaged in efforts to escape from it, but that they are doing so collectively. Patriarchy has typically split women from women, across generational lines, mother-in-law from daughter-in-law in the patriarchal family, mother from daughter, women isolated in one household from women isolated in another household, women of the ruling classes from those in the servant classes. It has taught contempt for women, which women have internalized as self-contempt and mistrust of each other. It has assumed that women do not like to be with each other, are competitive with each other, and value anything a male does more than what a female does. Any places where women meet and talk together are marginal spaces with no real access to power or information, so "women's talk" in such places will be "trivial."

This has never been entirely true. Women have bonded together as sisters, as adult women of the same household, as women of villages, and they have shared more than recipes and child-raising tips. They have also shared their dissatisfaction with male power. They have found ways to protect each other from abuse. The patriarchal male has never liked the spectacle of women talking to each other. Although he had not the slightest idea what women would say to each other, he has assumed that their conversation was not only idle gossip, a waste of time that kept them from their work (for him), but also, in some sense, subversive. Throughout patriarchal culture there reverberates the constant demand the women keep silent. Women should not speak, certainly in the company of men, but also not too much to each other. The repression of women, not only into marginality, but into silence; the deprivation of speech, of the capacity to articulate their own experience and communicate it; this is essential to the definition of women as objects rather than as subjects.

Thus the first step in forming the feminist exodus from patriarchy is to gather women together to articulate their own experience and communicate it with each other. Women assure each other that they really are not crazy, that they really have been defined and confined by systemic marginalization of their human capacities.

They develop words and analysis for the different aspects of this system of marginalization, and they learn how to recognize and resist the constant messages from patriarchal culture that try to enforce their acquiescence and collaboration with it. Distressing as it may seem to males who imagine themselves sympathetic to feminism, this process of consciousness raising must necessarily have a separatist stage. Women have to withdraw from male-dominated spaces so they can gather together and defined their own experience.

The need for a period of withdrawal from men and communication with each other is essential for the formation of the feminist community, because women, more than any other marginalized group, have lacked a critical culture of their own. Repressed ethnic and racial groups retained remnants of cultures prior to their conquest. They have also developed subcultures of resistance in modes of talk, song, and dance. Precisely because of women's isolation from each other, separated by patriarchal family structures, their deprivation of education, and even of speech, their cultural colonization by an education that incorporates them into a language that they have not defined, but which defines them as inferior and auxiliary to a male dominated world, women need separate spaces and all-female gatherings to form the critical culture that can give them an autonomous ground from which to critique patriarchy.

The need for a separate base in order to form a critical culture should not be confused with ideological separatism. By ideological separatism I mean that position assumed by some feminists that separatism should be total and permanent. This is generally accompanied by a dualistic anthropology that denies to males the capacity for authentic humanness, and that imagines ways in which women can reproduce without males and can form a totally separate society without them.[1]

It is understandable that some women come to this conclusion. As one contemplates the total history of patriarchy and begins to see all the ramifications of evil done by it, one necessarily goes through experiences of rage in which one concludes that males are to be avoided altogether. It is necessary for any woman who wishes to be authentically autonomous to pass through as least something of this rage. But to pass through it means not to translate it into a total ideology. One needs to come out to a firm ground of autonomous humanity as a female who can continually resist and refuse the snares of patriarchy without confusing this with the humanity of males. One needs to recognize one's own fallibility, one's own capacity not only to be victimized, but also to be victimizer, and, in the mature self-esteem, also be able to affirm the humanity of males behind the masks of patriarchy.

Thus we are not talking here about separatism as total ideology, but as a stage in a process, a stage that is absolutely necessary but not an end in itself, a stage toward a further end in the formation of a critical culture and community of women and men in exodus from patriarchy. We should be clear that when we talk about women withdrawing to collectivize their own experience and form a critical counterculture to patriarchy, for most women this means, at best, a few hours a week taken out of lives lived in the presence of males. Even women who are involved full time in feminist studies, and who are constantly engaged in communication with feminist women, still spent a large part of their lives interacting with males and male culture. This is hardly avoidable in a world in which most of the systems of daily life are male owned and male defined.

Only a very few women will have the desire, much less the means, to try to construct a female producer and/or consumer cooperative where all contact with males is minimized. And even this does not really remove them from many lines of dependency that link them with a male-controlled world. I support experiments with feminist working and living cooperatives as long as one does not succumb to a totalistic ideology that imagines males are going to vanish or wither away and one will not have to come to terms with males as one's fellow humanity.

Women-Church is the Christian theological expression of this stage of feminist collectivization of women's experience and the formation of critical culture. It means that women delegitimize the theological myths that justify the *ecclesia* of patriarchy and begin to form liturgies to midwife their liberation from it. They begin to experience the gathering of liberated women as a redemptive community rooted in a new being. They empower themselves and are empowered by this liberated Spirit upon which they are grounded (the two are not contradictory, since one empowers oneself authentically only by being empowered by the Spirit that grounds one) to celebrate this new community, to commune with it, and to nurture themselves and be nurtured in the community of liberated sisterhood.

How Women-Church might be transcended in a redemptive community of both men and women liberated from patriarchy remains to be seen. I assume that it should happen as the fulfillment and culmination of a process in which Women-Church is one stage. One can see this begin to happen as women shape a sufficiently clarified critical culture so that some men feel compelled to try to understand it on its own terms and not simply to try to ridicule or repress it. What is required for the development of a new cohumanity of men and women liberated from patriarchy is that men begin to critique their own dehumanization by patriarchy and form their critical culture of liberation from it in a way that truly complements the feminist exodus and allows the formation of real dialogue. I assume the name for this liberated humanity would then no longer be "Women-Church," but simply "Church"; that is, the authentic community of exodus from oppression that has been heralded by the traditions of religious and social liberation but, until now, corrupted by reversion to new forms of the *ecclesia* of patriarchy.

However, when I say that women-church is a stage in a dialectical process that must lead on to the cohuman church, a community engaged in liberation from patriarchy, I do not mean that Women-Church only needs to last a few years and then disappear into the great collaboration between men and women. Patriarchy is too old and too deeply rooted both in our psyches and in our culture and collective life to be quickly analyzed, rejected, and then overcome in new unity of men and women. We must think of Women-Church as a feminist counterculture to the *ecclesia* of patriarchy that must continue for the foreseeable future as an exodus both within and on the edges of existing church institutions.

Women-Church means neither leaving the church as a sectarian group, nor continuing to fit into it on its terms. It means establishing bases for a feminist critical culture and celebrational community that have some autonomy from the established institutions. It also means sharing this critical culture and sense of community with many women who are working within existing churches but who gather, on an occasional or regular basis, to experience the feminist vision that is ever being dimmed and limited by the parameters of the male-dominated institution. It means some women might worship only in alternative feminist liturgies; others might do so on a regular basis, while continuing to attend liturgies in traditional parishes into which they seek to inject something of this alternative; and some women might enter into these experiences only occasionally, such as at annual gathering of women pastors or feminist retreats, where women worship and celebrate their community together in the context of these occasional communities.

Only if some groups work intensely and exclusively on imagining an alternative culture in a way that cannot be controlled or limited by patriarchal culture, but also are in dialogue and interaction with women within the institutions who can then adapt and make use of what is being developed in alternative communities, does the possibility of a genuine transformational dialectic take place. One must refuse the institutionally defined options either of continuing on its terms or of cutting off all connection with it and becoming sectarian and hostile to those who are working within established institutions. This sectarian closedness, while it may appear "more radical," is actually the flip side of the demand that one stay in the institution on its terms. Both of these options are intended to cut off the creative dialectic between the exodus within and the exodus beyond the borders that can create real transformation and can, in effect, redefine the boundaries and the content of what it means to be Church.

We cannot quickly terminate this process of developing the feminist exodus and alternative culture and elaborating its autonomous ground, because we cannot assume that this transformation will be quick and easy; we cannot assume that, very soon, well-meaning males will understand and agree, and we can join each other in a new option. This is not to say that there are not many males of goodwill who do wish to understand and who very much wish to join with us. And so feminist theologizing and celebrating our exodus from patriarchy also needs to encourage parallel male groups, as well as mixed gender groups. But, to use the New Testament language, "We do not struggle against flesh and blood, but against powers and principalities" (Eph. 6:12). Many individual males may be ready at least to consider what feminism means for them. But institutionalized patriarchy does not wish to consider this because to do so would mean the dissolution of its structures of power. One can expect from patriarchal institutions and their defenders not only all the old lines of defense but ever new and more ingenious ones.

The feminist critical culture must continue to have an autonomous base precisely so that it can continue to unmask and rightly name these new strategies for the defense of patriarchy. It needs to be ready to face major repression aimed not only against feminist women, but also against their male collaborators, who will be viewed by patriarchy as the worst traitors of all. It is for this reason that Women-Church must form an ongoing commitment to establishing autonomous bases of community and cultural formation that are both in dialogue with the people of the churches, but outside their institutional control. This commitment must last for as long as it takes to defeat patriarchal power totally and transform all of its social and cultural expression; in short, we might say, until the coming of the reign of God/ess.

How did this concept of women-church begin? What are its roots? Perhaps its roots are as old as the idea of Church itself as an exodus community against structures of oppression. Wherever the liberating Church implied that its exodus included women (and it has always implied this), and women themselves identified with it as subjects of their own humanity (as they have, again and again), the seeds of women-church were present. For the very concept of Church as an exodus community that includes women implies an exodus from patriarchy. Women are not authentically included in Church unless Church means a community that seeks to overcome patriarchy as the root expression of oppressive relations between men and women, between generations, and between those who are powerful and those who are weak. Patriarchy means the elaboration of these natural distinctions into sources of privilege and dehumanization. The very concept of the Church as an exodus community from sin and evil, living in hope of redeemed humanity on a redeemed earth, implies the overcoming of patriarchy and its false sacralization as the *ecclesia* of patriarchy.

On the other hand, the explicit recognition that women must define this and must make clear that to be Church means an exodus from patriarchy is very recent. Most Christian women throughout the centuries have fought only for limited rights to participate in the church as it is. Even the first explicitly Christian feminists, such as Sarah and Angelina Grimké in the 1840s, who disputed patriarchal formulations of biblical anthropology and claimed to stand for the restoration of the true order of creation as a community of coequal men and women, only argued for the rights of women to preach in existing churches. Most struggles of women for ordination until the last decade assumed that it would be enough simply for women to have full rights as priests and ministers and then women would really be included. It is only after some decades of women's involvement in ordained ministry and theological education that the limits of the inclusion of women within male institutions and culture becomes evident. Then it becomes clear that we need to take a step beyond this kind of inclusion of women which changes nothing of the structures and cultural symbols of the *ecclesia* of patriarchy. I do not mean to repudiate the gains that have been made by such inclusion. Indeed, these gains are themselves the base that makes possible the new step beyond this type of inclusion to transformation.

American Protestant women have been included in ordained ministry in the past twenty-five years and in the last fifteen years have rapidly increased their numbers in theological seminaries. In many liberal Protestant seminaries women now make up more than fifty percent of the classes studying for the Master of Divinity or ordination degrees. The numbers of Roman Catholic women entering theological education have also greatly increased. This has happened not only at Catholic seminaries, which have been slow to open to women, but also at major nonsectarian theological schools, such as Harvard Divinity School in Boston, Union Theological Seminary in New York, the Divinity School of the University of Chicago, and the Graduate Theological Union in Berkeley. The large participation of Catholic women in such theological schools has largely gone unnoticed. Exactly why they are there and what they plan to do with a theological education which promises so little in terms of paid employment in their church is unknown.[2] In any case, it expresses one side of a major ferment among Roman Catholic women who seek to envision a feminist identity in theological terms and gain the educational and practical skills to do so.

Women-church among Roman Catholic women also has recent historical roots in the dramatic renewal of women's religious orders in America. This has created a strongly autonomous and feminist consciousness among sectors of these women, some of whom remain as members of their orders and many of whom have left their orders but continue to identify with larger movements of social justice having Catholic or ecumenical religious bases. In 1975, this Catholic feminist ferment gave birth to the Women's Ordination Conference, a major effort to work for the ordination of women in the Roman Catholic Church in a way that also implied a critique and renewal of ministry itself. In other words, it was clear that priesthood, as it had been traditionally defined, was symbolically and socially misogynist and hierarchical in a way that women found contradictory to the authentic meaning of Christian ministry. So women really could not be included in ordained priesthood without a fundamental redefinition of the way it was imaged and of the way it functioned.

In the ensuing decade this critique of the patriarchal nature of priesthood has deepened. To some extent this has created a contradiction in the very idea of an ordination conference, since ordination is only part of a much larger goal. Most Roman Catholic women neither can nor wish to be ordained within priesthood as presently defined. The possibility of splits occurred between women working for ordination into a priesthood pretty much as it is, women working to enter ordained ministry and to change it was they entered it, and women repudiating the idea of ordained ministry altogether. This potential split manifests the difficulty of bridging the different moments in a dialectic process of transformation. At the present time it has by no means been resolved. But as the immediate goal of ordination shifted more clearly to working for a larger cultural and institutional transformation, Catholic feminism formed a plurality of groups to express this. The National Coalition of American Nuns, the National Assembly of Women Religious (both of these being older organizations than the Women's Ordination Conference), WATER (The Women's Alliance for Theology, Ethics, and Ritual), Chicago Catholic Women, the Women's Ordination Conference, the Institute for Women Today, *Las Hermanas,* and the Quixote Center all work toward cultural transformation.

These groups formed into an open-ended coalition (not without difficulty and tension!), called the Women of the Church Coalition. In November of 1983, this group put on a major conference in Chicago which succeeded earlier gatherings sponsored by the Women's Ordination Conference in 1975 and 1979, but which also went beyond them. This conference was called "Woman

Church Speaks." It was the first effort to define and to collectively experience a new stance toward being feminists in exodus within the church. It defined a new theological and practical standpoint that intends to claim the authentic theological ground of being church, and no longer to be defined by the *ecclesia* of patriarchy nor to ask for inclusion to ministry or for the right to experience sacramental life in its terms. This assembly of some fifteen hundred people was ninety-five percent Roman Catholic, including somewhat more laity than women religious, a significant shift from the first Women's Ordination Conference in 1975, in which ninety percent were members of women's religious congregations.

There were only a small number of Protestants present and they were divided among many denominations. But these Protestant women banded together and petitioned the conference to recognize the Women-Church movement as ecumenical and not just Roman Catholic. I believe that this is, implicitly, already the case. That is, although the energies of most Protestant women are still absorbed in realizing the opportunities for ordained ministry that have been opened up to them, many such women already know that they need to supplement their struggles for change within their present denominations with an autonomous feminist movement that allows them to retain the critical perspective on patriarchy and on the larger goals of change that all too quickly disappears when one is involved all the time in institutional maintenance. Thus the two groups of women—those who have gained a foothold in ordained ministry and are struggling to change it, and those who have not and look at it from the longer perspective of its misogynist history—need to join together. They form, as it were, two sides of the necessary transformational dialectic, and they need each other.

The Woman Church conference in Chicago was basically liturgical in character. There were large group liturgies including a number of speakers, but these speakers were engaged more in giving sermons than lectures.[3] There were also many small workshops clustered around the three key divisions of feminist praxis defined as "spirituality," "sexuality," and "survival." Under "spirituality" there were workshops on such things as feminist theology, counseling, feminist retreat work and spiritual guidance, and, particularly, feminist liturgical communities. Under sexuality were considered such topics as sexual life style: celibacy, marriage, divorced women, lesbians, single women, reproductive rights, rape, incest, pornography, and prostitution. Topics under survival included women alone and poor with children, women on welfare, violence toward women, surviving patriarchal institutions as church workers, aging women, women refugees, militarism, unemployment, and organizing and networking.

There was a conscious attempt at the conference to model dialogue between racial, ethnic, and linguistic divisions. The conference was completely bilingual in English and Spanish. Conference sponsors made extensive efforts to find scholarships to allow poor women to attend. As a result many Hispanic women attended, including poor Hispanic women from Florida's migrant labor communities and from the barrios of New York. Because they were able to speak in their own language, these women not only were able to address the whole assembly, but to do so with a truly powerful eloquence. Thus it became dramatically clear that the communication between women across the divisions of class and race drawn by patriarchy is not insurmountable if women of resources reach across the divisions and provide the means, while, at the same time, really allowing the space for disenfranchised women to define their own experience.

I would like to conclude this chapter with the sermon I preached during one of the liturgical experiences at the conference. The sermon encapsulates the vision of Women Church that was emerging at this conference. The sermon reflects the high enthusiasm of a congregation that was collectively experiencing the possibility of standing on a new ground as Church together. The address ends by naming certain American Roman Catholic bishops as people invited to accompany us on our journey. The reason for evoking the names of these American bishops (although not the name of the pope, whose name is included primarily for the sake of irony) is because these particular bishops had, in fact, endorsed this conference and had sent contributions to it, so they were named in the conference brochure along with many other organizations, especially women's religious orders, as being among it patrons.

THEOLOGICAL REFLECTION ON WOMEN-CHURCH

What does it mean theologically to be Women-Church? That is what I want us to think together about. How can women, the excluded half of the human race, the excluded gender from the tradition of the Church claim to *be* Church, claim to speak as Church? Is this not, in the most basic sense, schismatic, sectarian, breaking the whole into only one of its parts, tearing the "seamless robe of Catholic unity," as the fathers are wont to say? I would contend today that we as women can indeed speak as Church, do speak as Church, not in exile from the Church, but rather that the Church is in exile with us, awaiting with us a wholeness that we are in process of revealing.

First of all, to speak as Women-Church means we speak to denounce, to cry out against the smothering of Church in the temples of patriarchy. We have a controversy with the representatives of patriarchy who claim to be the authentic spokesmen of the Church. We say that the temples of patriarchy have disfigured and hidden our true Mother and Teacher, and replaced her with a great mechanical idol with flashing eyes and smoking nostrils who spews out blasphemies and lies. What does this idol say? How speaks this monstrous robot of the temples of patriarchy? Let us recall the words that come from its mouth, the deeds that come from its hand.

This is the idol of masculinity, the idol of father-rule. And it claims all the earth as the creation and domain of father-rule. It monopolizes the image of God, claiming that God can only be spoken by the name of Patriarch, can only be imaged in the image of Father-rule. God is Sovereign, King, Warrior, God of Power and Might, who magnifies the rule of the powerful and abases the degradation of the lowly, who gives the scepter to the mighty and teaches the little ones of the earth to cower in fear and self-hatred. This God is not to be imaged as Mother, as Helper, as Friend, as Liberator. It cannot be imaged in the faces of women, or children, of the poor, of the timid and gentle creatures of the earth.

Men are the proper and fitting image of this mighty God, especially powerful men—rulers who command, warriors who kill, judges who punish. These are the ones who are most like God, who most exemplify the image of God. To see them is to see God. To obey their word is to obey the Word of God. To criticize their power, to rebel against their rule is to rebel against God. Women are not in the image of God. In themselves, women can only image that which is degraded, disgraced, that which is to be subordinate, that which is to be ruled over. Women image the body, the passions, the shameful bloody process of birth and death, of finitude and mortality, of corruptibility, of all those foul and stinking limits from which this mighty transcendent masculinity seeks to escape into eternal life and power forever and ever. Women cannot image God, the mighty and eternal One. They are the image of all that is *not* God, of all that must be crushed and reduced to silence so that men can be as God.

Let us hear further the blasphemies and lies of this great idol of patriarchy with its flashing eyes and smoking nostrils, its inhuman mechanical voice whirring out from its internal computer. "Christ has come, the great savior, for us *men* and for our salvation." Who is this savior and from what does he save us? This savior of men comes to free men from birth, from women, from earth, and from limits. This savior can only come in the image of the male. As God can only be imaged as male, as the male is the proper image of God, so the savior too must be male. Woman is misbegotten man, the defective and imperfect expression of the human species. Only the male represents perfect humanity.

In turn, only the male can represent Christ. There must be a physical resemblance between the priest and Christ, and this does not mean that the priest should look Jewish. No, it means that the priest should have balls, male genitalia, should stand erect as the monument of phallic power. Only the male can rise in the phallic pulpit to bring down the seminal word upon the prone body of the people, the women and children waiting passively below to receive it; only the male can confect the Eucharist with this same seminal power. Women are impotent, castrated, lacking in divine seminal power. They cannot act; they can only receive and should be grateful for what they receive.

Let us hear further what deeds come forth from the hand of this idol. "If women are not grateful, they shall be punished. Indeed, they have never been grateful, but have always been rebellious. In the very beginning woman was the cause of all of our troubles. It was she who brought sin and death into the world; she who caused us to lose paradise and to be forced to earn our living by the sweat of our brow. For this reason woman is to be punished through all of history. She is to be silent and to serve us in all meekness, knowing that this is her place and she deserves no better. If she talks back, she is to be muzzled, shamed, and ridiculed into silence. If she will not be shamed and silenced, she will be taught by force." A million women, twisted on the racks of Christian torture chambers, were bound in sacks and tossed into rivers, hung on gibbets or thrown into fires to teach them this lesson of shame and silence. In every minute of the day and night, women scream and stifle sobs of pain as they are beaten, stabbed, and raped in back alleys and in their own homes, to teach them this lesson, this lesson of shame and silence.

Women's bodies should be ever sexually available to those who own them, never sexually available to those who do not own them. Their wombs and ovaries belong to their husbands who impregnant them; to priests and doctors who make the rules of birth and death. Let women not think that they are in charge of their own bodies, that they may decide when to conceive and when not to conceive, when to give birth and when not to give birth. "If a woman dies in childbirth, it matters not, because it was for this that she was created by God." So spoke the great reformer, Martin Luther. And all the voices of patriarchy echo his teaching in ecumenical accord. Pope, patriarch, and prelate join hands in fraternal alliance over the prone body of woman. Solemnly they meet together to agree that woman is no part of their tradition. Her voice is not to be heard from their pulpits; her hands are not to be raised in blessing at their altars.

As Women-Church we repudiate this idol of patriarchy. We repudiate it and denounce it in the name of God, in the name of Christ, in the name of Church, in the name of humanity, in the name of earth. Our God and Goddess, who is mother and father, friend, lover, and helper, did not create this idol and is not represented by this idol. Our brother Jesus did not come to this earth to manufacture this idol, and he is not represented by this idol. The message and mission of Jesus, the child of Mary, which is to put down the mighty from their thrones and uplift the lowly, is not served by this idol. Rather, this idol blasphemes by claiming to speak in the name of Jesus and to carry out his redemptive mission, while crushing and turning to its opposite all that he came to teach. In its hands, his transformative redemptive mission is overturned or, rather, turned back to the ways of Babylon. The *first* shall be first and *last* shall be last. This is the way God made the world, and this is the way it shall ever be. The powers and principalities of rape, genocide, and war achieve their greatest daring by claiming to be Christ, to represent Christ's mission. The Roman Empire clothes itself in the mantle of the crucified and seats itself anew upon its imperial throne.

As Women-Church we cry out: Horror, blasphemy, deceit, foul deed! This is not the voice of our God, the face of our Redeemer, the mission of our Church. Our humanity is not and cannot be represented here, but it is excluded in this dream, this nightmare, of salvation. As Women-Church we claim the authentic mission of Christ, the true mission of Church, the real agenda of our Mother-Father God who comes to restore and not to destroy our humanity, who comes to ransom the captives and to reclaim the earth as our Promised Land. We are not in exile, but the Church is in exodus with us. God's Shekinah, Holy Wisdom, the Mother-face of God has fled from the high thrones of patriarchy and has gone into exodus with us. She is with us as we flee from the smoking altars where women's bodies are sacrificed, as we cover our ears to blot out the inhuman voice that comes forth from the idol of patriarchy.

As Women-Church we are not left to starve for the words of wisdom, we are not left without the bread of life. Ministry too goes with us into exodus. We learn all over again what it means to minister, not to lord over, but to minister to and with each other, to teach each other to speak the words of life. Eucharist comes with us into exodus. The waters of baptism spring up in our midst as the waters of life, and the tree of life grows in our midst with fruits and flowers. We pluck grain and make bread; harvest grapes and make wine. And we pass them around as the body and blood of our new life, the life of the new humanity that has been purchased by the bloodly struggles of our martyrs, by the bloodly struggle of our brother Jesus, and of Perpetua and Felicitas, and of all the women who were burned and beaten and raped, and of Jean Donovan and Maura Clarke and Ita Ford and Dorothy Kazel, and of the women of Guatemala, Honduras, El Salvador, and Nicaragua who struggle against the leviathan of patriarchy and imperialism. This new humanity has been purchased by their blood, by their lives, and we dare to share the fruits of their victory together in hope and faith that they did not die in vain. But they have risen, they are rising from the dead. They are present with us as we share this sacrament of the new humanity, as we build together this new earth freed from the yoke of patriarchy.

We are Women-Church, not in exile, but in exodus. We flee the thundering armies of Pharaoh. We are not waiting for a call to return to the land of slavery to serve as altar girls in the temples of patriarchy. No! We call our brothers also to flee from the temples of patriarchy; we call out brothers Maurice Dingman and Frank Murphy and George Evans; Raymond Hunthausen and Charles Buswell and Tom Gumbleton, and even our brother Karol Wojtyla and all our fathers and sons and husbands and lovers, to flee with us from the idol with flashing eyes and smoking nostrils who is about to consume the earth.

We call our brothers to join us in exodus from the land of patriarchy, to join us in our common quest for that promised land where there will be no more war, no more burning children, no more violated women, no more discarded elderly, no more rape of the earth. Together, let us break up that great idol and grind it into powder; dismantle the great Leviathan of violence and misery who threatens to destroy the earth, plow it into the soil, and transform it back into the means of peace and plenty, so that all the children of earth can sit down together at the banquet of life.

5. The Ecclesiology of Women-Church: Ministry and Community

Constructing a church liberated from patriarchy will require the dismantling of clericalism. To do this we need to understand the utter incompatibility of clericalism with a liberation understanding of ministry. Clericalism is the separation of ministry from mutual interaction with community and its transformation into hierarchically ordered castes of clergy and laity. The clergy monopolize teaching, sacramental action, and administration and turning the community into passive dependents who are to receive these services from the clergy but cannot participate in shaping and defining themselves. An understanding of ministry as originating from the community and continually based in it is suppressed in favor of ministry as "the ordained" who possess a heteronomous power beyond the capacity of the community.

In the official clerical mythology, an ordained priesthood is declared to have been established by Christ (as representative of God), who founded a hierarchy to pass down this divine power in a line of succession. Bishops dispense divine power to priests, and priests, in turn, dispense forgiveness, truth, and divine life to the laity, if the laity submits to the rules laid down by the hierarchy. In this way the entire teaching and sacramental life of the Church is turned into a power tool of the clergy over the people.

This clerical use of the powers of service is not only found in religious organizations such as the Church. We find the same deformation in other service professions such as medicine, psychology, teaching, and social work. In each case clients are made to feel a need that they are incapable of servicing through their own abilities or with the help of friends and peers. Indeed, the possibility of acquiring the knowledge, skills, and implements to do so is removed from access and made available only to those who are going to be the credentialed professionals. Having identified or created a need, people are turned into clients who must depend on a professional to service this need. In the process of receiving help from the professional, clients are progressively disempowered, made more and more dependent on the professional, and made to feel incapable of taking care of this need themselves.

Clericalism is built upon patriarchalism. The basic symbol and mode of the cleric's relationship to a layperson is that of an all-knowing father over a helpless child. The image of the patriarchal husband over the dependent wife is also used to image the relationship of clergy to laity, even though this image, drawn from Ephesians 5 in the New Testament (where it images the relationship of Christ to the Church) is not actually applied in the New Testament to the relationship of ministry to laity, because this hierarchy had not yet emerged in the Church.[1]

What we see in all forms of paternalism and clericalism is the relationship of a dependent adult to a dominant adult being assimilated into that of a child to a male parent. Because the power exercised by the father is presumed to be benevolent and wise, it is psychologically and culturally difficult to criticize it. Deep resonances of childhood guilt are evoked to keep such a relationship in place. The dependent person is made to feel both ungrateful and ostracized for rejecting paternal authority. Thus it is difficult to articulate the inappropriateness of such father-child relationships between adults and to name their function as disempowerment.

The symbolism of Christ as husband and Church as wife, applied to clerical-lay relationships, is an example of such an assimilation of adult relationships into father-child relationships. The "wife" in this relationship is not a peer or partner of her husband, but she is the dependent child-wife of classical patriarchy. The image of the laity as sheep and clergy as shepherds, an image drawn from ancient kingship imagery,[2] is also used to suggest a relationship of a herd of senseless animals to an all-wise guide. The identification of women with the dependent child-wife or sheep who are to be directed by the paternal clergy, functions as a powerful psychological bar to the ordination of women. The image of Christ as father-husband, Church as child-wife, applied literally to maleness and femaleness in the Church, has emerged as a key argument against the ordination of women in Anglican, Roman Catholic, and Eastern Orthodox polemic in recent years.[3] It is unlikely that women will be able to function in more than token ways in the ordained ministry, even in those denominations who have chosen to do so, as long as this patriarchal-clerical model of ministry is maintained.

The disempowerment of the people by clericalism takes place in sacramental life, in teaching, and in church administration. In sacramental life, all the symbols of the life of the community, as a life grounded in the divine and experienced together, are alienated from the people and made into magic tools possessed by the clergy through an ordination that comes from "above." We can analyze this in the various Christian sacraments of baptism, Eucharist, penance and, in a somewhat different way, in marriage.

Baptism should symbolize the overcoming of alienating and oppressive modes of human relationship, and the reunion with one's authentic potential for human life by entering into a community that represents redemptive human relationality. Clericalism instead turns baptism into a rite by which one rejects one's natural life, derived from one's parents at birth, and undergoes a rebirth to transcend that mortal and sinful birth bequeathed by the sexual congress of one's parents.[4] The theological key to the alienation of sacramental life is a quasi-Manichean Augustinianism that divorces nature and grace, creation and redemption. Once grace, or the participation in redeeming life, is defined as beyond nature, it can then be reified as a power possessed only by hierarchically ordered representatives of an institution that mediates this power.

The Eucharist should be the symbol of our nurture, growth, and participation in the authentic human life of mutual empowerment.

Yet it is the sacramental symbol that has been most radically alienated from the people and transformed into a clerical power tool. Classical Catholicism did concede that baptism was a sacrament that could be administered by the laity in a crisis situation when no priest was available. But the Eucharist is the sacrament most rigidly guarded as a clerical reserve and defined as an act that no lay person can validly perform.

The concept of supernatural power, descending from hand to head through an unbroken line of successive ordinations of bishops and priests going back to the apostles, who were in turn commissioned by Christ, focuses specifically on the power to preside at Eucharist.[5] Since the actual sacramental actions of the Eucharist are rather simple, and anyone could learn to do them in an hour, this is obviously not a matter of special skills or expertise. Rather, it is a matter of elevating this simple symbolic act of blessing and giving food and drink into the symbol of the power to control divine or redeeming life, a power that the clergy claim to possess in a way that is beyond the access of lay or merely "natural" human beings.

The logical corollary of this view of Eucharist is that the people cannot ordain their own clergy. If the people do not have the power to consecrate the Eucharist, they obviously cannot confer this power on their clergy. Here Protestant clericalism is more confused, particularly among Baptists and Congregationalists, since they revived the ancient Christian practice in which the local community participates in calling and ordaining the ministry. More clerical Protestant churches reserve this act for the clergy, and episcopally ordered churches declare that only bishops can ordain, since they are the primary exponents of the supernatural power that descends from the apostles through the succession of bishops. But the tendency to reserve the eucharistic actions for the ordained is found in most Protestant, as well as all Catholic churches, and it is the most typical expression of clericalism. Its function as a clerical power tool is seldom analyzed or questioned.

Rites of penance and forgiveness represent another area of the clericalizing of a simple act, in this case, admitting fault and becoming reconciled. Rites of purification were reserved for priests in temple Judaism, but the New Testament speaks of forgiveness as something that Christians should exercise one toward another.[6] But in the first centuries of Christianity, this question of forgiveness was complicated by the issue of apostacy under threat of persecution. Could someone who had repudiated his or her baptism be forgiven and taken back into the Church? Some rigorists would grant no second chance to those who had become traitors to their baptism; others would grant only one forgiveness.[7]

It was also believed that martyrs, or those who had refused to bend before persecution and had suffered for the faith, had acquired unique powers to forgive these weak brothers and sisters. The third-century Christian episcopacy consolidated its own centralized clerical power by wresting the power to forgive apostates from charismatics or martyrs and claiming that bishops alone possessed this power.[8]

Penitential rites developed into a public ritual in which Christians known to have committed various sins would be banished from the Eucharist for a number of years. Only after years of enduring this treatment were they readmitted to communion with the baptized in a public ceremony of reconciliation.[9] The Synod of Elvira in Spain in A.D. 306 revealed the importance of this emerging power of forgiveness as a tool of the bishops' control of clergy and laity. The synod passed a series of canons stipulating severe penances for a variety of sins, many of which allowed for reconciliation only at the end of one's life. The synod is important also for its emphasis on sexual sins, which are considered equally important with sins of apostasy. Since the synod of Elvira was the first to attempt to mandate celibacy for the clergy, a recent study of it has suggested that this was the first example of interconnecting sexual repression of the clergy with control over the sexuality of the laity as a key element in clerical power.[10]

Private penance developed in monastic practices and was then also applied to laity.[11] The private confessional developed as an even more elaborate way of extending clerical control over the life of the laity. Private confession was required yearly to remain in communion with the church, and monthly confession was recommended. Again, enforcing the power of the clergy over the sexual life of the laity became central to the ritual of confession. Not only repression of extramarital relations, but also control of sexual life within marriage, particularly in the forbidding of reproductive self-determination to women, became typical of such clerical control. Many Catholic couples in the 1950s remember their struggles with unworkable regulations on birth control as that of a pervasive power of the priest over one's marriage bed.

Marriage itself is a sacramental rite which traditional Christianity has treated with some ambivalence. Since marriage is the obvious expression of natural community and reproduction, classical Christianity was not sure that it could be a vehicle of the higher or supernatural power of sacramental life at all. For the first eight centuries theologians and spiritual teachers strongly suggested that those who aspired to the fullness of Christian redemptive life should not marry at all or should renounce sex and procreation within marriage.[12] Throughout the Catholic tradition the married were seldom regarded as capable of sanctity, or, if so, only after they had renounced sexuality through widowhood or voluntary separation from the marriage bed. In the ninth century, marriage was defined as a sacrament primarily to put it under clerical control.[13] Even though Protestantism reclaimed a more positive doctrine of marriage as the normal life of Christians, they also followed this classical doctrine of sacramental grace as beyond nature in rejecting marriage as a sacrament. Protestant theology thus further exaggerated the Augustinian split between nature and grace, creation and redemption.

Control over marriage as a sacrament has been a key element in Catholic clerical control of the personal and sexual lives of the laity. Rejection of divorce, and thus the denial of a second sacramental marriage to those whose first marriage has failed, puts large numbers of Catholics, de facto outside communion with the church. Attempting to go through official canonical procedures to annul a marriage and hence obtain a second sacramental marriage subjects both partners, but particularly the woman, to a demeaning examination of sexual life and even bodily parts.[14]

Again, we see here a system of clerical power in which a celibate or sexually repressed clergy expresses enormous need for punitive power over the sexual lives of the laity to whom sexuality is permitted for the sake of reproduction. One finds similar connections between sexual repression, sexual power over others, and clericalism in authoritarian sectarian groups. For example, in the Unification Church, a key element of submission to the power of Reverend Moon and his representatives is submission to strict control over one's sexual life, either by repressing it or else by exercizing it upon command and in ways dictated by the leaders.

The disempowerment of the people educationally is a second essential element in clericalism. The clergy monopolize theological education, removing it to a place inaccessible to the people. Theological education is also developed in a language unknown to the people. This may be either a foreign language, such as Latin, which traditionally the laity and even nuns were not taught, or else, in modern times, a learned jargon that most people cannot understand. Theology is turned into a specialized culture available only to the professional. The people are thus made to feel helpless and dependent on the clergy to interpret the Scriptures and to analyze theological ideas and symbols. Yet the laity are also told that the essence of the faith is simple and easy and is based on a docile acceptance of the rules of life given them by the clergy. So there is no need for them to think for themselves, but only to do as they are told.

Protestantism in the sixteenth century originally represented a major effort to declericalize Scriptural and theological learning. This aspect of Protestantism built upon centuries of populist movements in the Middle Ages in which the unlearned took back the Scriptures and empowered themselves to read them and to teach and preach.[15] This was particularly accelerated in the later Middle Ages with the development of vernacular translations of the Bible and the invention of printing, making copies of the Bible more accessible. However, this declericalizing aspect of the Reformation was contradicted in mainline Protestantism by the fact that its primary leadership came from university-trained teachers. They had imbibed the new exegesis and learning, based on recovery of ancient languages and the beginnings of historical-critical method. It was assumed by these teachers that no one could rightly understand the Scriptures unless they went through the sort of university education that enabled a person to be fluent in the ancient languages.

In Protestantism the clericalism of the university became the new form of clericalism. Not accidently, the clerical robes of Protestant churches are the robes of university professors rather than the vestments of priests. Today, despite remnants of the populist tradition about giving the Scriptures back to the people, Protestantism effectively makes correct Bible interpretation inaccessible to the unlearned. Most importantly, no effective method of lay theological education for older youth and adults is developed to share the tools of historical-critical method and modern exegesis with the laity. So, in a new way, a split culture is created that divides clergy from laity. This leads many of the laity to suspect that the clergy really do not believe the "simple faith" at all, simple faith being identified with precritical literalism. Some of the most rancorous conflicts in contemporary Protestantism, such as that which recently divided the Missouri Synod of the Lutheran Church in the United States, have been expressions of a fundamentalist lay culture, identified with firmness in the faith, that attack a university-based culture of theological education, which the educators had failed to share with the adult laity.[16]

However, fundamentalism also has become highly authoritarian. It is based on the notion that literal belief in a series of magical events and the repression of critical consciousness derived from history and science are the proofs of salvation. Metaphorical and paradigmatic ways of interpreting scripture, which had been well understood before the Reformation, are repressed in favor of a pseudoscientific literalism that interprets events such as the virgin birth as biological "facts."

Roman Catholic basic Christian communities, fed by the rediscovery of prophetic tradition in liberation theology, have recovered today an understanding of populist Bible reading.[17] Even though Roman Catholicism has been, until recently, suspicious of popular Bible reading, the new encouragement of biblical literacy in the Second Vatican Council allowed popular groups to discover Bible reading as a subversive activity, which had made the Bible a tool of liberation of the people from clerical and ruling class oppression in medieval times.

Clericalism in church administration is the third area of hierarchical control over the people. The most hierarchical churches, such as Roman Catholicism, give the laity no effective role in church administration at all. The laity neither ordain nor call their pastors nor their bishops. They are not elected to church councils on a diocesan, national, or international level. They do not participate in decisions governing the life of the church, either organizationally, doctrinally, or financially. The Second Vatican Council tried to change this stratified pattern of church government for a more collegial relationship of pope with national episcopacies, bishops with priests, and priests with laity.[18] But these changes were quickly resisted by the Curia in Rome, which had never really welcomed Vatican II.

At most, there has been some progress at the most popular level, in the participation of the laity on parish councils. But even here, the pastor holds the final decision-making power juridically and so is really only consulting the laity, always able to disregard their advice. Thus even at the parish level, the system remains despotic, even if softened by the personality of certain priests to appear democratic. Because ultimately there is no accountability to the people, this is basically a benevolent despotism, and not true democracy.[19] At the diocesan level bishops have resisted effective participation by the laity and even by priests. In the period after the Second Vatican Council, there was an effort by some priests to develop "priests' unions" that could enter into collective bargaining with bishops as independent organizations.[20] But this was quickly quashed in favor of in-house priest senates controlled by bishops.

Efforts to modify hierarchy at the international level have become even more the targets of Vatican backlash. Councils of bishops called to consult with the pope have been turned as much as possible into rubber stamps for decisions already made by the pope and the curia. Efforts by national episcopacies to develop a genuine collegial structure where the various constituencies of laity, priests, nuns, and theologians would gather in national synods for key decisions of church policy, and even election of bishops, were squashed when this appeared in the Dutch church in the 1970s.[21]

The Vatican strategy has been to use its power to appoint bishops to national churches to undercut any such efforts toward greater autonomy and accountability at the national level. In Holland, dioceses that were already small were further subdivided, introducing right-wing bishops uncongenial to most Dutch Catholics, who undermined earlier efforts toward a national church government. Right-wing bishops, appointed to key sees such as New York and Boston in the United States, have also been an important tool in keeping the American national church under Vatican power.

The most closely guarded secret in modern Roman Catholicism is the late development of this pattern of hierarchical government and its nondominical origins. Vatican power depends on promulgating the belief that the Roman hierarchical form of church government was literally founded by Christ and has been in place, virtually unchanged, from the beginnings of the church, although no one with even the most cursory understanding of church history could possibly believe this. It is significant that, in the recent admonition to the Brazilian liberation theologian Leonardo Boff, under fire from the Vatican Congregation for the Faith (former Inquisition), the primary warning focused on his teaching that Jesus did not found a historical institution.[22]

Liberation theologians breathed a sign of relief that other matters, such as Marxism and views on class struggle, were bypassed in this admonition. Boff quickly consented to retract his offending opinions. But there has been little discussion of why the Vatican regarded such a point about dominical founding of the church institution as the most important issue on which to hold the line against modern liberation theology. Clearly, what they are attacking is any whisper of doubt that Jesus Christ actually founded or intended to found a church institution with the sort of centralized autocratic structure of late nineteenth- and twentieth-century Roman Catholicism. By contrast, Protestant churches drew from the Reformation populist impulse in a way that more decisively declericalized church administration. Protestant churches have also shared an affinity with the democratic developments from medieval parliamentarianism. They have tended to structure their polities in ways that provide for elected lay delegates to regional and national decision-making bodies, as well as to lay councils on the local church level. Protestantism drew from medieval and early modern parliaments a concept of the laity as one of the "estates," comparable to the "commons." This means that the lay delegates are seen a representing the laity as a separate group in the church, rather than clergy themselves being seen as elected representatives of the whole people. This sense of clergy, laity, and bishops (in Episcopal churches) as separate orders tended to clericalize lay professionals and so, in a new way, prevented a real sense of the whole community consulting together as the base of church government.

This, of course, varies between the more hierarchical Protestant churches and the more congregational ones, where lay boards can sometimes hold a commanding influence over the local pastor. But the church institutions in general, perhaps like all human institutions, toward creeping clericalism, even in churches with a strong tradition of congregational power. The tendency is to delegate power to a few representatives of the laity in a way that disempowers the lay community as a whole. This is as much the responsibility of the laity as it is a result of the clergy's hunger for power. Many laity think of ministry as services that they pay professionals to provide, rather than a ministry in which they themselves must be involved on an active basis. Thus many prefer to cede decision-making power to the clergy and to the few laity who come forth to take church offices, rather than claiming collective responsibility.

Women-Church, as a community of redemption from pa-

triarchy, must take responsibility for a more radical reappropriation of ministry from clericalism. It must understand ministry as
the articulation of the community whereby the community symbolizes its common life, communicates it to one another, and engages in mutual empowerment. One place to start dismantling
clericalism is by theologically reenvisioning the relationship between nature and grace, creation and redemption. Women-Church
is rooted in what has been defined recently as "creation-based
spirituality."[23] This means that the grace of redemptive life is not
beyond nature, but grace or divine gift is the ground of being of
nature. Creation is itself the original grace or blessing. Evil and
alienation arise from the distortion and twisting of our true natures. One might say that the "first lie" is the naming of differences among humans of race, gender, and ethnicity as "good and
bad," "being and nonbeing." Upon this lie, power systems are
erected that further injustice and oppression and block our access
to authentic humanity and authentic relationships with our bodies, the earth, and God/ess. But this alienation does not mean that
authentic human life and relationship to the divine transcend
nature. It simply means that authentic life is contrary to these
alienated systems of injustice that falsely claim to be "nature."

The loss of contact with our good potential does not mean that
it is unavailable or has been destroyed. It means that we rediscover
our authentic capacities by turning around or changing our minds
(metanoia) to reencounter the true capacity for human life that
always remains with us and upholds our existence, even if we
"forget" or lose touch with it. *Metanoia* is not easy, because the
powers and principalities of alienated existence socialize us into
false consciousness.

A reencounter with original blessing is experienced as a leap to
a new state of being that breaks the hold of false power upon our
spirit. In this sense, it is psychologically experienced as something
beyond our present state of existence. But, at the same time, we
know it to be the most natural thing in the world, since, when we
encounter original blessing, we immediately recognize it as our
true selves—something with which we are already gifted, not

something we have to strive to achieve. This is the truth to the Protestant and Augustinian teaching about salvation by grace alone, without the works of the law. But this doctrine must be freed from the distorting, dualistic anthropology that identified the law of our alienated state with nature.

All the functions of church—the repentance by which we enter it, the Eucharist by which we commune with it, and the ministry by which we mutually empower it—are simply expressions of entering and developing a true human community of mutual love. The greatest possible distortion of church is to identify it with an ecclesiastical superstructure that distorts our true nature and has been created by competitive and oppressive hierarchicalism. The whole concept of ministry as an ordained caste, possessing powers ontologically above nature and beyond the reach of the people, must be rejected. Instead, ministry must be understood as the means by which the community itself symbolizes its common life to itself and articulates different aspects of its need to empower and express that common life.

If we understand clericalism as the expropriation of ministry, sacramental life, and theological education from the people, then women-church—and indeed all base Christian communities—are engaged in a revolutionary act of reappropriating to the people what has been falsely expropriated from us. We are reclaiming sacramental life as the symbol of our own entry into and mutual empowerment within the redemptive life, the authentic human life or original blessing upon which we stand naturally when freed from alienating powers. Theological education and teaching are our own reflections on the meaning of reclaiming our authentic life from distortion. Ministry is the active praxis of our authentic life and the building of alternative bases of expression from which to challenge the systems of evil.

We should then think of our baptism as the process of *metanoia* or turning around by which we see through the ideologies of alienated life and get in touch with the original blessing, which is the true ground of our being. This turning around may be experienced as such a gradual process that one has no sense of when it began, or it may be experienced as such a decisive breakthrough that one can date the day and the hour when new perception dawned. But the argument among Christians as to whether it is a decisive event or a gradual and ongoing process is a false one. It is both event and process. As long as the powers and principalities of alienated life are still in place in the world, it must necessarily be an ongoing and unended process.

Because true human life is communal, and not one of isolated individuals, this *metanoia* is appropriately expressed by entering into a community that affirms authentic life as the principle of our common humanity together. Needless to say, many people today, who have some intimations of this process of conversion, are searching for a community that represents the communal dimension of this life. But they are unable to find such a community, except perhaps in supportive affinity groups. Many lack even this community base and thus hover on the edge of thinking themselves unacceptable or mad.

Most institutional churches not only fail to become communities that nurture liberated being, but they in fact disallow it. They instead represent the sacralization of inauthentic, oppressive systems of power. Thus for many people, the process of conversion becomes also the process of leaving the church. This makes it all but impossible for many people who have left the church in the process of claiming their authentic humanity to recognize their process as conversion. Indeed, without a community that affirms redemptive life and names it as authentic humanity in communion with God/ess, such conversion remains truncated, lacking in a positive sense of newness of life.

The dismantling of clerical concepts of ministry and church organization might suggest an anarchism that rejects all leadership. Groups that reject patriarchal models of leadership often go through a pathological phase in which any talent or expertise is rejected and those who have such talents are sabotaged for exercising leadership. Confusion reigns in which nothing gets done because people cannot agree on delegating tasks. But once this phase is worked through, it becomes evident that dismantling clericalism does not do away with authentic leadership based on function and skills. This means that the community itself decides what expressions of liturgy, learning, and service it wishes to engage in as expressions of its growth in community life. It then becomes fairly easy to delegate various tasks to people who have the readiness to undertake these tasks.

A ministry of function, rather than of clerical caste, can allow the true plurality of the ministerial needs of the community to be defined and met. It can also draw on many people in the community who have a variety of skills or gifts and thus activate their gifts as ministries. Full community life needs a variety of enablers. Lumping all ministry into one ordained caste means that many of the community's needs go unmet, since no one person possesses all these skills and gifts. A congregation needs at a minimum: (a) liturgical creators: poets, artists, and choreographers who can bring forth in creative expression the community's symbolic life; (b) teachers who know the history of religious ideologies and their relationships to various social systems and can help the community critically reflect upon and reconstruct its inherited symbols; (c) administrators who are skilled at organizing and developing the material resources of the community; (d) community organizers who can critically analyze the different structures of social oppression and organize community power to make social change; (e) spiritual counselors who have deep wisdom in the inner life and its relationship to life with others in community, and who can be guides in this journey.

Every community that is engaged in a full community life should be engaged to some extent in each of these areas of liturgy, education, and theological reflection, organizing its own material and human resources, committing itself to some social praxis, and deepening its inner life. Communities need to find among their own members, or call into themselves, persons who have particular skills in these various areas. Such persons are designated as enablers or ministers in these various areas, but not in order to do these things for others, who will then simply passively consume their services. Rather, the function of the ministers is to be the helpers and teachers who equip the community itself to engage in these various activities.

One might say that the more the poets, artists, and choreographers liturgize, the more the teachers teach, the more the administrators plan, the more the community organizers generate effective action, and the more the spiritual directors deepen the inner journey, the more the whole community should feel empowered in these various capacities. Although no one need feel competent in all these areas, everyone should feel that they are learning to participate in these various spheres. Increasing numbers of the community members should become able to take leadership in one or more areas of the community's life. Thus it becomes more and more possible to rotate many roles, since many people feel somewhat competent in one or another area and are able to grow through exercising leadership in that area.

A community based on the ministry of function values and supports the talents of its members and knows how to empower these talents and to use them to develop the talents of others. Presiding at the liturgical gathering, which involves blessing the eucharistic symbols and administering them to others, requires the fewest special talents. This came home to me dramatically a few years ago when I had been asked to preach at Old Cambridge Baptist Church. The pastor of the community, a woman, asked me also to share in blessing the Eucharist and administering the cup to the community. She did not ask me if I knew how to do this; she simply assumed that I could do it without instruction. Having watched this act on many occasions, I readily joined in saying the words of blessing and then administrating the cup. It occurred to me as I did so that this particular ritual act hardly required long training or special skills! Yet it is precisely this act which the clerical ministry has most stringently reserved for itself to express its exclusive power to transcend the community.

Other skills of ministry, however, require great skill and much preparation. To be a creative poet and liturgical creator; to be able to teach from long acquaintance with the meaning of the symbols of a tradition; to have the tools of social analysis and community organizing; to be able to lead people into the inward journey of spiritual development: all these ministries are based both on special talents and on careful discipline to develop them. A community desperately needs these ministries to develop the fullness of its own life, but these are the skills too often missing in its ordained ministry. Yet it takes neither special gifts nor long training to bless and break bread and hand it to others, or to play other roles in the liturgy that have been planned by others. Thus it is actually the performance of these roles that could be most easily rotated on a regular basis. Communalizing these roles would say clearly that the use of sacramental roles as a power tool of the leadership over the people has been overcome.

The most important reason for designating one person to play a leadership role regularly for a certain period of time would be to symbolize the unity of the community. This may be an important reason to join leadership in liturgical and pastoral functions. But it should be understood that liturgical presidency does not mean that this person possesses a power to create redemptive life and mediate it to others, but rather that she or he sums up the redemptive life of the community in its symbolic unity. To closely associate several other members of the community on a rotating basis with this person, not only in distributing, but also in blessing the symbols of sacramental life, may be one way both to unify and to communalize this act.

I have been speaking here of a community that has a full life. The term *full* implies that a certain variety of functions makes up church life. One lives a full church life when all these functions are carried out within one's life. One of these functions is collective study. Study can take several directions. It may mean exploring the historical and sociological meaning of past traditions and symbols. The goal here is to deconstruct these symbols in their alienating form and reconstruct them in a form that reconnects with original blessing and authentic life. Study might also include consciousness-raising sessions where people collectivize their experience of patriarchal oppression and engage in critical analysis of it.

Study might also include other kinds of groups who are concerned more with psychological and spiritual counseling and the deepening of personal self-knowledge in the context of social relations. More specialized types of study groups focus on understanding a particular social problem, such as world hunger or homelessness or violence in the family. Such a group would explore the factors that cause and perpetuate social problems and the ideologies that legitimate them, as well as tools for criticizing and changing them, and commitment to carrying out some social praxis.

A second aspect of full church life is liturgy—collective prayer and celebration. I mention this second rather than first because it seems to me that a community must have some idea of its own identity as a witnessing community with some social praxis before it can begin to symbolize its collective life authentically. Most church liturgies are dead precisely because they have no real reference point in a community that has a collective sense of its identity and a social praxis that expresses that identity. It is important to have liturgical creators with special knowledge of the meaning of symbols, poets and song writers and artists who can give creative expression to the aspirations of a community. Yet all this is dead if the community lacks an authentic praxis as a reference point for liturgical expression.

When this praxis is present, although creative artists may express it powerfully, it is often enough to express it very simply and artlessly. I remember a summer spent in Mississippi in 1965, during the height of the civil rights struggle in the American South. An ecumenical group of Christians was based at the former Beulah College. Each person was involved intensively in some organizing work, often at great risk to personal safety. Once a week the group would assemble and express its gathering together and sending forth again in prayer. This took the form, as I remember, simply of sitting in a circle, recounting something of the events of the week, holding hands, and uttering some spontaneous prayers in the style of a Quaker silent meeting. Although there was little liturgical art to these assemblies, it was probably the most powerful liturgy I had ever experienced, precisely because the community reference point it expressed was so intense and powerful.

Third, a community needs to engage in some social praxis that makes it a community witnessing to a new option for human life beyond the circle of its own membership. This means it needs to focus on some key or representative issue around which it can mobilize its resources to be a force for change in society, even if only at a local or neighborhood level. It is important that communities be realistic about this choice and focus on some particular thing that they can accomplish effectively. This means that, even if the issue is a very big one, such as world hunger, they need to define some aspect of it that they can address concretely. They also need to be willing to limit themselves to only one or two particular issues (depending on the size of the group and the possibility of having several subgroups with different concerns), and not be pulled in a dozen directions at once.

Evils in the modern world have grown both so plural and so large in scale that justice communities have a tendency to become paralyzed, attempting to address everything in theory and yet doing very little in practice. This leads, finally, to frustration and withdrawal. By developing an analysis that understands the interconnections of different issues and then choosing a particular issue upon which to work, communities can find the appropriate fit between their resources and the possibilities of concrete action.

Finally, a community may decide to collectivize its life together at some level. This may take the form of a regular meal together. It may take the form of collectively sharing a part of their financial resources, which would be used for its social praxis and not simply for internal maintenance. It might be invested in either collective work projects, which might employ several members of the community, or collective living, with members sharing a common household or group of households. The extent to which a community wants to collectivize its life together should be carefully analyzed. Too much collectivization of all aspects of life—living in one family, engaging in community employment—creates a sectlike group that interacts too little with other networks. But certain kinds of collectivization—sharing housing, pooling money —can help overcome the contradictions of isolated and fragmented nuclear or single-parent households that make it difficult to focus on anything other than personal survival. When a few members collectivize their lives and others do not, the first group may appear as an ingroup that stands apart from others. Thus these dynamics need to be discussed in order to clarify what a group is trying to accomplish by bringing together particular parts of their lives.

This summary of different aspects of community life—study, liturgy, social praxis, and collectivization of work or family—does not mean that every group that wishes to identify itself as engaged in liberation from patriarchy need put all these aspects together in one community. Those who wish to underline the dialectical relationship between women-church as an autonomous community and the historical church institution may choose to limit their participation in women-church to a study group or a worship group that accompanies their participation in another worship assembly. Such persons would also connect themselves with a local church or other structures of a particular historical institution and try to feed the ideas generated in the women-church study or worship group into gatherings of the historical church.

Other persons may focus on some particular social praxis, such as work in a battered woman's shelter or a drop-in center for homeless women. This social ministry would then become central to their critical analysis of patriarchy and work for change. Some people working on projects might also join a feminist study group that is not made up of the same people as the social ministry, but that serves as a forum for reflection on this and other struggles for change. Some may also attend a feminist liturgy and/or a more traditional liturgy. In other words, instead of unifying all these activities in one community, richness may be found in experiencing them in a series of different communities, each of which links up with different, but perhaps overlapping, networks of people in a particular region who are working for social transformation.

Thus, when speaking of different aspects of community, one

speaks in an ideal way of church as one community where all these various aspects would flow from one coherent vision. But this demands a high level of intentionality that is both difficult and dangerous, although it can be rewarding as well. It is dangerous because the more a group brings together many aspects of its life into one system, the more tendencies it has toward closed-minded sectarianism and the misuse of power. So communities should engage in careful reflection on each new step toward communalization to be sure that personal initiative and autonomy is safeguarded.

In actuality, in the present transitional and fragmented situation, most will probably choose a variety of communities. For some people it may actually seem better not to put all their eggs in one basket, but to express different aspects of their communal life and transformational vision through different groups, thus interacting with a diversity of networks that reach out in various directions.

The second part of this book, which focuses on liturgical expression of women-church, does not presuppose one pattern of community. Rather, a variety of liturgical occasions are examined that could be developed and used by networks of people who have a variety of patterns of life together, ranging from study and liturgy groups within local churches affiliated with historical denominations, to autonomous communal-living groups, and many variations between these two extremes.

II. LITURGICAL LIFE AND WOMEN-CHURCH: HEALING OUR WOUNDS; CELEBRATING OUR LIBERATION

6. Women-Church Liturgies: Basic Perspectives

This section of the book will explore a variety of human occasions for liturgy or ritual action by which a community that engages in liberation from patriarchy might sacramentally express this journey and thus deepen and empower its own life processes. The liturgical ideas developed here are drawn from many layers of the Mediterranean and Western religious traditions: nonbiblical ancient Near Eastern tradition, Jewish tradition, and Christian tradition. I draw explicitly and consciously on all three layers of the tradition upon which Christianity itself stands not in order to be eclectic or syncretic. These words suggest an arbitrary bringing together of traditions that have nothing intrinsically in common. But these three layers of tradition have, in fact, been built one upon the other. One does not fully understand Christian traditions of the weekly Sabbath, the church year with its seasonal celebrations, or the patterns of crisis and renewal found in Holy Week and Easter without understanding the Jewish ritual week and year that underlie this Christian pattern. And similarly one does not understand the Jewish pattern without understanding the ancient Near Eastern pattern upon which it built.

The ancient Near Eastern patterns of our worship life were founded originally upon ritualizing the nature cycle of the seasons of the year. The cycle of the year ran from harvesting to new planting to harvesting again, from rainy season to the searing heat of drought that brought death to the vegetation of the parched land and back to the redeeming moisture that promised new life. This yearly cycle was experienced as the basic arena for the drama of death and new life. The nature cycle became, for the cultures of the Eastern Mediterranean, the sacrament of the struggle for life against death, for ordered cosmos against disordered chaos. In the symbolic sequences of the seasonal year, ancient peoples experienced ritually their basic struggle between the ordered world of settled towns and planted land, with its precarious hold on security and prosperity, and all the social and natural forces that could break in at any time, destroying the carefully constructed water channels, wiping out the planted fields that would feed the people for the coming year, even trampling the structures of human habitation and massacring the people or laying waste to towns and villages. The foes of this ordered world were both the precarious forces of nature—floods, droughts, high winds—and also hostile tribes who looked enviously upon the prosperity of a settled group.

In the rituals of the yearly cycle the community lived through these vicissitudes of threat from natural and human foes. They experienced themselves devastated by these foes and then rescued from them, with prosperity and security restored, peace and justice again firmly established in the land. Through this mimetic exploration of their life conflicts, they sought to strengthen and empower themselves in the real conflicts. By symbolically living through their own defeat and rescue, they assured themselves that they could survive real devastations and that life would win over death.

In this cycle of the year, ancient religion also saw the drama of the gods. In the dying vegetation and the parched land, and then the coming rains and new green rising from the earth, they saw mirrored the death and rising again of Lord Baal, who represented the powers of fertility in land and water as well as the king, political representative of the people. In the capacity of nature to fight back and overcome these threats of death and destruction they saw the Maiden Anath, warrior goddess who fiercely attacked the enemies of Baal and defeated them, midwifed his rebirth from the dead, and reunited with him in the Sacred Marriage that restored order to society and prosperity to nature.[1]

Upon this ancient cycle of year celebrations the Hebrews in the first millennium B.C. overlaid the commemorations of their historical story: the Exodus from bondage in Egypt, the march through the desert, the giving of the Law at Sinai, entrance into the Promised Land. The ancient Hebrew ritual year evolved over more than a thousand years and drew on preagricultural strata of nomadic sheepherding rites in festivals of new moons and sacrifices of the firstlings of the flock. In Canaan some of these rites fused with agricultural rites drawn from Canaanite practices. The three most important ritual periods of the year are all built on key agricultural festivals, but each has been reinterpreted to become a commemoration of Israel's historical story.[2]

Passover, or the Feast of Unleavened Bread, is rooted in the celebration of the barley harvest in which the new grain is made into massoth, or unleavened bread. This is interpreted as a commemoration of the flight from Egypt, the unleavened bread becoming a symbol of the bread made in haste for the journey. The Feast of Weeks or Pentecost is the festival of the wheat harvest, in which the loaves of bread made from the new grain are waved at the gods in thanksgiving. This becomes the commemoration of the giving of the Law at Sinai. Finally, the Festival of Booths is a thanksgiving celebration for the grape harvest. It is characterized by the construction of huts from leafy boughs, representing agricultural huts in which the community would live and feast during the harvest.

The Feast of Booths became elaborated as the turning point of the year. It is preceded by the Day of Atonement, rooted in ancient Near Eastern ritual of New Year when the sins of the community are ritually purged. The Feast of Booths which follows is interpreted as the tents in which Israel dwelt during its sojourn in the desert. The New Year also became associated with messianic expectations—the defeat of the enemies of Israel and the reenthronement of Yahweh as king—anticipating that ultimate reign of God when all evils will be defeated and God's justice and peace will dwell on earth.

The Hebrew historical story adds another dimension to the Canaanite story of rescue from cyclical vicissitudes of nature and periodic incursions of foes. It suggests a new kind of God, a God who makes a historical choice for a nobody people, a people in slavery under the great empire of the ancient Near East. This God adopts this nobody people and makes them "his" people, rescues them from slavery, covenants with them, and guides them on a journey to a new land. For the Hebrews, God does not just participate in and ratify the periodic conflicts of life and death, but God intervenes and transforms the patterns of social reality. In alliance with this God, who overthrows existing social patterns and creates new ones, the Hebrews looked forward, not just to periodic rescues from foes, natural and social, but to a decisive rescue from evils, a definitive establishment of peace and justice in the land.

This change will come about, not simply through petitioning the gods, sacrifices, or mimetic participation in divine struggles, but through ethical response of the people to God. God commands justice and righteousness. Historical vicissitudes now are interpreted as expressions of God's righteous wrath and punishment of Israel for wrongdoing and unfaithfulness. Restoration and new hope hinge on repentance and collective moral struggle to obey the commandments. Thus Hebrew religion introduces into ritual new elements of historical transformation through ethical action. However much feminists may wish to prescind from certain aspects of this vision—its patriarchalism and ethnic exclusivism, its punitive view of God—our fundamental hope for historical liberation, and indeed the hope of all modern liberation movements for moral transformation of society, is rooted in this Hebrew redefinition of religion.

Upon this pattern of the ritual year Christianity overlay the commemorations of messianic expectation and fulfillment. The October New Year festival of Hebrew faith, with its expectations of the kingdom of God, became the Christian beginning of Advent, the preparation both for the birth of Christ, and also the expectation of the return of Christ in the final redemption of history. The Hebrew Passover became the Christian Easter, and the Feast of Weeks or Pentecost, when Jews remembered the gathering of the *ecclesia* of Israel at Sinai, became the Christian celebration of the foundation of the Christian church with the dispensation of the Holy Spirit.

Christianity also proved very facile, not only in assimilating and transforming the Hebrew year cycle, but also in assimilating many key festivals and holidays from the cultures that it proselytized in the Greco-Roman world, then the world of northern European paganism, and then in new continents, such as Latin America. The Roman celebration of the Winter Solstice, the festival of the birth of the invincible Sun, a festival adopted by the Roman emperors to celebrate their power, became the Christian Christmas, the birth of the messianic King. In Coptic Egypt the three agricultural festivals of sowing in mid-December, harvest in mid-May, and vintage in mid-August became a cycle of Marian feasts, thus supplanting the old Mother Goddess who used to bless these days with the Christian Mother of God.[3]

The commemoration of the Annunciation and, later, the Immaculate Conception in December, the dedication of May to the crowning of Mary as Queen of Heaven, and the mid-August celebration of the "falling asleep" or the Assumption of Mary became the core of a cycle of Marian feasts that would be carried into Europe. One could elaborate an endless list of such takeovers and transformations of older festivals, both into the calendar of the Church universal, and also into the feasts of local regions.

Although Christianity developed many historical commemorations in its calendar, particularly of the historical events of its Lord, and also of Mary and the saints, the core of the Christian calendar is eschatological or messianic. It builds upon the future dimension of Hebrew hope. But it also sees itself as already empowered by the advent of this final deliverance of the world from sin and death, even while still looking forward to its future completion. This element of a foretaste of things to come is the key dynamic of Christian ritual. One cannot understand the yearly reenactment of advent expectation, leading to the messianic birth, the Lenten preparation for the final passion and resurrection of Christ, and the feasts of Christ's ascension into heaven and the outpouring of the Holy Spirit "in the last days," unless one understands that these are not simply remembrances of events completed in the past. Rather, they look back to experiences which themselves point forward to that final time when the bondage of evil and mortality is lifted from humanity and from all creation and the fullness of God's reign of peace is established.

In the organization of liturgical ideas found in the following chapters there is a conscious reappropriation of all of these three strata of our tradition. From our Hebrew heritage we particularly reclaim sensitivity to historical injustice and the longing for historical redemption that tended to be spiritualized or suppressed by a Christian misinterpretation of the belief in a salvation already embodied in a Christ of the past. Christian liturgical consciousness can be greatly enriched by new contact with the Jewish heritage of Passover, the Sabbath meal, the hallowing of Sabbath, and even by limiting consumption according to rules of kosher. This particularly becomes possible because of the renewal of liturgy, study, and intentional community among American Jews.[4]

Like Christian basic communities, these Jewish renewal communities closely interconnect prayer and study with struggle for social justice. From them the ancient Jewish rites have taken on new life, reconnected with the issues of social justice of today. This movement has also been the setting for a birth of Jewish feminism which is religious and not simply secular.[5] Jewish feminists are struggling with great pain, but also with deep faith, to explore the deep roots of the traditions that have so long marginalized them. They seek authentic ways to transform these traditions into words that speak to women's fullness of humanity as Jews.

The liturgies of this book also reappropriate the hallowing of nature and cyclical time of ancient pre-Judeo-Christian traditions. Remembering that the word *pagan* does not mean "devil-worshipers," but rather the religion of the "paganus," the rustic or country people, we must affirm the need for a new rapprochement between the historical and eschatological rituals of the Jewish and Christian traditions and the religions that have remained close to nature and have sought to fit humanity into the rhythms and disciplines of nature. Biblical religions have exaggerated the trajectory of linear, historical time and transcendent finality. This has resulted in teaching contempt for the wisdom of the cycles of renewal in nature and the "pagani" who reverence their relationship to these cycles.

However much historical religion has taught us to stand out from nature and to look forward to deliverance from nature, the actual existence and survival of humanity is still based on the cycles of nature. Decomposition of vegetation creates rich soil; evaporation and precipitation bring life-giving moisture from which grows the new harvest. Day and night, the seasons of summer and winter, the turning of our planet and the movement of the planets around us—these are the processes that sustain our life. To deny these rhythms is to deny the concrete foundations of our continuing life. To teach contempt for these interconnections is to create a culture and technology that has brought us perilously close to destroying the very earth, air, and waters that sustain our being. By reclaiming in our ritual observance the natural cycles of night and day, the lunar cycle, the year cycle, and our own life cycle from birth to death, we also accept our finitude and our chief historical task, which is to sustain human and natural life in harmonious interconnection in our time, so that it can be passed on in a viable form for our children.

Although it affirms the pagan or country-folk layer of our tradition, the understanding of liturgy developed here differs from the pagan feminist movement of recent years (although I believe that this movement is motivated, not only by concern for the liberation of women from sexism, but also for the reharmonization of humanity with nonhuman nature discussed above). The chief difference between pagan feminists and the perspective of this book is that such feminists wish to dissolve entirely the Jewish and Christian stratas of ritual and religion and return to a religion of nature renewal. They explore Jewish or Christian traditions only to recover the pagan or matriarchal strata that they see lying hidden behind it. They regard the religion of nature renewal, centered in the great Goddess of nature, as sufficient to provide both a religion fully affirmative to women, and also a religion that will reconnect us with nature.

This dissolving of historical and messianic religion into nature religion results in several problems, in my opinion. First of all, it lacks a sense of real historical roots, of a historical community whose accumulated wisdom one values, even as one criticizes it and seeks to renew it. Whatever religious teachers of ancient nature religion may have once existed, they have long since been cut off. The actual connections between these earlier religions and their later survivals are cloaked in obscurity. Modern pagans tend to exhibit an impatience with historical accuracy in these matters, a desire to make do with myths that serve their present purposes, such as an easy equation between worship of ancient Goddesses and a feminist religion that empowers women as autonomous persons.

But, more important than these unhistorical tendencies, is a romanticism that suggests that a world without sin can be easily recreated simply by reverencing and celebrating nature cycles. In a sense nature religion refers us back to a prefallen world of "dreaming innocence" where happy men, women, and children live in harmony with nature. It is a world in which historical responsibility has not yet ejected Adam and Eve from paradise. One may question whether, in some primordial era, life for humanity with nature was ever so happy. But, in any case, our historical consciousness, as well as the rise of systems of oppression and alienation, have long since ejected us from this state of innocence. To try to go back to it in purely ritual or cultural ways is escapist.

If we are really to reclaim a healthy relationship between our minds and our bodies, between humans and nonhuman ecology, we cannot shirk the task of historical responsibility. We need not only to imagine such a harmony in cult, but to do it as a historical, ethical task of dismantling the systems of oppression and shaping new ways of living between human groups, and between humans and nature. It is not that several exponents of Goddess-nature religion lack a sense of ethical protest and social action, but rather that their theology proclaiming that "all that is is good" lacks an understanding of historical sin and a willingness to be accountable for social systems of evil.[6]

Situated in the context of acknowledging our split from good nature and our struggle to reshape our relationships to the beings around us, the celebration of vernal equinoxes or lunar turns ceases to be cultural escapism and becomes a part of an ethical faith of critical judgment and historical hope. Such nature celebrations become a prophetic sign of a once and future world that we must come to know again in order to survive on earth. Thus it seems to me that the historical and messianic strata of our tradition are vital to a realistic understanding of where we are. But we must transform these historical and messianic dimensions of our faith from contempt for the natural cycles of renewal. We must convert them and so convert ourselves to the tasks of shaping a just and sustainable universe, a world without rape, genocide, and war.

The following presentation of liturgy is divided into four chapters, which represent four different sequences of liturgical observance. No single community will appropriate all these liturgical occasions on a regular basis, but rather, they may select those which are meaningful and relevant. Authentic liturgy, which is done with real intentionality and meaning, requires a lot of energy. This means that it takes considerable time both to prepare it and also to assimilate it afterwards. Liturgy means lifting up a particular human moment and making it paradigmatic of all moments, focusing in the mimetic reenactment of this moment all our accumulated fears and hopes for this type of event. We should properly be both exhilarated and exhausted when we have truly worshiped. The fact that most people experience liturgy as dead is the terrible testimony to the way it has been both routinized and transformed into a tool of alienation and domination.

The first sequence of liturgies in Chapter 7 focuses on the formation of church as a community of liberation from patriarchy and all oppression. These liturgies do not belong to the natural life cycle, although they have sometimes been confused with them by adding life-cycle rituals to the Christian sacraments. Thus baptism is confused with birth ritual, confirmation with puberty rites. Rites of marriage, the anointing of the sick, and and the *viaticum* for the dying all refer to the life cycle rather than the Christian community. The rites of entrance into and building up of liberated community is messianic, rather than based either on historical commemoration or cycles of nature. It represents our break or conversion from historical systems of oppression and the embarking on redemptive life. It points ahead to a new future of which we have a foretaste in our experiences of conversion and liberated community in the present.

Christianity has been wrong in identifying the formation of church or messianic community with rejection of nature or rejection of Jewish tradition. It is not past human tradition or nature that we reject when we enter messianic community, but rather their corruption. We reject the corruption of human tradition into a tool of alienation and oppression. In rejecting ideologies and social systems of oppression, we also reclaim our true relationship with somatic reality, with body and earth and with the Great Goddess that sustains our life in nature. For Women-Church, entry into messianic community means, particularly, conversion from patriarchy as ideology and social system. It means the formation of a critical culture and community of liberation from patriarchy. It means our nurture and growth in our new and true humanity as women, and as men and women together.

The second sequence of liturgies in Chapter 8 deals with rites of healing from particular occasions of violence and crisis. These rites would be performed once only, since they are shaped for a particular community or person and related to a particular act or history of violation. Each rite would be unique to that person, time, and situation. Yet, since unfortunately these types of violations occur all too frequently, the rites of healing sketched here need to be developed in many communities for many hurting people in our midst. In fact, sometimes it is not easy to decide which liturgy belongs to rites of healing and which to life-cycle rites, since these acts of violence, and the need for healing from violence, occur so regularly in most of our lives.

I have, for example, included divorce as a rite of healing rather than a life-cycle rite, not because divorce is not all too expected in many of our lives, but because it is always experienced as failure and hurt, the final acknowledgment of a long history of violation and hurt. It thus contradicts everything that we hope for when we enter into committed community. I also put in this section a rite for the coming-out of a lesbian or homosexual, because in homo-phobic society this event cannot be seen as the simple affirmation of a God-gifted sexual preference, but as the repudiation of past guilt and repression that have denied one's nature and a crying out against the homophobic society that has created this guilt and repression.

The rites found here have been entirely neglected by Christian ritual, and indeed all historic ritual, as far as I know. And yet they represent occasions where people most desperately need rites of healing. Not only has the church neglected such rites, but, in promoting sexism and homophobia, it has directly contributed to the violence from which people seek healing. This is why violated people generally turn away from—if they are not actually turned away from—the churches on these occasions. They seek out thera-pists and other professional healers. While professionals are im-portant at these moments, they are often beyond the financial means of violated people, and and they also fail to address the deeper dimensions of such crises—the sense of being alienated from human communities of meaning and of being rejected by God. Thus healing from violence demands a deeper liturgical di-mension that enfolds violated people in a supportive community of meaning and assures them of divine love.

These rites of healing include liturgies for a woman who has been raped, for a woman who has been battered, and for a woman or man who has been the victim of childhood battering or sexual abuse. One might also ask about rites of forgiveness of and recon-ciliation with a repentant batterer, rapist, or abusive parent. I will not explicitly develop liturgies for this category, but it should not be excluded from consideration. In our present society, victims of abuse in childhood or even in adult life are often shut up for many years in fear and shame. Only after a long period of time, when they have actually separated from the abusive situation, are they able to acknowledge its existence and come to terms with the deep levels of their hurt. Thus many of these rites will be retrospective, the final stage of a long journey of coming to terms with violence in one's past.

I also include in this section liturgies of healing from miscarriage or from abortion. Although the first has been seen as natural, and the second as a sin or crime, both of these terminations of pregnancy leave women with deep feelings of loss. Life has begun and has been snuffed out again, either by forces in one's body beyond one's control, or else because the pregnancy itself was unwanted and could not be sustained personally and socially. Both of these situations, in somewhat different ways, call for healing, for reconciliation with oneself and others, for ritual closure that allows one to continue one's life.

One might also include rites of healing from less intimate forms of violence, such as violence that occurs suddenly from strangers, or even violence from natural disasters, such as fire. Although these kinds of violence are less likely to give the victim traumas of internalized self-blame, as is the case with rape and family violence, they nevertheless leave us deeply off balance, not able to trust the streets or the security of our homes or environment. Thus I might have included rites of healing from mugging and robbery on the street, from burglary or burning of one's home, and from the loss of a job, when there is no immediate expectation of new employment.

The third sequence of liturgies in Chapter 9 contains rites of the life cycle. These rites are intended to carry us through our life from birth to death. I start here with the naming celebration for a newborn child (rather than with the actual birth of the child, which I take to be a rite in which the mother, rather than the child, is the primary subject). This rite would include not only giving the child the name by which it will be commonly known, but also a second name that will be revealed to it at puberty. The child would also be signed with the hopes of baptism, although not fully baptized, since we take baptism to be a rite that must be appropriated fully only by an adult who is making a conscious choice of conversion from systems of evil. The naming celebration would also include forming a parenting community for nurturing the child.

The second major life-cycle rite is puberty, where sexual maturity is celebrated. Since in our modern societies there is a big gap between sexual maturity and social maturity, these rites would celebrate the beginning of a new stage of more mature, but still dependent social life in adolescence. It would allow the female particularly to claim menstruation as a positive mystery of her life-creating potential. It would be a time of instruction in, as well as affirmation of, dawning sexuality, how to appropriate one's own sexuality and one's sexual relations to others responsibly. As the young person takes the major step of social maturity by leaving home to live at college or in one's first apartment, a rite of coming of age might be appropriate. This could be more of a party than a formal rite, a time of good wishes and also of assurances of some elements of continuing help from the familial community.

Marriage is the next major stage in the life cycle, when two people come together to build a relationship that will be a new family for them. We include here both the conventional marriage celebration of a heterosexual couple, who may or may not intend to have children, and also of a homosexual couple who, although they will not create children together, may still become parents, either of children from a previous heterosexual relationship or else of children by adoption or artificial insemination. Although in fact many such family covenants break down in our society, the basic hope of such a covenant celebration is that it is permanent, in the sense of being a lifelong covenant with another person that will provide one with a second family through the adult years and relate one to the next generation that one helps to parent, biologically and/or socially.

Pregnancy and the process of birth become the drama of that next stage of life in which new life is created from the sexual and social union of a couple. In recent years women have learned new exercises to help prepare their bodies for birth. The husband also has been involved in these exercises to prepare him to assist at the birth. Although these have been treated as medical exercises, they are in fact a new kind of rite where males are linked into the processes of pregnancy from which they are biologically excluded. Men learn to identify with the pregnancy and therefore also become bonded with the coming child. The revival of ancient birth chants that assisted the birthing mother (linked with the Mother Goddess as creatrix) would be a significant way to empower the woman in labor by linking her with the religious meaning of her labor of creation.

Next we consider various liturgies to guide us through key moments of transition in our lives. These include embarking on a new career, leaving one employment to return to school to prepare for a new career, or moving from one house and neighborhood to a new house and neighborhood. Women who have accepted the traditional pattern of domestic work and child raising might need a rite that would affirm a mid-life turning point, when they have decided to go back to school or seek a job outside the home to develop other aspects of their potential. With fewer children and greatly extended life expectancy for women, no woman can look upon child raising as a lifelong vocation. To affirm the transition into a new stage of life for women (and eventually for men and women as coparents) as a normal part of the life cycle would help us recognize this fact.

Finally, we consider those rituals that guide us on our course, not toward new growth and increase, but toward decrease, cessation of fertility, cessation of paid employment, sickness, dying, and death. In our rites of the life cycle we need to acknowledge that human life is not all movement from strength to strength, ever onward and upward. Such a model of endlessly self-actualizing life, promoted by middle-class male psychologists, implicitly denies our finitude and mortality. The expectation that every day in every way we should be getting better and better leaves us feeling inadequate at every stage of life, constantly repressing our real insufficiencies. But it particularly leaves us unprepared for the decline of our physical and social powers, for sickness, for the incurable limits of our potency, for dying.

By accepting our finitude, we can also learn to live fully at whatever stage of the life cycle we are in, rather than feeling alienated from our present time because it is not yet or will never be the full realization of our ideal self. We can also learn to exchange old physical potency for new pleasure in lessening business, the cultivation of wisdom, the passing on of inherited wisdom to grandchildren. Our present society has truncated the life cycle into two stages: childhood and adulthood, the first understood as dependency on parents and the second as independency or self-sufficient autonomy. This not only fails to link adults, particularly adult males, with parenting, but it entirely cuts off a proper appreciation of old age as a social as well as biological state of life. Once the elderly cannot take care of themselves, we hide them away in retirement homes so that we will not have to witness their declining physical powers. Thus we deprive both the elderly and children of the mellowing appropriate to the autumn of life. The elderly become bitter and crochety, or confused and senile, or else they try to emulate a new adolescence in retirement. They are not allowed to gather up the threads of their life in a meaningful whole, to pass on their learning to the new generation of children, and thus to prepare themselves for that final surrender of their powers to the Great Goddess, the divine matrix out of which we have all come and to whom we must all return.

In the fourth sequence of liturgies in Chapter 10, I discuss seasonal celebrations. I recognize here four different seasonal cycles of our lives: the cycle of the day and night, the cycle of the week, the cycle of the month, and, finally, the cycle of the year. In the cycle of day and night I include blessings for the rising of the sun and the beginning of day, and also blessing for the setting of the sun and safekeeping through the night. We also have a blessing for meals, particularly the meal that a community or family may take together in the course of the day. This offers us an opportunity not only to give daily thanksgiving for food, but also to reflect on the ethics of our consumption. Some new understanding of kosher eating—avoiding the foods of oppression and exploitation—would be a way of connecting our daily food with mindfulness of the just distribution of food to all other people and the sustaining of the food-making powers of earth.

The second seasonal cycle of the week is not based on a natural cycle at all, although it may have originated in marking the quarters of the moon. But the week, hallowed particularly in Hebrew tradition, is preeminently a work and rest cycle or a social cycle. In biblical thought, the week also mirrored the cycle of historical time and redemptive time, the six days of God's work in creating the world and the seventh day of rest. Later Jewish and Christian thought also linked the week to messianic time, to the six millennia of world history, the time of struggle between good and evil, and the final Sabbath at the end of history. For Christianity, the seventh millennium of the world history, the thousand years of messianic blessedness that will culminate historical time, has been superseded by the eighth day, the time of eschatological blessedness, in which we are delivered not only from evil, but from death itself. Thus Christians observed as their day of worship and rest, not the seventh day of historical justice, but the eighth day of eschatological deliverance, which they observed on Sunday, the first day of the week, although it is actually not in time, since it falls outside the time sequence of the week.

In the celebrations of the week I lift up two particular elements. First, the Sabbath or Sunday meal becomes a way of gathering family and friends for at least one meal together, in lives that are often too busy and fragmented to have a daily meal together. Even for families who do share a daily meal, this would be a time to eat together in a particularly unhurried manner, to spend several hours eating and talking around the table. It is appropriately begun and ended with blessings and special prayers and symbols that lift up its meaning, both as a time of rest, and as a time of expecting a final rest from toil and deliverance from historical evil. Each "week-end" meal should become a foretaste of the messianic banquet.

Secondly, the Sabbath or Sunday needs to be reclaimed as a real day of rest. This is not meant in a repressive sense as a time of grim quiet, as in a puritan Sabbath. Indeed, we assume that prayer is never grim in Women-Church. Rather, it is a time to affirm that living, not work, is our real goal. We work to live; we do not live to work. Work itself should become increasingly unalienated and expressive of creativity. But, in unredeemed time, we still live in an age where much of the work by which we live is alienated work. Sabbath or Sunday becomes the time to celebrate unalienated work, those activities by which we recreate ourselves, whether that be conversation, lying about and reading, playing games, or even puttering in our gardens, workshops, or kitchens. Since we live in a world of addiction to work, it takes great discipline and commitment to refuse to work on Sabbath or Sunday. We need to make firm resolutions to do nothing on the Sabbath except what we really enjoy doing, for only in this way can we re-create ourselves and the world. Without the regular celebration of the Sabbath, the world sinks totally into alienation. Through learning to keep the Sabbath, we may redeem the world from alienation, or, as the rabbinic tradition puts it, if Israel can keep fully two Sabbaths in a row, they would bring in the messianic age.

The monthly cycle is particularly a ritual cycle of women, since it links the lunar cycle of the moon with the monthly cycle of their bodies by which their powers of life making wax and wane. This may include a new moon celebration, as well as some way by which women mark the monthly processes of their bodies. In patriarchal culture, menstruation, the ebb time of the cycle after it peaks in ovulation, has been particularly turned into misogynist contempt for women's bodies. Thus new ways of affirming the period of bleeding and cleansing of the body from the old potency, in order to make way for the new, are particularly good for women.

The architectural design for a Women-Church center (pp. 147, 148) pays particular attention to this dimension. A dry and a steam sauna, a hot whirlpool, and a cool plunge offer a repertoire of experiences of cleansing and renewing of the body. One might imagine women on a regular basis taking one or more days out at this time of the month to be more meditative, to take a walk alone or with a few friends, to withdraw into oneself and come into contact with the deep layers of one's embodied mind. When women bond together in close community, they often synchronize their menstrual cycles, so we might suppose that, in Women-Church, women who are closely connected with each other would find themselves having the same monthly cycle. They might then observe this time of withdrawing together, communicating in the conversation circle after or during saunas and dips in the pool. Women-Church also provides several small retreat houses with a bedroom, a living room, and bath, where a woman might get away by herself for a few days to read, study, or meditate.

The fourth cycle of seasonal celebrations is the yearly cycle. As we have shown in the earlier part of this chapter, the seasonal cycle of the year is the oldest way of developing ritual that links humanity with the renewal of the earth and the Gods. In our tradition the planetary cycle of the vernal and autumnal equinoxes and the winter and summer solstices, the cycles of planting and reaping, heat and cold, dry and wet seasons (which vary in the regions of the earth), have been the hinges upon which the yearly cycle of life, death, and new life has been hung. Upon this framework the Hebrews overlaid their cycle of historical commemoration and the Christians their cycle of eschatological observances.

In this sketch of possible annual rites, we do not wish to choose between the natural, the historical, and the eschatological, but to experience consciously all three layers of this heritage. The four turning points of the yearly calendar are still midsummer and midwinter (the summer and winter solstices), and midautumn and midspring (the autumnal and vernal equinoxes). On this four-season plan we also connect key historical observances, both the foundation points of our historical tradition, such as Passover in the Jewish calendar and Christmas, Easter, and Pentecost in the Christian calendar. We also lift up in each season a key moment of observance of a great historical tragedy, both remembering the tragedy itself and also pledging ourselves never to let such a thing happen again. In the fall this rite focuses on the burning time, the history of the holocaust of women, not only those killed as witches during the time of the Inquisition, but also the whole of patriarchal history which has turned women's lives into a burnt offering to reproduce the species.

In winter the historical commemoration might focus on the December 6 remembrance of the martyrs of El Salvador, the four women martyrs, the thousands of unnamed Salvadorans, and the martyred Archbishop Romero. This might be more appropriately a rite for U.S. Americans and Latin Americans, rather than for peoples less connected with the tragedy of Central America. Other nationalities might choose to focus on South Africa or some other region. But we envision this remembrance as dealing with the issue of colonialism and the tragedy of exploitation of poor peoples of the earth for the profits and wealth of the few.

On April 19 we turn to the remembrance of the Holocaust under the Nazis, recalling the six million Jews and the millions of others who died in that great massacre of modern times. This is also a time to dedicate ourselves to stopping new massacres and genocides of people by the infernal technology of modern life. Finally, in summer, on August 6, we commemorate Hiroshima Day, repenting not only of that horror by which two whole cities were incinerated in the first testing of atomic bombs on human flesh, but also the inauguration of the nuclear age with its demonic nuclear arms race that may incinerate us all. Summer is a time to celebrate the life powers of earth, the growing of the new plants for food, the warm days and lush fields of vegetative bounty. This it is also a time to dedicate ourselves to preserving our mother, the earth, and all human, plant, and animal life that depends on her, from the final holocaust of fire that would scorch all flesh, fill our soil, air, and water with deadly radiation, and blot out our sun.

In addition to these four pointers of historical memory and recommitment to life, we also have rites appropriate both to the natural and to the messianic significance of each season. In the autumn we mark the time of new beginnings, the New Year of both the Jewish and the Christian liturgical calendars. Judaism made this a time of corporate penance, a time of purging the community of its sinful deeds. Christians have dropped the rite by which the Church as a whole repents, and they created instead a Lenten season of repentance that focuses primarily on individual purgation and renewal. I suggest here a rite of repentance for the sins of the Church. Here Christians would remember their historic sins against Jews, against "heretics" or religious deviants, against other races, against women, and against the poor. Some may prefer to locate this rite at the beginning of Lent, or on Ash Wednesday, thus setting a tone for a corporate, as well as an individual, meaning for the season of penance.

Fall is also a time for recovenanting celebrations, appropriately following a rite of repentance for the sins of the Church. Recovenanting means that communities of liberation recommit themselves to each other and decide how they will make these commitments real in the coming year. Fall is also the time for harvest celebrations, feasts of plenty, and thanksgiving for the fruits of the earth. Along with harvest celebrations we should also recognize the many people who do not enjoy such prosperity but go hungry through the combined disasters of destruction of nature and social distortion. These two observances of plenty and of want should be related but not combined, because there is a time to be sober about the starving and also a time to enjoy and celebrate plenty. The feast of plenty not only allows us to be grateful for our own prosperity, but also allows us to imagine a world where all have plenty, rather than one in which the prosperity of some is built on the impoverishment of many.

Winter is the time of both winter solstice and Christian holidays. I suggest that these two should be distinguished, rather than confused, as they have been. The winter solstice celebration is a pause in the time of coldest days and shortest hours of light, particularly for peoples in northern climates. The decorated evergreen tree, covered with bright lights, lifts up the hope for the rebirth of the sun which from this point will grow again into lengthening days and the promise of new greenery with the return of spring. It is a time of festivity, gift giving, and parties. Related, but not confused with it, is Christmas, the memory of the child born in a stable and the hope for the birth of the messianic child of the new humanity delivered from bondage to evil.

Springtime is the most intense season of the ritual calendar, since overlaid upon it are the rites of nature renewal, historical memories of deliverance from slavery, and messianic hope of final deliverance from sin and death. It begins with Ash Wednesday, leading into the Lenten season. Forty days of fasting and preparation become a time both of trimming off the winter fat from our bodies (for those in affluent nations and classes), and also *metanoia* or turning around of our minds. It is a wilderness period for throwing off our attachment to idolatries of power, wealth, and fame, and reconnecting ourselves to the true foundations of creation and new creation. In Christianity it has also become a time of renewing adult catechumenate, preparing for baptism or confirmation at Easter.

Celebration of Passover at the vernal equinox is also the time to remember past deliverance from slavery and to become again the people of promise, committed to delivering all people from slavery into the promised land of our earth. Several kinds of seders might be chosen during this period. There are more traditional seders, new more universalist seders of liberation, and also seders of reconciliation between estranged peoples, such as the Seder for the Children of Abraham that was intended to bring Jews and Palestinians (and Arabs) into a commingling and sharing of their antagonistic and mutually exclusive stories of victimization and hope.[7]

Stations of the Cross on Good Friday have become an important time of ritual marches for social justice. In the downtown area of major cities (this works particularly well in Washington, D.C., but it is possible in other major American cities, and probably other capitals of the world), places symbolizing the issues of injustices, where peoples of the world are being crucified today, are marked out on a map within walking distance of each other. A march is then organized from station to station, with rites of remembrance of the particular evils at each stop on the march.

The Easter liturgy in its renewed form—its dramatic birth of the new fire in the midst of darkness; its rehearsal of the creation of the world and the prophecies of liberation, redemption, and community; its blessing of the baptismal waters by imitating the rush of the divine Spirit over the primal waters at creation and the lowering into them the paschal candle; the welcoming in of new members to the community in baptism and confirmation; the fruit of a renewed adult catechumenate; and finally the paschal Eucharist—is so powerful that liturgical creativity has nothing to add, but only to use its talents to bring out the prophetic and inclusive meaning of this great rite of deliverance from bondage to sin and death.

The occasion of Pentecost, in which Judaism celebrates its founding in the giving of the law, and Christianity its foundation in the dispensation of the prophetic Spirit of the messianic age, is an appropriate time to focus on the meaning of salvific community —both the disciplines by which we need to walk and the prophetic Spirit that must inspire us. For Women-Church concerned with a prophetic ministry including women and a church committed to liberation from patriarchy and all oppression, it would be a good time to reflect on and renew that vision of ministry and community. The commissioning of ministers, particularly for special ministries of enablement, might take place at this time.

Summer is a quiet time liturgically. It is a time to descend from the intense memories and hopes and to cultivate our gardens, to live in ordinary time. I suggest several celebrations that would in different ways focus on our responsibility to care for the earth. One might be a summer solstice celebration that would exorcize the demons of pollution from our earth, air, and waters and plant the tree of life. The ritual might then continue into the night around a bonfire that signifies the light of the sun that lingers far into the night on this longest day of the year, with feasting and dancing under the open sky. A second observance in summer is Hiroshima Day on August 6, which I have already mentioned.

In perusing the following four chapters, with their various liturgical ideas, it is important to keep in mind that it is in no way my intention to provide a prayer book with fully developed rites that can simply be repeated. In some cases very few actual prayers are provided, but instead only suggestions of symbolic actions or themes from which liturgies could be generated. In other cases more developed prayers, chants, songs, and symbolic actions are presented. But, in either case, the intention is primarily to interpret the meaning of these occasions from which liturgy might come forth.

Any group interested in developing a liturgy around such an occasion needs to enter into its own process of reflection. It should ask, Does this ritual express the meaning of this event or not? What are the key themes about this occasion that emerge from our own experience? Only after having worked through the group's own interpretive stance with some depth can a liturgy that is truly contextual grow. Thus what follows are not rites to be performed, but a compendium of ideas and resources from which groups might create their own work of liturgy. This must happen in communities who are engaged in their own journey of exodus from patriarchy and formation of liberation church. In this context they can decide how they want to represent these processes of liberation to themselves in order to empower and celebrate their ongoing journey.

7. Creating Women-Church: Rites of Community Formation

In this chapter I discuss liturgies that midwife the formation of Women-Church and nurture its growth. In these liturgies a community of women or of women and men shape and develop their life together as a community of liberation from patriarchy.

COVENANTING

FOUNDATIONAL COVENANTING

When a group of people decides they wish to gather together to form an exodus community from patriarchy, they should first spend some time together thoroughly discussing the meaning of their action, theologically and ecclesially, and setting goals together. This might take the form of evening discussions over several weeks, culminating in a covenant-forming retreat where the kind of community they want to form is agreed upon and celebrated. Discussion should include questions like these: Do we want primarily a discussion group or a consciousness-raising group? Will we share our stories and reflect on our personal experience? Will we try to study the structures of patriarchy and locate our experience in a more systemic way? Should we also become a counseling and support group for one another in our personal problems? Should we become a theological study group? Do we want to become a worship community? What kind of liturgical life do we want, how often would it take place, and how would the liturgies be developed?

Another question that might be discussed is the relationship of the group to the historical church institution. Some persons may want the group to be a full liturgical community. Others may want it to supplement their attendance at a church affiliated with an established denomination. Some may be profoundly alienated from historic Christianity, needing expressions of religious community that depart radically from it. Others may see the group as a house church in continuity with their membership in the historic church. It should be possible to affiliate with the group from a variety of perspectives. But it is important to talk these differences through in depth in order to establish the basis of the group's common life.

A third area of discussion should be life style commitments. Do the members want to share some part of their money to fund community projects? How do they want to organize responsibilities? Do they want to have a regular community meal? Do they want to live in community together, sharing housing? What areas of life do they want to keep autonomous, and what areas do they wish to collectivize? Do they want to commit themselves to certain disciplines? Here the Shakertown Pledge, with its commitments to an ecologically sound life, simple living, world citizenship, and occupational accountability, might be a starting point for discussing specific commitments.[1]

Finally, the members should discuss how they want to engage in particular projects of social witness. Should this take the form of a specific project that the whole community would support, both financially and with their own participation, or would this mean sharing and supporting projects in which members are already involved with other groups? As the community decides what sort of study, worship, and action elements it wishes to incorporate in its life, organizational plans can be developed. Tasks can be defined and particular people selected to take responsibility for various roles. The discussion time should result in a credal statement about how the group members understand the church they plan to form together and its organizational design.

COVENANTING CELEBRATION

A Book of the Covenant can then be created. In this book are entered the basic credal statement and description of the theological vision of the community. The organizational design of the community will also be specified: who will take responsibility for what tasks during the first year of the covenant. The covenant celebration might begin with a renewal of baptism (or first baptism for those who have not been baptized or do not feel they can identify with their former baptism). In this ritual the group recites the Exorcism of the Powers and Principalities of Patriarchy, signs one another with water and oil, and shares the eucharistic cup of milk and honey (see baptismal rite). The community then recites together its credal statement.

The community reads its commitments from the Book of the Covenant, and all members enter their names in the book. If the community is large enough that it feels certain people should be selected for particular roles as coordinators, teachers, community organizers, or liturgists, the names of these persons can be called out, and the community will lay hands on each in turn, commissioning them for their particular job for that period of the covenant. The covenant celebration ends with the community members passing the peace and linking arms to sing a final song.

A community covenant should last for a specific time period, such as a year. This means that periodically the community will renegotiate its covenant, perhaps in the fall, when many people begin a new year. Each year the community would again spend some time in retreat. They would decide whether they want to change anything in the previous covenant. Have their theological ideas evolved so they need to alter elements in the creed? Do they want to change elements in the community organizational plan? Do particular people want to bring forth proposals for particular projects or commitments? What are the necessary tasks and who will do these tasks for the coming year? These new decisions are entered into the Book of the Covenant. The retreat concludes with a recovenanting rite. The creed is read together, new decisions are read from the Book of the Covenant, and all enter their names in the book for this year. New leaders are commissioned.

BAPTISM

Baptism signifies a decisive turning away or *metanoia* (changing of one's mind) from the powers and principalities of personal and systemic oppression. It means not only that we personally reject these powers in our minds and hearts, but also that we break the hold of these powers over our lives. We need to recognize that the powers of evil go beyond our conscious control. They have entered into the deep layers of our unconscious, so we continue to accede to them without realizing it. They are expressed in political, economic, and social systems that we neither control nor can entirely escape, as long as they continue to exist. So our exodus from the powers of patriarchy is a continuing journey, both inwardly to our own consciousness, and outwardly as a social struggle. Baptism signifies our disaffiliation from patriarchy and all its claims to social necessity and divine legitimacy, and our commitment to a new order.

Traditional theology has recognized both an objective and a subjective side of baptism. The objective side is God's liberating grace, which is given to us as an unmerited gift from beyond our historical nature and which transforms the self into a new being in communion with God. The subjective side is the process of personally appropriating baptism by making this journey of *metanoia* and transformation meaningful in one's own life.

Catholic and mainstream Protestant churches have emphasized the objective side of baptism. They have believed that it could and should be administered to infants and children, since it is a divine gift beyond one's own powers to choose and to change oneself. Mainstream Protestants have also encouraged the subjective appropriation of baptism in a conversion experience that takes place as one approaches adulthood. Sixteenth-century Anabaptists, or radical Protestants, rejected infant baptism. They stressed the personal conversion experience as the basis of baptism and thus discounted the validity of any baptism imposed on infants or children before they themselves are capable of repenting as a voluntary decision. For Anabaptists the rite of baptism had no efficacy of its own, but it rather expressed and proclaimed one's conversion experience.[2]

The Anabaptist view of baptism was based on a theological anthropology that affirms the essential goodness of the self. Anabaptists rejected the Augustinian tradition of original sin as a state of depravity into which the infant is born as a result of the corporate sin of the human race, and which is transmitted to the child through sexual reproduction. Anabaptists believed that the good human nature, grounded in the Holy Spirit, is still present. Alienating forces are at work in the world, but the capacity to choose good and evil is intact, and so it is possible to repent of sin as an act of personal choice. God's gift of grace and personal choice are not mutually exclusive, as they are in the Augustinian hierarchical theology of nature and grace, but grace and free will work together.

This is also the theological anthropology of this book. Conversion and *metanoia* are experienced as a power that breaks in from beyond our past situation, empowering our transformation. But the transcendence of grace is not beyond the human nature given to us in biological birth. Rather, it is beyond cultural consciousness and the systems of unjust power that have shaped us. We have been socialized in patterns of culture designed to justify patriarchy and to make it appear natural and divinely ordained. In this sense conversion, whether happening gradually as a slow waking up to a larger and better self, or in a dramatic moment of insight, is experienced as beyond one's past historical self. But this does not mean it is beyond our natural potential. Rather, transformation is possible precisely because it is grounded in our original and authentic nature and potential.

Conversion is breaking free of the alienating and oppressive socialization that has distorted our consciousness into accepting the normalcy of victimization. Conversion is a leap to a new consciousness that renounces the ideologies that sought to justify these systems of oppression and seeks an alternative world where truthful and good relationships prevail. In a sense, one can speak of it in the Augustinian words as "breaking the bondage of the will,"[3] but not in the sense that one's original free will was abolished and no longer exists, but rather that one's free will had been put into bondage by socialized mystifications. In conversion, one's will breaks free of this bondage and exercises decisive choices against systems of oppression and falsehood.

This means that, as the Anabaptist tradition asserted, the decisive rite of baptism should take place as a proclamation of adult conversion. It is only then that the full reality of baptism is existentially present. This does not mean that one can routinize it in some particular age such as late teens and demand that everyone experience conversion on schedule. In our society, young people in their teens are not usually ready to make genuine adult decisions of faith. In the early twenties at the earliest, when young people are sufficiently emancipated from parental dictates, can they begin to shape their own understanding of life. For most people a genuine conversion experience probably takes place even later, in the period of older adulthood, when conventional *personas* shaped by socialization break down and people begin the process of more authentic individuation. Even though some may experience decisive moments of insight that turn around their whole lives, conversion is still always part of a growth process, a clarifying of important values in life, and a journeying into fuller appropriation of those values.

Traditional churches have displayed an excessive desire to take control of people's lives from infancy. This means that the process of growth in converted life is identified with conventional socialization into patriarchal values with a Christian veneer. This leaves no real place for adult *metanoia* and disaffiliation from unjust ideologies and social systems. Therefore, deep rethinking of conventional socialization is typically identified both by the church and by the individual as "leaving the church." To understand the church as the community of liberation from patriarchy, and baptism as the decisive change of consciousness by which one disaffiliates with patriarchy, one must locate the ritual expression of *metanoia* in adulthood. Thus the rite of baptism is this liturgy will be geared to the adult turning point in one's consciousness, since the churches we have inherited have confused patriarchy and Christianity.

This does not mean that, as children are born into communities of people committed to the journey out of patriarchy, there might not also be a rite in which such a child is signed with the hopes of baptism. But the rite of signing (which might take place at the same time as the naming ceremony for a new child) would not be understood as the completion of baptism. Rather, it would be understood as claiming the child's life for the journey into freedom, with the understanding that the child itself would have to own and appropriate this claim at some time in the future when it has become a self-determining adult.

RITE OF BAPTISM

Baptism might be preceded by a period of reflection of several weeks. During this period the person seeking baptism would reflect on the meaning of this turning point in their consciousness and life commitments. Several people with skills in theological and social analysis might act as guides in this process. The person would enter into reflection on the meaning of the cultural patterns from which they seek liberation. What are the roots of those patterns? How have they shaped one's own life? How have they shaped our social institutions? What does it mean, realistically, to seek to disaffiliate from them and commit oneself to the journey into freedom? How will this change one's manner of living, one's relations to others, one's vision of the future?

As a result of this period of study and reflection, the person seeking baptism would develop a statement of faith that interprets theologically the meaning of this conversion experience. How does conversion affect one's relationships to ultimate reality, to society, to nature, to oneself, to the future? The initiate would also develop a life history that would contextualize the meaning of conversion in terms of one's own past and future. The initiate might also choose a new name or a new interpretation of a given name to fit the emerging identity.

The community would assemble in a semi-circle around the person to be baptized. They ask the initiate what her (or his) new name is. The initiate reveals the new name and its meaning, and the community welcomes the person by this name. The initiate then reads her (or his) life story and statement of faith. Together, the community and the initiate stand and recite a litany of exorcism from the powers and principalities of patriarchy. One person holds a candle during this rite, and a bell is rung at the conclusion of each statement of exorcism. Such a litany of disaffiliation from patriarchy might go as follows:

— Powers of corruption of our humanity, which turn males into instruments of domination and shape women to be tools of submission, begone!

— Powers of militarism, which drain our money and resources for weapons of destruction, while withholding food, education, and medical services from the poor, begone!

— Powers of domestic violence, which assault children, women, and the weak and elderly in the home and hold them in bondage to fear and self-hatred, begone!

— Powers of violence in society, which lock up each home against the others and make us afraid to walk outdoors at night, begone!

— Powers of racism, which make us believe that only those who look like ourselves are valuable, and which prevent us from seeing and loving the human personhood of others who appear different from ourselves, begone!

— Powers of wealth and exploitation, which give leisure, luxury, and power to the few, while leaving the multitude in poverty and in hard, uncreative labor, begone!

A bit of salt is placed on the tongue of the initiate with the words: "Let your eyes always see the truth and your lips always speak the truth."

A basin of water is then brought with a towel, or, if there is a pool of water available, the community would process to it. Water is poured three times on the head of the initiate. Or, if a pool is available, the initiate descends unclothed into it and is submerged three times. With each pouring or submersion, these words are spoken:

"Through the power of the Source, the liberating Spirit, and the forerunners of our hope, be freed from the power of evil. May the forces of violence, of militarism, of sexism, of racism, of injustice, and of all that diminishes human life lose their power over your life. May all the influences of these powers be washed away in these purifying waters. May you enter the promised land of milk and honey and grow in virtue, strength, and truthfulness of mind. And may the oil of gladness always anoint your head."

The initiate rises from the waters and is clothed in a white garment. Their forehead is anointed with oil and a candle is put into their hands. A brightly embroidered stole is put around their shoulders. The baptized is then led in procession back to the celebration circle.

Following the baptism, the new community shares a Eucharist of milk and honey. A cup of mingled milk and honey and sweet cakes are blessed with the words:

This is the loaf of the beloved community, which had been scattered in the world of patriarchy and now gathers together into a new people to anticipate a new world liberated from oppression. This is the cup of salvation, the taste of the good land flowing with milk and honey, which is our true and promised home.

The loaf and cup are given first to the baptized and then shared by the whole community.[4]

The liturgy ends by exchanging the kiss of peace and singing a final song, while the community stands with linked hands. The community then has a party.

RITES OF RECONCILIATION

Much of the understanding of sin in patriarchal religion is inauthentic. It has adopted myths of the origin of sin, such as the stories of Eve and the apple, which blame the victim and serve to justify patriarchal oppression of women as deserved punishment for women's fault in the "fall of Man." The biblical and historical role models of female saints and sinners also serve to model masochism and to repress female power and critical thinking. Women are blamed for rape and for prostitution, rather than being seen as the victims of a sexually violent and pornographic culture. It is the woman, not the male partner, who is "taken in adultery" and stoned. The Gospels begin to criticize this unjust trashing of women by expressing leniency and forgiveness toward women stigmatized as prostitutes or adulteresses, but this direction is quickly reversed by a male ascetic Christianity hostile to female sexuality.

Any discussion of the meaning of penance and reconciliation in Women-Church must begin by naming sin correctly and disaffiliating from false definitions of sin that justify evil and blame the victims. These structures of patriarchy were not invented by individuals living today. They have been built up over many millennia and have become entrenched in social institutions and cultural ideologies. So the first task in the right naming of sin is to demystify these social institutions and their cultural ratifications.

Women, although they have been the primary victims of patriarchy, are not thereby only innocent victims. Nor is it true that women are naturally more loving and males naturally more violent and combative. These gender stereotypes have been socially constructed by patriarchy. They serve to make male violence appear natural and inevitable and to shape women to be its scapegoats and its mollifiers in privatized altruism. Confession of sin does not mean simply rejecting the evils of social systems or stigmatizing evildoers "out there." It is true that the sort of people that would choose to affiliate with Women-Church are probably not the primary movers in the pornography industry, in the research and development of military weapons, or the owners of factories that pollute the environment; nevertheless, confession of sin means little if it merely criticizes the sins of others. We must ask ourselves how we have collaborated with these evils.

All people are not equally sinners. There are indeed evildoers in the world who have gained great power in unjust systems, and who daily make decisions to perpetuate and expand the deeds of oppression. Yet even those who have little direct power in such systems are not completely absolved. The systems of oppression reach into our daily lives. At work, at home, in the streets, and in our patterns of consumption and play, they define a world with which we are called to agree and cooperate. All of us, to some extent, have cooperated with systems of sexism, racism, class privilege, neocolonialism, and militarism. We have cooperated with them by accepting them as normal. We have taken aspects of these systems into our own egos and have gained some advantages thereby. A confession of sin must examine and name these structures of sin and also indicate, in concrete ways, how the people of this community have been accomplices in these systems. Statements of confession need to be constantly rethought and rewritten as the consciousness of the community about these issues changes and develops.

Guidelines for a rite of confession for the evils of sexism may be drawn from Andrea Dworkin's chapter on Antifeminism in her book *Right-Wing Women*. [5] In this chapter she speaks of pornography as the basic ideology of patriarchy. By pornography, she means all the cultural symbols that picture women as existing primarily for sexual use or, conversely, defining them as "good" only when they are asexual. Dworkin views prostitution as the outward expression of patriarchy. By prostitution, she means all the actual practices of sexual exploitation of women. Within this she describes four categories of crimes against women: (a) economic exploitation of women by gender-based work, both unpaid housework and low-paid wage labor; (b) violence against women in the home: incest, marital rape, and battering; (c) violence against women outside the home: mugging and rape, and (d) reproductive exploitation or denial of women's sexual and reproductive self-determination. These categories in Dworkin's chapter might be used to develop a rite of confession of one's collaboration with sexual exploitation.

Rite of Mind-Cleansing from the Pollution of Sexism

This rite takes the form of holding up a series of symbols that represent different aspects of sexism and naming what they represent:

— (Holding up makeup kit) This represents the role of the coy girl who learns to flirt and display her body as a sexual object.

— (Holding up a can of cleansing powder) This represents the role of the household drudge who does all the housework by herself without demanding that all who share in the household share in the work of the household.

— (Holding up broken pen) This represents all those women who were willing to discard their aspirations for careers and education because they accepted the message that women's place was in the home.

— (Holding up a picture of a woman with a taped mouth) This represents the failure of women to protest every time they hear sexist language and sexist innuendoes in conversation because they are afraid they will be condemned as pushy bitches.

— (Holding up stuffed wallet) This represents the hierarchical violence between middle-class white women and poor women of color; the economic power of privileged women over working-class women, and the attitudes that make privileged women feel superior to the secretary and the cleaning woman and assume that such work suits them.

— (Holding up flag with feminist symbol on it) This represents the lateral violence between liberal and conservative women, the assumptions of conservative women that feminists are not feminine, and the assumptions of feminists that conservative women are merely stupid and unenlightened; the inability to meet each other as persons struggling with complex problems of survival.

— (Holding up gold ring) This represents the lateral violence between heterosexual and lesbian women, the feelings of suspicion and fear generated among heterosexual women in a homophobic society toward lesbian women.

— (Holding up crossed sticks) This represents lateral violence between separatist and liberal feminists, the feelings of hostility and anger toward another woman who is more angry or less angry at patriarchy than I am, the inability to encounter each other's experience and to accept our different places on the journey.

After each statement, the group spends some time in silent meditation in which each person reflects on how this statement applies to themselves. A word or symbol is written down on pieces of paper given each person. At the end of the reflection each woman deposits her paper in an urn of fire in the center of the group. One person says, "Let these fires kindle our good anger and purify our destructive hostility turned on ourselves or others, so that our energies may as clean, as bright, and as powerful in their own right intent as these flames."

The women turn in pairs to each other. Placing their hands on each other's heads, they say to each other, "The Wisdom-Spirit forgives us, frees us, and empowers us to grow and change. I too forgive, free, and empower you to grow in strength and truth." Each then embraces the other, and the group joins hands for a final song.

Such formulas of penance should not become routine. They need to be rewritten constantly to make real contact with our growing edges. Also, real conflicts may arise among the members, which are not being dealt with through ordinary channels of communication. Groups might have some process by which a member of the community could call for a meeting of reconciliation. During this meeting the parties to the conflict would lay out their differences, and they would try to work it through to a real point of consensus and reconciliation. At the point where reconciliation is achieved, a simple liturgy of mutual reconciliation in laying hands on each other could take place.

LITURGIES OF WORD AND SACRAMENT

Christian liturgy is compounded of two main elements: the Jewish synagogue liturgy of the word, which consisted of song, Scripture reading, and sermon, and the fellowship meal of bread and wine.[6] Around this core other elements have been added: litanies, processions, and creeds. I will discuss various examples of these elements, which could be put together in different kinds of liturgies focusing only on word or combining word and sacrament.

TEXTUAL READINGS AND SERMONS

Women-Church is not confined to the texts of the Hebrew Scripture and the New Testament for its readings. It may draw from a variety of texts, both ancient stories and modern poets and writers, particularly feminist writers. But when a text is read in liturgy it becomes more than an inspirational reading. It becomes a paradigmatic text. It becomes a place where we expect to encounter the transforming Spirit speaking to our own lives. Therefore it is critical to the identity of Women-Church whether or not it decides to make biblical texts an important element in its study and proclaimed word.

Since, as Elisabeth Schüssler Fiorenza has pointed out, all biblical texts are androcentric, they must be accompanied by a feminist hermeneutic for hearing and interpreting them. Fiorenza says that we should accept as Holy Word only those texts that have a discernible intent of liberation. Yet since these texts are also androcentric, their intention toward liberation is not consciously feminist. Therefore, even these texts must be studied in order to recontextualize their liberating intention as one of liberation from patriarchy. I would suggest that Women-Church could also study texts that consciously intend to repress women, such as the story of Eve or 1 Timothy's dictum that women should keep silence. But the purpose of this study would not be to give authority to these texts, but rather to discern the evidence of women-church—the presence of women as subjects of ecclesial life in those times—which repressive texts are attempting to decry and vilify.

Scriptural study in Women-Church would take the form of small study groups that would focus on such key texts. They would seek to understand the liberating or repressive intent of the text in its original context, sometimes examining the way in which that text, in turn, is a commentary on an older text in another context. Through this study they would seek to recontextualize liberating texts and liberate repressive texts through writing a new *midrash* on the text (see my book, *Womenguides: Readings Toward a Feminist Theology*)[7] This study would then be used as the basis for proclaiming the text in the liturgy of the word. The original text and its new *midrash* would be read, and the study group would comment on their conclusions. The community could then interact with the textual work of the study group.

Since patriarchal texts have exercised such coercive influence on our lives, although perhaps more so among Protestants who give primary authority to Scripture, it is useful as one Women-Church ritual to exorcize patriarchal texts and thus to break their oppressive power over their lives. This does not mean that one would never study biblical texts again, but rather that one can study them in the full freedom of the Spirit, taking the goal of liberation from patriarchy as our norm. The following exorcism of patriarchal texts was constructed as part of a feminist liturgy that was done in several places: at Immaculate Heart College in Los Angeles and at the Pacific School of Religion in Berkeley, in the summer of 1984, and at the ancient cathedral in Lund, Sweden, in September of 1984.

Exorcism of Patriarchal Texts

A small table with a bell, a candle, and the Bible are assembled in the center of the group. A series of texts with clearly oppressive intentions are read. After each reading, the bell is rung as the reader raises up the book. The community cries out in unison, "Out, demons, out!"

Suggested texts in need of exorcism:

— Leviticus 12:1–5 (uncleanliness of women after childbirth)
— Exodus 19:1, 7–9, 14–15 (shunning of women during giving of the Law at Sinai)
— Judges 19 (rape, torture, and dismemberment of the concubine)
— Ephesians 5:21–23 (male headship over women compared to the relation of Christ and the church)
— I Timothy 2:11–15 (women told to keep silence in church and to be saved by bearing children because they are second in creation and first in sin)
— I Peter 2:18–20 (slaves exhorted to accept unjust suffering from their masters as a way of sharing in Christ's crucifixion)

At the end of the exorcism, someone says, "These texts and all oppressive texts have lost their power over our lives. We no longer need to apologize for them or try to interpret them as words of truth, but we cast out their oppressive message as expressions of evil and justifications of evil."

Scripture is not the only source of oppressive teachings. We also share a tradition of misogynist theology which continues to deeply affect the Christian church and the society influenced by it. Thus another liturgy of disaffiliation from patriarchal theological tradition can be constructed around readings from patriarchal theologians.

Litany of Disaffiliation from Patriarchal Theology

Let us reflect on the history of inferiorization and marginalization of women by Christian theology.

1. You are the Devil's Gateway. It is you who plucked the fruit of the forbidden tree. You are the first who deserted

the divine law. You are the one who persuaded him whom even the Devil was not strong enough to attack. All too easily you destroyed the image of God, man. Because of your desert, that is death, even the Son of God had to die. . . . Therefore cover your head and your figure with sackcloth and ashes.   Tertullian, *On the Dress of Women*[8]

2. Why must a woman cover her head? Because, as I explained before, the woman does not possess the image of God in herself, but only when taken together with the male who is her head, so that the whole substance is one image. But when she is assigned the role as helpmate, a function that pertains to her alone, then she is not the image of God. But as far as the man is concerned, he is by himself alone the image of God, just as fully and completely as when he and the woman are joined together into one.
                                    Augustine, *On the Trinity*[9]

3. As the philosopher says, 'Woman is a misbegotten male.' Yet it is necessary that woman was made in the first production of things as a helpmate. Not indeed as a helpmate in any other works than procreation, for in all other works man can be more effieciently helped by another man than by a woman, but as a helper in the work of generation. . . . The woman is in a state of subjugation in the original order of things. For this reason she cannot represent headship in society or in the Church. Only the male can represent Christ. For this reason it was necessary that Christ be incarnated as a male. It follows, therefore, that she cannot receive the sign of Holy Orders.   Thomas Aquinas, *Summa Theologica*[10]

4. When a woman thinks alone she thinks evil, for the woman was made from the crooked rib which is bent in the contrary direction from the man. Woman conspired constantly against spiritual good. Her very name, *fe-mina* means 'absence of faith.' She is insatiable lust by nature. Because of this lust she consorts even with Devils. It is for this reason

that women are especially prone to the crime of witchcraft, from which men have been preserved by the maleness of Christt.   *Malleus Maleficarum* (fifteenth-century manual of the Dominican Inquisitors against witches)[11]

5. Eve originally was more equally a partner with Adam, but because of sin the present woman is far inferior creature. Because she is responsible for the Fall, woman is in a state of subjugation. The man rules the home and the world, wages war and tills the soil. The woman is like a nail driven into the wall, she sits at home.

    Martin Luther, "On Marriage"[12]

6. The covenant of creation dictates a certain order, a relation of priority and posteriority, of A and B. Just as God rules over creation in the covenant of creation, so man rules over woman. He must be A; he must be first. She is B; she must be second. He must stay in his place. She must stay in hers. She must accept this order as the right nature of things through which she is saved, even is she is abused and wronged by the man.   Karl Barth, *Church Dogmatics*[13]

7. It is the unbroken tradition of the Catholic Church that women have never been admitted to Holy Orders, with which the Orthodox tradition also concurs. Jesus Christ did not call any woman to be part of the twelve, even his own mother. The apostolic Church faithfully carried out this exclusion of women from priesthood that was instituted by Christ. Moreover, it should also be said that the maleness of the priest reflects the sacramental mystery of Christ and the Church. As representative of the Head of the Church, the bridegroom, the priest must be male. There must be a 'natural resemblance' between the priest and Christ. For Christ himself was and remains a male.

    Vatican Declaration on Women's Ordination, 1976[14]

After each reading, the community says in unison:

"From the evil power of this tradition, O Holy Wisdom, deliver us."

The group then kneel and say together the following prayer:

> God and Goddess, we gather here
>> in your name
>> and in our name
> We have heard the tradition of the centuries
>> Some of the words that have condemned us to
>> reject ourselves and one another in your name.
>
> We have been raised
>> to be distrustful of ourselves
>> suspicious of other women
>> limited in our hope
>> confined in our love.
> We acknowledge that
>> we have learned this lesson well
>> from our brothers and husbands
>> lovers and friends
>> and we have learned this lesson
>> from one another as well.
> And all of this in your name
>> We bring the layers of our history
>> and our life together
>> and pray to you, God and Goddess, who are both
>> Mother and Father to us
>> for the courage to shake the
>> dust of oppression from our well-worn sandals
> For the strength to say "no more"
>> to the wedges that
>> have kept us separate from one another
> For the love that will
>> fertilize our lives
>> so that
> We might be reconciled with
>> one another.

LITANIES OF REMEMBRANCE

Many litanies can be constructed to recall into our presence those who are absent or dead. This recalls the Jewish *Kaddish* or remembrance of the dead. It also recalls Christian litanies of the saints, which summon the "cloud of witnesses" of past forerunners to be present with us in our assembly. The following are two models of such litanies, one a remembrance of the victims of genocidal massacres, and the other a litany of women foremothers.

Litany of Remembrance of the Dead

"We who are the survivors of many massacres of sisters and brothers, let us remember our dead."

— Let us remember the millions of people, most of them women, who twisted on burning fires in Medieval and Reformation Europe and were called witches.

— Let us remember the American Indians, men, women, and children, who died from diseases, hunger, cold, and forced marches as they were driven out of their ancient homelands.

— Let us remember the Africans, who died in the middle passage and under the lash as slaves in the colonies of South and North America.

— Let us remember the six million Jews who died in Nazi concentration camps while Christians on both sides of the conflict averted their eyes.

— Let us remember the many other victims of the Nazi holocaust: Communists, resistance fighters, homosexuals, the mentally ill, the handicapped, gypsies, and Slavic peoples, who lost their lives to the Hitler death machine.

— Let us remember the victims of the first nuclear bombs who were torched in the cities of Hiroshima and Nagasaki. May their deaths serve as witnesses to avert that final holocaust of technological fire and destruction from which none of us, human, animal, nor plant, may survive.

After each statement, the community resonds: "Let us forget, never, never again."

Litany of Remembrance of Foremothers

"Let us celebrate our foremothers whose history we reclaim as we seek to create a new humanity."

— We remember Miriam, who, together with Moses and Aaron, led the people of Israel out of Egypt.[15]
— We remember Deborah, who judged the people of Israel in truth and righteousness.[16]
— We remember Huldah, the prophet, who confirmed the word of God to the people.[17]
— We remember Bruria, rabbi, who interpreted the law for her generation.[18]
— We remember Mary Magdalene, apostle to the apostles of the good news of the resurrection.[19]
— We remember Phoebe, the deacon, leader of the church at Cenchreae, who was a messenger of the gospel to the churches.[20]
— We remember Priscilla, who, together with her companion, Aquila, labored in the service of Christ and risked her life for her fellow apostle, Paul.[21]
— We remember Thecla, commissioned by Paul to preach the gospel and to baptize.[22]
— We remember Prisca and Maximilla, prophets of the ongoing presence of the Spirit.[23]
— We remember Paula and Melania, founders of communities of prayer and service for women.[24]
— We remember Julian of Norwich, teacher and mystic who revealed the mother nature of God and Christ.[25]
— We remember Catherine of Siena, who called popes and kings to repent and be faithful to their true tasks of serving the people.[26]
— We remember Sor Ines de la Cruz, whose brilliant gifts of science and poetry were hidden beneath the veil of culture and religion.[27]

— We remember Margaret Fell, who established the right of women to be vehicles of the Spirit and preachers of the word from the Society of Friends.[28]

— We remember Antoinette Brown, first woman to be accepted into the ordained ministry of a Christian church.[29]

— We remember Sojourner Truth, who became the living embodiment of the power and beauty of black women.[30]

— We remember Amanda Berry Smith, who carried the gospel of liberation to her sisters and brothers in America and Africa.[31]

— We remember Georgia Harkness, who won the right of full ordination for her Methodist sisters after a one-hundred-year struggle.[32]

— We remember Sally Preisand, who carried the promise and the burden of being one of the first American women rabbis.[33]

— We remember Carter Heyward, Alison Cheek, and others of the Philadelphia Eleven, who suffered much to pave the way for ordination for their Episcopal sisters.[34]

— We remember Theresa Kane, who dared speak words of pain and hope to Pope John Paul II in Washington.[35]

There can now be added names of important women in the lives of the assembled group. After each statement of remembrance, the community responds, "Be present with us."

CREEDS

Credal work is an ongoing process in Women-Church, a way of continually reflecting on our basic theological affirmations. Covenanted communities should work out a basic credal statement which they revise at each recovenanting. This could be recited together at liturgical gatherings.

In more spontaneous gatherings that meet for a retreat or a study seminar and that wish to conclude with a liturgy, a credal statement might be developed for the occasion. The following creed was written for a liturgy celebrated at the conclusion of a class on feminist theology at the Pacific School of Religion in

Berkeley, California, in the summer of 1983. "We are the believing community who confess our sin of blaming victims and denying pain. We choose to be a community which encourages each one to remember her/history and to listen carefully to those who suffer. We are the believing community who honor vulnerability of the individual in order to honor the complementary beauty of all the divine tapestry of creation. We are the believing community, filled with the bread of life, who seek to share bread in its many forms: rice, sweet potatoes, corn, beans. We have a glimpse of the light and seek to share truth and understanding in relationships of loving solidarity and inclusiveness. We have been washed by forgiveness and seek to share freedom and justice, tempered by loving concern. We have tasted the wine of sacrifice and seek to share peace and reconciliation in a world terrorized by annihilation and the threat of war. We are the believing community who focus intensely on all these needs by means of prayer that we may have coherence and courage as we go out into the world together.

BLESSINGS OF SYMBOLIC FOODS

Women-Church affirms the importance of the symbolic foods of bread and wine, which stand for the staple food of humanity (bread) and the drink of the fermented grape, which is both the ordinary meal beverage of Mediterranean people, but which also points to the element of intoxication and ecstasy of heightened life experience in communion with God/ess. (Nonalcoholic juice can be substituted.) In the Christian tradition we see these as key symbolic foods of our sacramental fellowship meal with the martyred rabbi and messianic prophet, Jesus of Nazareth. They also point us toward that messianic meal where all humanity can sit down at the banquet of life, freed from war and injustice. This meal stands for our collective body and blood, which comes to us from the source of all being and is renewed in redemption.

There are many eucharistic blessings in the Christian tradition. In early Christianity such blessings were thought of as the particular charismatic work of prophets and prophetesses and were spontaneously developed at each Eucharist. Women-Church should feel free to continuously reshape such blessings. The following is a simple blessing drawn from ancient Christian tradition but adapted to contemporary concerns for justice.

Blessing of Bread "As these grains were once scattered on the hillsides and plains and now are brought together into one loaf, so gather your people, O Wisdom-Spirit, into the community of justice and peace. May the world of patriarchy vanish away and the new age of love and joy between sisters and brothers arise.

Blessing of the Cup "We are the new wine of life that flows in the branches of the vinetree. We remember our brother Jesus, who poured out his blood to water the roots of this vine. We also remember the many brothers and sisters who have died that a new world might be born: Oscar Arnulfo Romero, Martin Luther King, Ita Ford, Dorothy Kazal, Maura Clark, and Jean Donovan, whose blood fertilized and gave new growth to this vinetree. In sharing this blest cup, we share our lives with one another for the sake of the beloved community. We pledge to continue their struggle until all humankind can sit down together in peace and joy at the table of life.

The bread and wine are shared with the salutations,
"The bread of life"; "The cup of salvation."
Women-Church is not limited to bread and wine in its eucharistic foods. In the baptismal liturgy we drew on an ancient Christian tradition of a cup of milk and honey used for the baptismal Eucharist. Women particularly need to claim and bless the symbol of the apple, since this innocent and good fruit has been absurdly turned into a symbol of evil and an assault against women as the source of evil. Thus a Eucharist of blessing and sharing the apple is particularly appropriate.

Blessing the Apple This is the apple of consciousness raising. Let the scales of false consciousness fall from our eyes, so that we can rightly name truth and falsehood, good and evil.

ARCHITECTURE FOR WOMEN-CHURCH

Although most Women-Church groups will gather in each other's houses, some groups may have the means to band together to shape a particular building suitable for the various needs of feminist communities. I envision various purposes of such a center. One space that is needed is a place for liturgies that is both centering and elevating. I envision a round room able to hold as many as 150 people, but comfortable with only a dozen or so. It would have no immovable furniture and so could be adapted to various types of gatherings: conferences and talks, collective meals, and liturgies. It would have a dome of natural light in the center of the ceiling and panels of colored glass in rainbow hues around this center, standing for the plurality and unity of all good things in creation. There would also be narrow tall windows around the circumference of the wall. The building and windows would be oriented to catch the light at the winter and summer solstices. Under the celebration center there would be a round crypt, accessible by stairs at the center of the room or at the side. This crypt chamber would be used particularly for rites connected with birth and death.

Attached to the celebration center would be a kitchen to cook collective meals. This area would lead into a second building that would contain a conversation circle for study and discussion gatherings. This building would be egg-shaped. The conversation circle would be divided by an indoor garden from another area, containing a hot tub, a cool plunge, and dry and steam saunas, as well as toilets and dressing rooms. The garden would have roses and various herbs for healing and bracing teas. The saunas and hot and cool baths would be used for general relaxation, as well as for rituals involving bathing, such as puberty and menstrual rites and baptisms. This room would also be covered by a domed glass ceiling to bring in the natural sunlight.

The celebration center should, ideally, be set in some area of pleasant meadows and woods. It would have several small cottages scattered about, with sleeping and creating spaces, where women could stay for several days to meditate, read, and write. A circular outdoor meadow area for outdoor celebrations of May Day and summer solstice would also be desirable. The land should have an outdoor pool of water or a running stream. The cottages can also be used for extending the functions of the center, such as the providing a play center for children, a weaving or pottery center, or a library.[36]

· Elevation ·

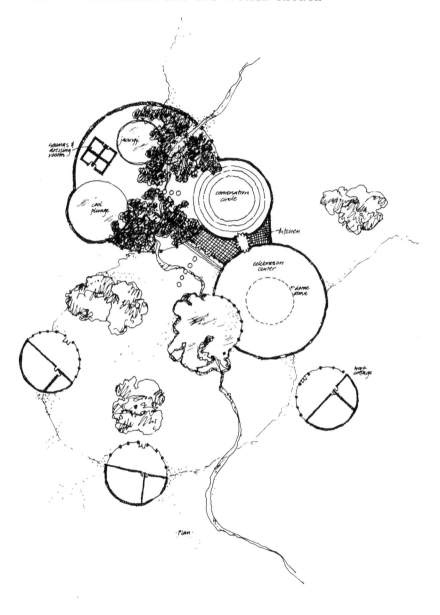

saunas &
dressing
rooms

jacuzzi

conversation
circle

cool
plunge

kitchen

celebration
center

dome
above

work
cottage

·plan·

8. Healing Our Wounds: Overcoming the Violence of Patriarchy

Healing is one of the most ancient aspects of religion. In the New Testament, Jesus acts primarily as an exorcist and healer. His power to break the hold of the demonic upon people's spirits and bodies and to heal them of illnesses, such as blindness, lameness, and hemorrhage, was understood theologically as an essential part of his identity as the Christ, the presence of God's healing and redemptive power. Christians have followed this tradition in various practices of healing ranging from pilgrimages to holy shrines where miracles of healing take place, to the charismatic preacher who heals through laying on of hands. Although this has lent itself to charlatanry, it also has indicated the depths of human need for expressions of healing that integrate the physical, the psychic, and the spiritual.

Western culture has divided reality into various zones, giving physical healing over to the medical doctor, psychic healing to the psychiatrist, and spiritual healing to the priest. While the skills of modern medicine and psychiatry are not to be rejected, this division tends to reject a holistic perspective. Medicine focuses only on the part of the body that is considered problematic, neglecting the body as a total system and the mind-body-spirit relationship.

Traditionally, women were the primary healers in society. Their healing arts combined herbal with psychological and spiritual lore. Modern elite male medicine, which originated in the universities and among the guilds of surgeon-barbers, systematically deprived women of the right to practice healing arts, culminating in the male medical takeover of midwifery. The professionalization of medicine has also meant a disempowerment of all forms of popular healing. People are made to feel that they are incapable of healing themselves and each other and must depend on specialists whose knowledge is beyond their reach and cannot be questioned.

Recently the women's health movement has begun to challenge much of this tradition of male professional medicine, particularly in the area of gynecology. Here male medicine shows a startling history of misinformation and misogyny, which has often resulted in destructive practices toward women. Women have sought to take back control over their own bodies, particularly in sexual and reproductive matters, and to relearn traditions of holistic medicine.[1] My own view is that modern medicine is not to be rejected, but rather combined with more holistic traditions. Traditions of psychic and spiritual healing, as an essential part of total well-being, need to be recovered.[2] The healing liturgy proposed here is a general one, designed to symbolize healing as a purification from death forces in the self and an opening up of the self to the healing life forces of creation and redemption. It is done by a small group of friends, together with the one seeking healing, indicating that an essential aspect of healing is love communicated through touch.

RITE OF HEALING FROM DISTRESS OF MIND OR BODY

A few friends surround the one seeking healing, seated in a circle around her. With eyes closed, she locates the various parts of the body where she feels pain and distress and also talks of the anxieties, angers, and stresses that may be connected with this physical distress. The women put their hands on these parts of her body, with one in front of her placing her hands on her temples. In a guided meditation, the woman is led to imagine these death forces of pain and psychic distress draining out and flowing away into a great pool of water that flows into the earth. If possible, this meditation might then be followed by immersion in warm water. The woman is then led back into the group wrapped in a warm cloth. With hands placed on all sides of her body, the group invokes the Wisdom-Spirit of original blessing and redemptive power. An aura of redemptive energy, welling up from the source of all life and renewal of life, is called to surround the woman. She meditates on opening all the channels of her being to this life force, letting it flow all through her, reconnecting and harmonizing her own life energies with the great life energy of God/ess. At the end of the healing meditation all come together in a hug.

RITES OF HEALING FROM VIOLENCE

In addition to this general liturgy of healing from physical and psychic distress, I include in this chapter many liturgies of healing from various kinds of social violence, particularly violence created by patriarchal hatred of women, which assaults women sexually. I include also healing liturgies for abortion, miscarriage, or stillbirth. Divorce affects both women and men, but women are far more likely than men to end in poverty as a result of it, particularly if they become the primary parents of children.

Florence Hayes has written the liturgy for divorce in this chapter, which includes a renaming ritual. Kate Pravera also contributed her renaming ritual, which she wrote for herself after her divorce. Such a renaming liturgy indicated the extent to which women have been deprived of self-naming in patriarchal society and have lost their mother's names through the generations. Thus renaming takes on special significance for women, who have lost their names and have been named by others seeking to control them. The final liturgy in this chapter is a coming-out liturgy for a lesbian and might be called "a healing from homophobia" rite.

RITUAL OF HEALING FOR AN INCEST VICTIM

It has been estimated that one in three females are sexually abused as children by their fathers or other male relatives or friends of the family. Freudian psychology has turned this situation upside down, blaming the child for sexually seductive thoughts toward the adult, rather than recognizing the sexual abuse of children. This has profoundly reinforced the victim-blaming pattern toward children in sexual abuse situations, and it further prevents children from speaking about such incidents. Sexually abused children carry the guilt and shame of these experiences much of their lives, and it is probably one of the biggest factors in female mental illness.

The following ritual was developed by a female incest victim who had been abused much of her childhood by her father. He also abused her younger sisters as well, but she was his main target. Her father played the role of the secret seducer, while the mother, who refused to recognize the situation directly, took out her anger against the father on the child, constantly attacking the child verbally as a "filthy, vile creature." The girl grew up feeling that she was dirty and evil, and she became promiscuous as a teenager. Later she repressed all memory of this history, but when she attended seminary these experiences surfaced again. She went through a period of near collapse, but, with the help of a sympathetic therapist, she was finally able to come to terms with this experience and bury her feelings of self-hatred.

About the time she was nearing the conclusion of therapy, she discovered in the attic of her home a black toy cat she had owned as a child. When she had been abused by her father, she would creep into her room and abuse the cat by pulling its ears and fur and stabbing it in what would be its vagina, if it had had one. She decided to do a burial ritual for the cat as the symbol of her own burial of her history of abuse and especially of her feelings of self-hatred that had resulted.

Order of Celebration

First the woman dug the grave in the woods. She worked alone, giving her time to reflect and to work up a sweat. The liturgy took place at midnight. The mourners arrived, one with a cross lashed together, another with a bowl of water, others with flowers or clover, some wearing black coats and hats. Mourners included her therapist and the people who had been her close supporters during her recent struggles. The therapist read Psalm 27. Midnight, the cat, lay in her open shoebox casket, and all could see how battered and torn she was. Another friend, also an incest victim, read the tenth reading from the Tao Te Ching on newness, birthing, and wholeness. The survivor then gave a eulogy for Midnight. Here she reflected on how many other women were living through dark experiences that needed to be buried: homeless women, battered women, rape victims, other incest victims. She reflected on the terror in which so many women live their lives and how we need to bury that terror. She committed herself to work for the cause of these women. Then Midnight was interred in the grave, and all participated in heaping earth over the box.

Then the survivor was baptized by each person. The bowl of water was passed from hand to hand and, as each person sprinkled her with water, they made statements of affirmation and support. The levity rose, until finally by the end the whole bowl was dumped on her head. An e.e. cummings poem was read: "i thank you god for this most amazing day." The survivor reflected on the effect of this ritual a year later. The ritual served to provide closure to the experience of incest. She still grieves for what was lost and what she never had in her childhood, but this grief has a different quality to it. It is "gentler, wiser, and easier to bear." She feels stronger and is no longer frightened. She promised herself to visit Midnight's grave "once the trees are a little greener."

RITE OF HEALING FOR WIFE BATTERING
(Litany compiled by Carol Adams of Richardson, Texas.)

The community gathers in a circle, with the woman seeking healing in the center. A presider stands and makes an introductory statement:

Marriage, the joining of men and women in a family-building covenant, has been held up to women as our supreme goal and the source of our highest happiness and fulfillment. But in reality, under patriarchy the marriage contract has too often been a license for legalized violence against women. It has been said that rapists are the shock troops of patriarchy, while wife batterers are the army of occupation. The greater physical strength of men compared to women, and the physical training of males for aggression and the training of women in passivity, are the foundations of a system that treats all women as wives—as property and servants of men. Religion has too often justified this violence, both legitimating the male right to beat their wives and directing women to accept it as the means of their redemption. A theology of victimization turns the crucifixion of Christ into a spirituality of sadism for men and masochism for women. We are here to repudiate this violence to and violation of women. We reject its legal sanctions, its cultural acceptance, and its religious cover-up. We cry out against it. We pledge ourselves to make it visible. It must be stopped. Here, in this place, it will be stopped.

We come together particularly in mourning and healing for our sister _____, who has suffered this violence, who has decided to resist it, who seeks the healing of her soul, her mind, and her body from its poisons and its blows. Let us pray together this prayer of lamentation:

(The following prayer integrates Psalm 22 with the "Letter from a Battered Wife" in Del Martin, Battered Wives.[3] The male language of the psalm is retained as an expression of the ambivalent resource a patriarchal God presents for the woman subjected to violence. It could be recited antiphonally.)

First Group: I am in my thirties and so is my husband. I have a high school diploma and am presently attending a local college, trying to obtain the additional education I need. My husband is a college graduate and a professional in his field. We are both attractive and, for the most part, respected and well liked. We have four children and live in a middle-class home with all the comfort we could possibly want. I have everything except life without fear.

Second Group: My God, my God, why have you abandoned me? I have cried desperately for help, but still it does not come. During the day I call to you, my God, but you do not answer. I call at night but get no rest.

First Group: For most of my married life I have been periodically beaten by my husband. What do I mean by beaten? I mean that parts of my body have been hit violently and repeatedly and that painful bruises, swelling, bleeding wounds, and unconsciousness and combinations of these things have resulted.
I have been kicked in the abdomen when I was visibly pregnant. I have been punched and kicked in the head, chest, face, and abdomen more times than I can count. I have been slapped for saying something about politics, for having a different view about religion, for crying. I have been threatened when I would not do something he told me to do. I have been threatened when he has had a bad day and when he has had a good day.
After each beating my husband has left the house and remained away for days.

Second Group: But I am no longer a person; I am a worm, despised and scorned by everyone! All who see me make fun of me: they stick out their tongues and shake their heads.

First Group: Few people have ever seen my black-and-blue face or swollen lips, because I stayed indoors afterwards, feeling ashamed.
Now the first response to this story, which I myself think of, will be "Why didn't you seek help?"

Second Group: You relied on the Lord, they say. Why doesn't he save you? If the Lord likes you, why doesn't he help you?

First Group: Early in our marriage I went to a clergyman who after a few visits told me that my husband meant no real harm—he was just confused and felt insecure. I was encouraged to be more tolerant and understanding. Most important, I was told to forgive him the beatings just as Christ had forgiven from the cross. I did that, too.

Second Group: It was you who brought me safely through birth, and when I was a baby, you kept me safe. I have relied on you since the day I was born, and you have always been my God. Do not stay from me! Trouble is near, and there is no one to help.

First Group: Things continued. Next time I turned to a doctor. I was given pills to relax me and told to take things a little easier. I was just too nervous. I turned to a friend, and when her husband found out, he accused me of either making things up or exaggerating the situation. She was told to stay away from me. She didn't, but she could no longer really help me. Just by believing me she was made to feel disloyal. I turned to a professional family guidance agency. I was told that my husband needed help and I should find a way to control the incidents. I couldn't control the beatings—that was the whole point of my seeking help. At the agency I found I had to defend myself against the suspicion that I wanted to be hit.

Second Group: Many enemies surround me like bulls; they are all around me, like fierce bulls from the land of Bashan. They open their mouths like lions, roaring and tearing at me.

First Group: I called the police one time. They not only did not respond to the call, they called several hours later to ask if things had settled down. I could have been dead by then.

Second Group: My strength is gone, gone like water spilled on the ground. All of my bones are out of joint. My heart is like melted wax. My throat is as dry as dust, and my tongue sticks to the roof of

	my mouth. You have left me for dead in the dust.
First Group:	I have nowhere to go if it happens again. No one wants to take in a woman with four children. Even if there were someone kind enough to care, no one wants to become involved in what is commonly referred to as a "domestic situation."
Second Group:	O Lord, don't stay away from me! Come quickly to my rescue.

Reflection Prayer (by presider):

"We have heard the anguish of a battered wife. We have also heard the cry of lamentation from our biblical faith. We have cried out to the God of our Fathers, but we have not been heard. The patriarchal face of this God has shut up the bowels of mercy from us and left us in humiliation, guilt, and despair. Too often the victim herself has been made to feel that she is the cause of the problem. We must begin anew. We must strip off the masks of patriarchy from our God and Goddess and unlock the well-springs of justice, healing, and hope. Let us hear the story of our sister."

Story Telling: The battered woman gives an account of her story, the history of violence against her in her marriage, the things that locked her into this situation, and how she has begun to resist and seek freedom and a new life.

Balm of Healing: Several women surround the battered woman. Each one anoints parts of her body with perfumed ointment. As they anoint her they say, "This (face, hand, chest, back, leg) was created to feel and enjoy life. It has been made the object of violence and the seat of pain. Throw off this pain. Cast off this humiliation. Be healed." The women then surround her and lay hands on all sides of her and hum in a rising and falling incantation. This might move into a song, such as "Sometimes I Feel Like a Motherless Child." The battered woman stands and joins in a circle with the other women. Together they say:

We are here to end the violence. Yes, we will!
We are here to break the terror. Yes, we will!

We are here to heal the wounded. Yes, we will!
We are here to help each other. Yes, we will!
We are here to make a new beginning. Yes, we will!
We are here to change the system. Yes, we will!
We are moving out together. Yes, we are!
We are creating a new world that is safe and happy. Yes, we are!
Where women, men and children can live together without fear. Yes, we will!
The end of the old, the beginning of the new. This is the time!
The end of terror, the beginning of safety. This is the place!
The end of silence. The beginning of protest and change. We are the ones, and we will do it. Yes, we will!

The group may then do a round dance together with appropriate music and song.

RITE OF HEALING FROM RAPE

Women assemble in a circle, with the woman who has been raped inside the circle and others facing her. Someone says:

"We are here because our sister (name) has been violated. Her body, her feelings, and her spirit have all been gravely injured. We are here to mourn with her and also to cry out in anger with her. We are outraged—outraged at the hostility to women and the distortion of sexuality into violence that are all around us in patriarchal society, taking the most extreme form in rape. We are filled with grief because we don't know when the violence will end and how we can repair the damage that has been done. But we refuse to give up. We will not be defeated. We will not be intimidated and turned into fearful people unable to claim our freedom to go where we please and do what we wish."

A second person says:

"We love and affirm our sister (name) who has been hurt. Although she has been injured, she is not destroyed. Although she has been demeaned, yet she has not lost her integrity. Although she has been subjected to ugliness, yet she is still beautiful. Although evil has gripped her, yet she is still good. Although lies may seek to impugn her, yet she is still truthful. We affirm her wholeness, her goodness, her truthfulness, her integrity, her beauty. We dispel the forces of destruction, of ugliness, of violence, and of lies, which seek to make her their victim."

The woman may now choose to say something about her experience, or she may prefer to remain silent or express herself in nonverbal ways.

The group now leads the woman to a ritual bath. The bath is filled with herbs and sweet-smelling flower petals. Her body is immersed and massaged with sprays of warm water. She is dried and anointed with fragrant oils and clothed in a festive dress with a crown of sage leaves and a bouquet of flowers and herbs. Reassembling in a circle around the woman, one woman facing her says:

— (With hands on abdomen) From violence to your body, be healed. (Others repeat) Be healed.
— (With hands on breast) From violence to your feelings, be healed. . . . Be healed.
— (With hands on forehead) From violence to your mind and spirit, be healed. . . . Be healed.
— (All together) The Mother-Spirit of Original Blessing surrounds you, upholds you on all sides, flows round about you, caresses you, loves you, and wills you to be whole. Be whole, sister, be whole.

If the rape has taken place in the woman's home, her house or apartment should be purified and rededicated, with special attention to the room where the rape took place and the door or window by which the rapist entered. (See liturgy of rededication of a house after violence.)

REDEDICATION OF A HOUSE AFTER A BURGLARY OR OTHER VIOLENCE

The ritual begins with the persons who live in the house standing in front of it, surrounded by friends. An opening statement is made by one or several of those who live in the house:

"This house is our home, the place of our rest and our security. We have looked forward to return to this house so many times to find the place where we relax, seek shelter and security. This our home has been violated. Instead of a place of security and peace, it has become a place of fear. Its integrity has been broken. Its peace has been shattered. We now start up with fear when we hear unexpected noises, wondering if it is another assault . . ." (Some details of the burglary and its effects on the various members of the household may then be described.)"

Isaiah 24:4–12 is read responsively by two persons, while others moan softly. This passage of Isaiah says, among other things:

"The city of chaos is broken down, every house is shut up so none can enter. Desolation is left in the city, the gates are battered into ruins."

Members of the household then say together:

"We will not succumb to fear. Holy Wisdom is our strength and our protection. We will once more make this house into a home, the place of security, peace, and love. We will go on living here, drawing strength and protection from our mutual love."

Led by the household members, the group then encircles the house, some bearing fragrant branches, one swinging a pot of incense. As the group circles the house, a pointed stick traces a furrow around the house, and a trail of grain is left in this furrow to symbolize a circle of life. The group stops at various points around the house saying together,

"Wisdom is our security and our protection. We shall not be afraid."

The group then enters the house. Each door and window in the house is sprinkled with some leaves from the fragrant branches. The group says:

"Let this door (window) no longer be a place where fear prowls. Let us look out at pleasant vistas and beckon in sweet breezes and welcomed guests."

The ritual concludes with the group gathering around the dining room table. The incense pot is put in the center, with the branches in vases around it. The group joins hands, saying,

"In the power of Holy Wisdom, we join together to be strength and protection for each other. Let that power and strength flow from hand to hand, from touch to touch, glance to glance, word to word. Let us bind up the wounds of this house, and each other's wounds. Peace and love be with us all, every one."

RITE OF HEALING FROM AN ABORTION

Community Prayer: O great Mother and Father, power of all life and new life, we are sorrowful this day. We are saddened by the conflicts we often experience between life and life, between the affirmation of a potential new life which was barely begun and the ongoing life that we must nurture and sustain, our own ongoing life and the ongoing life of those to whom we are committed to uphold and sustain. We are more than sad, we are also angry that we are faced with such choices, for these are choices in which there is no wholly good way; these are choices between two bad things, choices against a potential life or against existing life. We don't like to have to make these choices. We would like to arrange our lives so that we don't have to make these choices, but this is not always possible. We are surrounded by fragmentation and insufficiency, mistakes of judgment, and sometimes by coercion in those choices we would like to make freely. We are surrounded by a world of coercion and violence and stifling of the kind of knowledge and self-understanding that would allow us to make better choices, to think and plan better in advance. We are surrounded by a world in which vast numbers of people go to bed hungry and where many children come into the world unwanted and without the most minimal opportunities for love and development. We don't want to create life in that way. We want to create life that is chosen, wanted, and can be sustained and nourished. Our sister has made her hard choice. We don't want to pretend that this choice was easy or simple, without pain and hurt, but we also trust her that she has made the best choice that she could make. We affirm her and uphold her in her ongoing life, as she gathers her life together and centers her energies on how she is going to continue to sustain her own life and the lives around her which it nourishes.

The woman who has had the abortion speaks. She reflects as long as she wishes on what the decision means to her and her ongoing plans for her life.

A group of women surrounds the woman seated in the center and lays hands on her saying;

Be healed sister, be whole!

Then one of the women brings a flower pot with new soil in front of her and scatters seeds in it, saying;

Life is broken, life dies, but life is reborn, life continues. We do not look back to the past, but to the new futures that arise each day with the new rising of the sun, with the fresh dews on the grass and the sunshine of new possibilities. Let these seeds symbolize the new possibilities of life that open up before us, even as we mourn the flickers of life that are not to be.

The woman in the center takes a watering can and waters the seeds, and the flower pot is presented to her.

The group may then choose to continue conversation in the pools of water.

RITE OF HEALING FROM A MISCARRIAGE OR A STILLBIRTH

Community Prayer: O great Mother and Father, power of all life and new life, we are sorrowful this day. Our sister (name) and brother (name) were anticipating the birth of a child into their lives. Already expectations, preparations, and plans had been formed around this new child. But this potential life that had begun to grow and develop has been snuffed out. We are left with empty arms and an empty heart where the thoughts of this coming child had been. We are saddened by the insufficiency of life, our inability to shape life to our wishes, and make a life that had begun to grow to fruition in a newborn child. We would like to rail against heaven, to be angry at the blind forces that end so quickly the fragile beginnings of our hopes. But we don't know who or what to be angry with. Should we be angry at you, the source of life, who have deprived us of this life? Or are you, too, subject to the insufficiency and limitations of life as you struggle to bring new beings to birth? Are you, God and Goddess of life and new life, also unable to control the forces of death that circumscribe your creative work? Do you too mourn and sigh with us at this quick snuffing out of the spark of being that had begun in us? Can we weep and mourn together, humans and God/ess, for the little one who was and now is not and shall not be?

Yet we must go on, we and you. We must continue our struggle to support life, both the lives of those who are around us and depend on us, and our own lives. Failing in our hopes to nurture a new life, we turn to nurture the lives that already exist and need our help. Heal our sister (name) and brother (name) from their sorrow. We turn our energies to them and affirm and uphold them in their ongoing life, as they gather their lives together, center their energies on how they are going to continue to sustain both their own lives and the lives of those around them.

The woman (or the couple) now reflect on feelings about the miscarriage or stillbirth and hopes for taking up the threads of life. The group surrounds them, lays hands on them, and says,

Be healed of sorrow (names), be whole.

The rest of the liturgy continues as in the liturgy of healing for an abortion.

A RITUAL OF DIVORCE, *by Florence Perrella Hayes*[4]

Participants: The couple and two friends who join them in reading the service; also the children (if there are children) and other close relatives and friends.

Symbols: A large goblet filled to the top with wine, and a bowl of earth; If there are children, two red roses for each child.

Actions: 1. Greeting and invocation
2. Remembering the vision
3. Reaffirming the parental covenant (if there are children)
4. The vision darkened, expressions of sorrow and forgiveness
5. Emptying the cup
6. Pronouncing the names
7. Blessing

Each of the seven steps begins with an appropriate reading from Scripture or poetry or song, and each concludes with a few moments of silence before moving on. (All quotations in this service are taken from the Jerusalem Bible.)

Greeting and Invocation

1st Friend: Welcome to all who have been drawn here out of love for _____ and _____ . We, their family and friends, join them today to mark the completion of their married life, and to ask God's blessings upon them as they face the challenge of a new journey. May the Holy One grace them now and with loving kindness in the days to come.

Remembering the Vision

2d Friend: "Now the earth was a formless void, there was darkness over the deep, and God's spirit hovered over the water. God said, 'Let there be light,' and there was light. God saw that light was good, and God divided light from darkness" (Gen. 1:1–4).

1st Friend: Falling in love is a blow of divine knowledge, a crack of light in the darkness.

2d Friend: Falling in love is a foretaste of the Kingdom and a return to the Garden.

She: We begin to create the world all over again!

He: We honour that vision we shared, and the good work of our life together.

He and She: (Each, in turn, names a positive memory or a satisfying work done together.)

She: To affirm these things and bond them to our hearts forever, we drink from this common cup.

(Each tastes from the cup.)

Reaffirming the Parental Covenant

1st Friend: "Your children sit round your table like shoots round an olive tree" (Ps. 128:36).

He: Our love continued the work of God's creation. We honor these new persons, our children, who now grace us and challenge us and extend our horizons. (Mention each one by name.)

She: They are the enfleshment of our love, the wonder and the joy, the consolation and anguish of our lives. We affirm our commitment to them as long as we live.

He: We continue to be parents and children even when we are no longer husband and wife. As a sign of this unbreakable covenant, we share this final taste of our common cup.

(Parents and children all taste from the cup of wine, leaving some left at the bottom.)

The Vision Darkened

2d Friend: Opposite evil stands good,
opposite death, life;
so too, opposite the devout person
stands the sinner.
This is the way to view all
the works of the Holy One;
they go, in pairs by opposites.

She: Love once called us together,
now life demands our separation.

In sorrow, I ask for your forgiveness
for growing in a way unlike your own.
Forgive me the daily betrayals.

He: Forgive me for not listening.
Forgive me my failure to understand.

She: Do not remember the stubborn, crowding weeds,
those faults I neglected to uproot.

He: Do not remember my fear,
and the dishonesty in which I hid.
Remember me with love.

She: Remember me with love.
A kiss of peace is exchanged or a handshake.

Emptying the Cup

1st Friend: "There is a season for everything, a time for every occupation under heaven:
a time for giving birth;
a time for dying;
a time for planting;
a time for uprooting what has been planted" (Eccles. 3:1–2).

He: There is a time to link our lives together and there is a time to sever.

She: What is holy about separation?
What is holy about the ending of a dream?

2d Friend: It is the holiness of letting go, of admitting there is nothing and no one we possess.

1st Friend: It is the holiness of blessing one another's freedom. It is the refusal to consume the one we once desired.

He and She: It is to accept our limitations.
(Both lift the cup together)
As the remainder of this cup is emptied, the remainder of our marriage is poured out upon the ground.
(Together, they pour the wine onto the earth.)

Change of Name

In Quebec, where this liturgy was written, no legal steps are necessary when a divorced woman desires to resume her maiden name. If, however, she would like to adopt an entirely new name, she will need the help of a lawyer. The purpose of the naming in this ceremony is simply to mark the event among one's friends.

2d Friend: "The man named his wife Eve because she was the mother of all those who live" (Gen. 3:20).

1st Friend: "And there was one that wrestled with him until daybreak, who seeing that he could not master him, struck him in the socket of his hip, and Jacob's hip was dislocated as he wrestled with him. He said, 'Let me go, for day is breaking.' But Jacob answered, 'I will not let you go unless you bless me.' He then asked, 'What is your name?' 'Jacob,' he replied. He said, 'Your name shall no longer be Jacob, but Israel, because you have been strong against God, you shall prevail against men' " (Gen. 32:26–28).

2d Friend: Who are you? What have you done? A name should be an expression of our essential selves. That name may be revealed to us slowly in the process of our lives. It may be spoken by others only after we die, or it may remain forever hidden with God.

1st Friend: Where have you come from? Where are you going? In the meantime, we wear a public name, infuse it and shape it, a key for those who care and a mystery to all others.

To mark the beginning of your new lives, you will be known as _____ and _____ from this day forward. Your children's names will remain the same as their relationship to their parents remains the same. Each parent gives each child a red rose.

Blessing

All lift hands to bless the pair. They may simply receive the blessing or they may lift hands to bless one another.

2d Friend: We lift our hands in blessing to _____ and to _____ . May they find the strength and courage to forge their individual lives in serenity and good health.

1st Friend: May they be deeply familiar with satisfying work, joyful friendship, and their children's love.

All: May they grow in the wisdom and breath of God. (Each guest goes to the pair and makes a personal gesture of blessing, such as resting hands upon shoulders, a handshake, or a kiss.)

RITE OF NAMING

Florence Hayes's liturgy presupposes the ability of both partners to meet in a liturgy of reconciliation. But, too often, this is not the case. So a divorce liturgy as a liturgy of healing for one member of the former couple with friends may be needed. This might take the form of a renaming ceremony.

This rite of naming was written by and for Kate Pravera,[5] and it took place on May 7, 1981. It represented her claiming of a new identity as she moved from her marriage and also from earlier prefeminist self-understandings.

Gathering Music: Excerpts from Bolling's "Suite for Flute and Jazz Piano."

Readings: The Power to Name Is Ours

The simple act of telling a woman's story is a revolutionary act: it has never been done before. A new language must be created to express women's experience and insight, new metaphors discovered, new themes considered . . . As women share their naming of experience and insight, they forge connections to other women who hear their own unnamed longings voiced, their perceptions of the world and its powers given form.[6]

What is happening is that women are really *hearing* ourselves and each other, and out of this supportive hearing emerge new words.[7]

Women have had the power of *naming* stolen from us. We have not been free to use our own power to name ourselves, the world, and God. The old naming was not a product of dialogue—a fact inadvertently omitted in the Genesis story of Adam's naming the woman. Women are now realizing that the universal imposing of names by men has been false because partial. That is, inadequate words have been taken as adequate. . . . To exist humanly is to name the self, the world, and God. The "method" of the evolving spiritual consciousness of women is nothing less than this beginning to speak humanly—a reclaiming of the right to name.[8]

Part I: The Experience of Nothingness

I Was Once a Smiling Girl
who walked with her laughter
through a city that was hers.
I was once a woman poet
who came out with a poem
as one goes out with a child
to show and enjoy it.
I was once the mother of two beautiful daughters
and walked secure in my joy
defying the wind and other things.

Now,
I am a woman who does not know the land where she lives,
without love, nor laughter, nor nicaragua,
I am a poet
who writes in secret
in serious offices and boarding houses,
I am a girl who cries under an umbrella
when memories sting,
I am a mother who yearns for her daughters' happiness:
Now,
I am a song of rain and of melancholy,
I am of absence.
            —Gioconda Belli, written in prerevolutionary Nicaragua[9]

Readings:

In the anthropology of the Church Fathers, maleness and femaleness are treated as expressions of the body-soul split. Women are defined as analogous to body in relation to the ruling mind: either obediently subjugated body (the wife), or sensual bodiliness in revolt against the governance of reason (the harlot). Women are assimilated into the definition of sin. The bodily principle is seen as so intrinsically demonic that the high road to salvation demands the spurning of bodily life altogether for the ascetical virgin state.[10]

Women's intense perception of their own nothingness sometimes gives them acute perception of the larger forces of nothingness, domination, death, and destruction that operate in men's world. They may have very clear visions of the ways in which the destructive power of men operates not only in their personal lives, but also in the larger worlds of nature and society.[11]

Strike

I want a strike where we all go together.
A strike of arms, legs, heads,
a strike born in each body.

I want a strike   of doves
of workers   of flowers
of chauffeurs   of children
of technicians   of women

I want a huge strike,
encompassing love,
A strike where everything stops
the clock   the factories
the school   the colleges
the bus   the hospitals
the highway   the ports

A strike of eyes, hands, and kisses.
A strike where no one breathes,
A strike where silence emerges

to hear the sounds
of the fleeing tyrant.[12]

Part II: Wakening and Insight: A Coming of Self

Awakening often occurs through mystical experiences in nature or with other women. "Awakening" is perhaps a more appropriate term than "conversion" for describing women's mystical experience, because "awakening" suggests that the self needs only to notice what is already there. Awakening implies the ability to know or see is within the self, once the sleeping draft is refused.[13]

For women, awakening is not so much a giving up as a gaining of power . . . It is a grounding of selfhood in the powers of being, rather than a surrender of self to the powers of being. In this context, you are invited to participate in the following self-blessing ritual.

Self-Blessing Ritual: The Seven Powers of Self-Determination

At this point, salt is passed around. Sprinkle it on the ground where you are standing. Salt here symbolizes the salt of the earth—wisdom—so we are standing on our wisdom.

Group 1: In blessing our foreheads . . .
         (all touch their foreheads)
Group 2: We claim the powers of reason.
Group 1: In blessing our eyes . . .
Group 2: We claim the power of vision, to see clearly the forces of life and death in our midst.
Group 1: In blessing our lips . . .
Group 2: We claim the power to speak the truth about our experiences; we claim the power to name.
Group 1: In blessing our hands . . .
Group 2: We claim our powers as artisans of a new humanity.
Group 1: In blessing our wombs . . .
Group 2: We claim the power to give birth, as well as the power to choose not to give birth.

Group 1:   In blessing our feet . . .

Group 2:   We claim the power to walk the paths of our coura-
geous foremothers, and when necessary, to forge new
paths.

The Seventh Blessing:

You are invited to reflect for a moment on a power that you
would like to claim in your own life. After you have decided,
go to the center of the circle and remove a flower for yourself,
as a sign of claiming that power. Feel free to share with the
group.

The Blessing Continues:

While standing in the circle, all join palms and say,

In blessing each other, we claim the power that rests collectively
in our shared struggle as women.

Next, all bend to place palms flatly on the earth and say,

Invocation:

We bless the earth in all its fruitfulness. In so doing we claim
the powers of life that rest in the earth. In touching the soil, let
us feel the energy of all who struggle this day to rise from their
oppression. We remember those who work the land in every
corner of the earth. From Southeast Asia to Central America,
they rank among the most exploited of all the earth's peoples.
But there is hope. There is a movement of energy across the face
of this earth which refuses to die. As Archbishop Romero
claimed, in solidarity with the campesinas and campesinos of El
Salvador, "They (the junta) can kill me, but I will not die." Let
us claim the collective power that is ours!

Song: "We Shall Overcome"

Part III: *The New Naming*

There is a sense in which naming is not complete unless a name
is used by others. At the center of today's rite lies the claiming
of the power to name myself: Kate Pravera, "she who practices

truth." To complete the ritual, I will state my new name, which shall be used from this day forward. You are then asked to repeat, one by one, "You are Kate Pravera."

Closing Song: "We Are Dancing Sarah's Circle"

COMING-OUT RITE FOR A LESBIAN

Prepared by Rebecca Parker and Joanne Brown [14]

This rite is designed to celebrate the new birth that occurs for a woman who comes out to herself and her community and affirms her identity as a lesbian woman. It is based on the tradition of baptismal renewal rites, with the understanding that a woman who comes out experiences the birth of a new identity, or a return home to an original identity that had been lost. Discovery and affirmation that one's sexuality is the good gift of God/ess provides the basis for celebration. The following rite begins with giving thanks to the Author of all life for the creation of the universe, and it moves to focus on giving thanks for the woman whose life is being celebrated this day. Divine Wisdom is invoked as the link connecting the personal and the Holy One, and as such, Wisdom dwells within her.

Water is poured on the head of the woman being celebrated, to symbolize her blessed birth, the implicit holiness and goodness of her being. Appropriate words of blessing and affirmation are said, and the one being blessed is welcomed into the community.

The rite concludes with prayers of concern for the protection of all life, and for the liberation of all who are oppressed. A final psalm and hymn give thanks to the Source of justice and liberation.

Gathering and Preparation

Gathering Statement

Celebrant: Dear friends, all life is a sacred and blessed gift. We are here today to give thanks for the gift of life and to bless the life of _____ , who has invited us to join her in celebrating her affirmation of herself as a lesbian woman. In this time when lesbians and gay men are rejected and oppressed, our gathering here is a protest against unjust persecution and false judgment. We renounce the homophobia of the church and proclaim the sacred worth of every child of the Holy One, as we welcome with this sister with joy.

Let us prepare outselves for this time of celebration by pray-
ing together:

Prayer for Truth

All: O God of truth and justice, the evasions and deceits we
practice upon others and upon ourselves are many.

We long only to speak and to hear the truth, yet time and
again, from fear of loss or hope of gain, from dull habit or from
cruel deliberation, we speak half-truths, we twist facts, we
silent when others lie, and we lie to ourselves.

Those of us who are lesbian or gay often feel forced to pretend
to be that which we are not, to present ourselves in ways which
are not truthful, and sometimes with outright lies.

But as we stand before You, our words and our thoughts
speed to One who knows them before we utter them. We do not
have to tell untruths to You as we are often forced to do in the
straight world. We know we cannot lie in Your presence.

May our worship help us to practice truth in speech and in
thought before You, to ourselves, and before one another; and
may we finally complete our liberation so that we no longer feel
the need to practice evasions and deceits.

Eternal One, purify our hearts to serve You in truth.

Thanksgiving for Life

Hymn of Praise

Joyful, joyful we adore thee
Source of glory, Source of Love,
Hearts unfold like flowers before thee
Opening to the sun above,
Melt the clouds of sin and sadness;
Drive the dark of doubt away;
Giver of immortal gladness,
Fill us with the light of day!

All thy works with joy surround thee,
Earth and heaven reflect thy rays,

Stars and angels sing around thee,
Center of unbroken praise;
Field and forest, vale and mountain,
Flowery meadow, flashing sea,
Chanting bird and flowing fountain,
Call us to rejoice in thee.[15]

Litany in Praise of Wisdom (To be recited antiphonally)

The sand of the sea and the raindrops,
and the days of eternity, who can assess them?

The height of the sky and the breadth of the earth,
and the depth of the abyss, who can probe them?

Before all other things Wisdom was created,
shrewd understanding is everlasting.

For whom has the root of Wisdom ever been uncovered?
Her resourceful ways, who knows them?[16]

The woman coming out responds:

It was Wisdom who gave me true knowledge of all that is,
who taught me the structure of the world and the properties
of the elements,
the beginning, end and middle of the times,
the alternation of the solstices and the succession
of the seasons,
the revolution of the year and the positions of the stars,
the natures of animals and the instincts of wild beasts,
the powers of spirits and the mental processes of human
beings,
the varieties of plants and the medical properties of roots.
All that is hidden, all that is plain, I have come to know,
instructed by Wisdom who designed them all.[17]

Everyone joins in praise of wisdom:

For within her is a spirit intelligent, holy,
unique, manifold, subtle,
active, incisive, unsullied,
lucid, invulnerable, benevolent, sharp,
irresistible, beneficent, loving,

steadfast, dependable, unperturbed,
almighty, all-surveying,
penetrating all, intelligent, pure,
and most subtle spirits;
for Wisdom is more mobile than any motion;
she is so pure, she pervades and permeates all things.[18]

The Celebrant adds:

In each generation Wisdom passes into holy souls,
she makes them friends of the Eternal and prophets;

She is indeed more splendid than the sun,
she outshines all the constellations;
compared with light, she takes first place,
for light must yield to night,
but over Wisdom evil can never triumph.
She deploys her strength from one end of the earth
         to the other,
ordering all things for good.[19]

Baptismal Renewal and Blessing

Song Invoking Wisdom

Be thou my vision, the joy of my heart;
Naught be all else to me save that thou art.
Thou my best thought, by day or by night,
Waking or sleeping, thy presence my light.

Be thou my wisdom, the lamp to my feet;
Thy word, like honey, to my lips is sweet;
Thou my delight, my joy, thy command;
My dwelling ever, be the palm of thy hand.[20]

Prayer

O Wisdom, beloved One, why are you so far from us?
Our world suffers from your absence.
No one seeks to be faithful to you,
No one searches for you.

We, your children, are rejected because people are so quick
to believe false images, or so bound to seeing what they

want to see they can't face the truths in front of their
eyes.

You shall know the truth, and the truth shall set you free,
it has been said.
What is the truth about ourselves?
Is it not you who have made us?
Are we not, each one of us, your handiwork?

We look around at the beautiful creation, so filled
with diversity and complexity. Yet everything has a place
and a purpose. You have made all things to work together
for good.

The tree's breathing creates the air we need to breathe.
The fish find their way to their spawning grounds
by the rhythms of the currents in their home streams.
The wind sets free the thistle down and sows the seed.
Is there anything in all creation that is not fitting?

And we ourselves, each one of us, in our uniqueness, and
diversity, and complexity, are not we, each one of us,
a part of the whole and valuable as we are?

O Wisdom, come to us!
Teach us to see the goodness of ourselves.
Teach the prejudiced to see the truth of human worth.
Infuse the obstinate with your mobility.
Give the human family open minds, open hearts,
eyes of wonder, and a will attuned to the good.
Amen.

Self-Blessing *The woman coming out recites these words:*

Holy One, you examine me and know me,
you know if I am standing or sitting,
you read my thoughts from far away,
whether I walk or lie down, you are watching,
you know every detail of my conduct.

The word is not even on my tongue,

Holy One, before you know all about it;
close behind and close in front you fence me around,

shielding me with your hand.
Such knowledge is beyond my understanding,
a height to which my mind cannot attain.

Where could I go to escape your spirit?
Where could I flee from your presence?
If I climb the heavens, you are there,
there too, if I lie in Sheol.

If I flew to the point of sunrise,
or westward across the sea,
your hand would still be guiding me,
your right hand holding me.

If I asked darkness to cover me,
and light to become night around me,
that darkness would not be dark to you,
night would be as light as day.

It was you who created my inmost self,
and put me together in my mother's womb;
for all these mysteries I thank you:
for the wonder of myself, for the wonder of your works.[21]

Renewal of Baptism

The celebrant and other friends pour or sprinkle water on the woman coming out, and address her with any or all of the following words, or other spontaneous words of blessing.

Born of woman, beloved of woman, lover of woman, you are blessed.
You are the light of the world.

Words of Welcome

All those gathered welcome the woman who is coming out by saying these words, or by their own spontaneous greeting.

We welcome you, sister and friend, into this community. With you we make a commitment to integrity. We promise to oppose injustice, and we embrace with joy the gifts that come to us from the Holy One's hand.

A Time of Singing and Sharing

Concluding Prayers

Prayers for Liberation and the Protection of All Life

Throughout history, there have been oppressed people. Even today the list of oppression builds longer and longer, with no end in sight. But the oppressed people who endure are those who have faith in their cause, themselves, and in their Creator. The Falashas, the Black Jews of Ethiopia, have lived lives of oppression for hundreds of years. They have a prayer of unity, of hope, and of faith, that we would like to share with you:

Do not separate me, O God, from your people, from the joy, from the light, from the splendor. Let me see, O God, your light, and let me listen to the words of the just while they speak about your law. O Holy One, Eternal Ruler whom I praise, be merciful to me. By day, be my shepherd, and my guardian at night. When I walk be my guide, my refuge when I sit.[22]

Let us pray together as a community of sisters and brothers. Let us mediate for a few moments on the prayer of Radclyffe Hall:

God we believe; we have told you we believe . . . We have not denied you, then rise up and defend us. Acknowledge us, O God, before the whole world. Give us the right to our existence.[23]

Concluding Psalm

God, give your own justice to our rulers,
Your righteousness to the rulers of the land.
So they may rule your people rightly,
And your poor with justice.

Let the mountains and the hills
Bring a message of peace for the people,
Uprightly they will defend the poorest,

They will save the children of those in need,
and crush their oppressors.

Like sun and like moon, justice will endure,
Age after age,
Welcome as rain that falls on the pasture,
As showers to the thirsty soul.

In our days justice will flourish,
A universal peace till the moon is no more
shall stretch from sea to sea,
From the river to the ends of the earth.

They will free the poor who call to them,
And those who need help,
They will have pity on the poor and feeble,
And save the lives of those in need.

Grain will be everywhere in the country.
Even on the mountain tops.
Abundant will be the harvest,
Luxuriant as common grass.

Praised be the Eternal, Our Creator,
Who alone performs these marvels.
Blessed be the glorious name of the Holy One,
Whose glory and justice fills the world.
Amen, Amen![24]

Hymn
This or another hymn or song can be sung to conclude the rite.

Now thank we all our God,
With heart, and hand, and voices,
Who wondrous things hath done,
In whom this world rejoices,
Who from our mother's arms,
Hath blessed us on our way,
With countless gifts of love
And still is ours today.

O may this bounteous God
Through all our life be near us,

With ever joyful hearts,
And blessed peace to cheer us,
And keep us all in grace,
And guide us when perplexed,
And free us from all ill,
In this world and the next.[25]

9. Celebrating the Rites of Passage: Liturgies of the Life Cycle

These rites of the life cycle carry members of Women-Church from birth to death through many stages and periods of transition. Certainly there are other points of transition, which are left unmarked in this collection. I do not intend to provide rites for every possible occasion, nor rites that are universally applicable to everyone even in a particular population, such as young people leaving home. The leaving-home rite provided here may apply to young people who have amicable relations with their parents, but not to young people who do not have happy parental relationships. Thus, again I stress that this is a resource book with some ideas, but finally any ritual needs to be shaped and contextualized for a particular community and occasion.

These rites also concentrate mostly on the female life cycle. There are some liturgies that apply equally to males, such as namings, baptisms, birthdays, leaving home, covenantings, moving to a new house, dying, and funerals. Other rites allow for males as participants, such as the birthing liturgy. Yet there remain important areas where specifically male rites of passage need to be written, such as puberty rites for young males and retirement of older males. These I believe must be written by men. The formation of a new perspective on these critical points of male development awaits the rising of communities of males who are engaged in their own exodus from patriarchy in solidarity with feminist women.

NAMING CELEBRATION FOR A NEW CHILD; SIGNING
WITH THE PROMISE OF BAPTISM

The following naming celebration was adapted from that done for Genevieve Beatrice, daughter of Marilyn Gherashe and Michel Trudel, on April 6, 1985. It was not followed by a baptism. A "signing with the promise of baptism" celebration has been added here, since these liturgies are understood as being done in the context of Women-Church. By signing with the promise of baptism, the community conveys the belief that we are to grow up, from the first moment of life, with the promise of freedom from evil. But it is a signing with the promise, rather than the fulfillment of baptism, because each person must claim that promise for themselves as adults as they enter into and define their own journey into freedom. Freedom means here both freedom from deforming ideologies and practices of the society, including those of one's parents, and also a claiming of the good values and practices of the society and one's parents, but contextualized in one's own adult journey.

A naming and signing celebration should be preceded by the formation of a parental support community for the mother and father of the child. This support community of several "life-parents," both men and women, should meet together with the parents several times to discuss the values they believe should shape the raising of a child at the present time. What values of the society do they reject, and how would they shape the household practices to try to eliminate evil practices, such as war toys celebrating violence? What values do they try to teach, and how would they shape the household practices to inculcate these values? The meetings should culminate in the shaping of a covenant document in which the parents pledge to work toward this kind of household. The life-parents pledge to help them and to become an extended parental community for the growing child, where the child can turn for supplemental or sole parenting, if the parents should die, separate, or otherwise become unavailable to the child.

Naming Celebration

Gathering into a Dedication Circle:

All present are welcomed. Relatives are identified in terms of the parts of the bloodline of the child they represent. A tree of life, salt, water, oil, and a candelabra with seven candles is present in the center. A book is passed around in which all can enter their names and a message of good wishes, to be given the child at the time of her (his) puberty rite.

Lighting of the Candles

by the mother:

> May the light we now kindle inspire us to use our powers
> to heal and not to harm, to help and not to hinder,
> to bless and not to curse, to serve you, Spirit of Freedom.[1]

The child is held and blessed with the words:

> In the beginning was God,
> In the beginning the source of all that is,
> In the beginning God yearning, God moaning.
> God laboring. God giving birth, God rejoicing.
>
> And God loved what she had made, and God said,
> "It is good." And God, knowing that all that is good
> is shared, held the earth tenderly in her arms.
> God yearned for relationship. God longed to share the
> good earth. And humanity was born in the yearning of God.
> We were born to share the earth.[2]

The Naming

The parents explain the name(s) chosen for the child and their meaning: who in the family or in history has held these names before, and what these persons represent as prototypes of the promises given to the child. The names will include one secret name which is pronounced in a whisper after the other names and which will be revealed to the child at the time of her (his) puberty rite.

The Promises

spoken by the hostess of the gathering:

Friends, as we participate in this naming and signing celebration, we affirm our commitment to (name) in a community of love. We accept her (him) into our community and accept our responsibility as extended family to nurture and care for her (him), to teach and to learn from her (him).

You, (naming parents), are the most important people in the life of (name). You are the primary conveyors of love and learning, strength and commitment, hope and trust. Will you, as parents, share with her (him) your faith and the stories of spirit-filled people? Will you provide a home and surroundings which will awaken in her (him) a capacity to love and a desire for peace and justice?

Parents: We will.

Addressing the Life-Parents by Name:

You, (names), together with (names of parents) have pledged to become an extended family for the parenting of (name of child). You have reflected on your commitments together. What pledges have you made?

The life-parents read the covenant they have drawn up with the parents, with their understanding of the values they hope to nurture and the kind of household they will help to develop to express these values.

After this reading the covenant document is placed in the book to be given to the child.

The life-parents are addressed:

You have pledged to help (parents' names) nurture this child. Do you promise to share with her (him) your wisdom and experience, to give her (him) comfort and encouragement and to be available to her (him) in time of need, so that she (he) can turn to you when your help is desired?

Life-parents: We will.

To the community: Will you all promise to surround (parents' names) and (child's name) with your love and support?

Community: We will.

186 / LITURGICAL LIFE AND WOMEN-CHURCH

Signing With the Promises of Baptism

Life-parents hold the child, while both they and the parents say together:

(name), we sign you with the sign and promise of freedom. This sign of freedom is our promise to model the ways of life and eschew the paths of lying and death. But we are not perfect. We will fail to do this in some ways. With this sign we affirm your own journey into freedom. We affirm that journey by which you will reject some of what we have given you and accept other things, each in your own way. May you be able to reject only those things which are death-bearing and affirm those things which will promote life, your own life and the lives of those around you. May your eyes see the truth and your lips speak the truth.

The child is touched on the tongue with salt.

With this water we commit you to that journey into freedom, the washing away of the history of sexism, racism, classism, military violence, and all those evils which stain our human story. We send you forth in the waters to claim the promise of newness of life, the reclaiming of the original blessing and harmony of humans with humans, humans with plants and animals, humans with the Wisdom-Spirit who brought forth all things.

Water is poured over the child's head.
The child is anointed with oil on the forehead, with the words:

May you have courage for this journey into freedom and may the oil of gladness always anoint your head.

The candelabra is placed next to the Tree of Life, with these words:

This Tree of Life stands for original blessing, the harmony of all living things with each other and with Holy Wisdom. It is the beginning, the end, and the center of our journey. Keep the vision of the Tree of Life always before you on this journey and let these lights of seven-fold wisdom always light your path.

Gifts:

Symbolic gifts may now be presented to the child by different persons present, symbolizing the qualities and hopes with which that person would particularly like this child to be gifted. Baby gifts may also be given on this occasion. Finally, the book with the wishes and the covenant document is held up and the promise is made to present this to the child at the time of her (his) puberty, at which time the secret name will be revealed to the child.

BIRTHDAYS

Birthdays are one of the most widely practiced forms of secular and family ritual. They are usually celebrated in our culture by the giving of gifts and a party with friends or an outing to do something especially desired by the one who has the birthday. The party culminates in a cake with lighted candles for each year of the person's life. Friends sing a song while presenting the cake, and the birthday person blows out the candles while making a secret wish.

Special festivities on a birthday are an important way of affirming that each person is unique and is loved. It is not mere childishness when people, even in middle age, say they feel depressed and unable to continue their life if no one remembers their birthday. Even businesses today make a practice of remembering employees' birthdays with a card, present, and sometimes a party.

One might think of some ways to focus even more this attention to birthdays and their significance for affirming each person's life. A cup of blessing might be hallowed with an invocation of the Mother-Spirit of original blessing, through whom all life comes and is renewed. The cup is passed first to the birthday person and then to the guests. A book of memories and hopes could also be developed, starting with first birthdays in childhood, and then passed on to the person to continue as an adult. In this book a photo from each birthday might be entered, together with some wish or hope for the future. As the book builds through the years, it becomes a record of past birthdays and renewed possibilities that can be looked at and added to each year.

PUBERTY RITE FOR A YOUNG WOMAN

This rite takes place after the first menstruation of a young woman. It begins with a gathering of women, including her mother, and friends whom the girl regards as confidantes. They may be of various ages, but they must themselves have begun to menstruate. These women bathe together, perhaps by taking a sauna and a swim together. The women discuss with the young woman her questions about sexuality, ways of caring for menstruation, sexual intercourse, how to choose or avoid conception, and the understanding of sexual relations.

After this experience of bathing and discussion, the young woman is brought into an assembly, where the women sit around her in a circle. She is clothed in a bright dress, and a multicolored sash is put around her waist and a crown of flowers on her head. The women hold up various symbols for women's body and care for women's body, reciting a chant together with her:

My eyes are not objects of control over me. My eyes are the way I see the world. They enable me to look in all directions, to take in the beauty and the excitement of all visible things.

My lips are not objects of control over me. My lips are the way I speak and sing and eat and kiss and express my love and delight.

My legs are not objects of control over me. My legs are the way I walk and run and dance and move wherever I wish to go.

My breasts are not objects of control over me. My breasts are the way I express my mothering powers, to make milk, perhaps someday to feed a baby with my milk.

My body is not an object of control over me. My body is me. It is my being, my acting and my being present wherever I want to be. Let my body always be the joyful expression of myself. Let it never be used as a means of power and control over me.

At each incantation, the young woman is anointed with scented oil on different parts of her body.

The women then say to the new member of the community of women:

You are becoming a woman. You are no longer a child. Your body is ripening, becoming more alive to sexual feeling and able to conceive and bear children. You are also becoming more independent of your parents, preparing yourself for independence, learning to decide for yourself what is right and what is wrong, how best to use the powers of your mind and body. To symbolize your growing independence, we give you this key to the family house.

A live baby (or baby doll) is put into the young woman's arms. The women say to her:

This baby represents the child that your body is becoming able to conceive and bear. You are now able to become a mother. But you are not yet ready to take responsibility for caring for another human life, a life that will be weak and dependent on you to feed it, wash it, clothe it, and teach it how to walk and talk and grow. You must be in control of this wonderful life-making power of your body: Do not use it until you are ready to take responsibility for caring for another life; choose to use it when you decide that you are ready to become a mother. You are the decision maker. You must decide when you are ready to use your body for love and when you are not; when you are ready to create a new life and when you are not.

The young woman hands back the baby, and an egg is put into her hand. She holds the egg while she recites with the women:

This is the mystery of life and the renewal of life that happens in our bodies. Every month an egg is born and grows and makes ready for the creation of a new life. If I do not choose to create a new life, this egg falls away and is washed out of my body with the purifying blood. Then a new egg is born and grows, and so the cycle continues, the great cycle of the power of creation of which we are all a part. This great power of life lies in my hands. I am responsible for it.

Then girl breaks the egg into a bowl.
The circle of women then say to her:

You are now one of us. We welcome you into the community of women.

They put into her hands the covenant book from her naming celebration and a bound book with blank pages where the young woman can write her secret thoughts. On the first page is inscribed her secret, symbolic name given to her at her naming ceremony and revealed to her now at her puberty. She pronounces the name: "My secret name is _____ ." All the women respond, "Welcome, _____ ." The rite then ends with a party.

COMING OF AGE: A RITUAL FOR A PERSON LEAVING HOME, *by Adele Arlett*[3]

Parents and friends of the young person gather, if possible at the parents' home. Each person brings a long strand of yarn or ribbon of different colors and textures, and one cut flower. The parents provide the vase and greenery to hold the flowers.

As the vase fills with flowers, people gather around a large bowl of water placed in the center of the room. The parents step forward, stir the water with their hands, and begin to reflect:

I am reminded today of the waters of your birth, of the excitement of new life, of new love entering the world. (They may then relate some story of the conception or birth or their coming into relationship with the person leaving.)

When we give birth we know it is just a beginning. As some animals carry their young in a pouch, even so we humans enfold our young for many years in layers of love and protection from the greater world. Now, at the time of emergence, we feel again the excitement of new birth.

All come forward to the water, dip hands in, and lift arms high so the water runs down the arms to drip from the elbows. They circle the emergent person and lay hands on her or him, saying:

We praise the living water of our many births. May we always welcome it, that we may have life and have it to the full.

The person responds:

I leave the home of my childhood rejoicing, with mind and heart open to the new. Yet may all I have been remain with me in who I shall become.

A friend says:

As you have been loved in this home, so may your home become a new center of love for the world.

Another:

As you have been nurtured, so may you nurture others.

Another:

May you maintain a home that will be center of joy and life for all humankind.

Presentation of gifts:

We bring you hand soap (a harsh variety such as mechanics would use) so that you may never be afraid to get your hands dirty in the service of your neighbor.

We bring you lotion, so that those hands may be soft for touching with love.

(Parents): We bring you powder for your feet. May they carry you far, but never so far they cannot bring you home again.

The parents take their long strand of yarn in their hands (one end of which is being held by the young person) and cut the person free. Friends all extend their yarn to the young person and to each other, tying a wild net of knots and connections.

The emergent person then turns to the parents and ties a deliberate and strong knot, uniting her or his own yarn in a new tie with theirs, saying:

Remembering both our joy and pain, I choose you, my parents, as part of my adult community of mutual love and support.

Someone says:

As our many connections make up the web of human life encircling this planet, we welcome you to the responsibility and the joy of supporting that life.

Another:

And in turn we offer you this small gift as a sign of our love and support for you. (This can be an address book with the names and phone number of those who are present and any others who wish to be included, each name entered in the person's own hand, along with a collection of money to help the young person get started.)

The celebration may then end with an appropriate joyful song and a party.

COVENANTING CELEBRATIONS FOR CREATING NEW FAMILIES

Official Christian ethics rejects both premarital and extramarital sexuality, attempting to make the first sexual intercourse ("deflowering") of the female coincide with her wedding night. Throughout much of Christian history, the church forbade contraception for married couples. The woman was expected to be sexually available to her husband on demand; she was not allowed to define her own sexual needs. Marriage was expected to be permanent, and divorce was rejected by most Christians until recently. All these values are in disrepute at the present time, yet there continue to be both a great need and a longing for committed and faithful relationships that can build new families and provide stability for people throughout their lives.

I believe that adult society should overcome its hostility and hypocrisy toward the sexuality of young people. On the one hand, we should expect that young people in the late teens and early twenties (this should not be forced on pre- and early teens) will enter into sexual experimentation. Adults should help them begin linking sexual experience with genuine caring and affection for the other person, overcoming sexual objectification and exploitation typical of our culture. Women particularly should be helped to have the courage to reject sexual demands by males when these are not linked with real friendship and concern, but are depersonalized and exploitative assertions of control and domination. When a young woman decides to become sexual, she should know how to use contraceptives and be clear about the necessity of using them until she decides to bear and raise a child.

Since there is an increasing gap in modern society between sexual maturity (puberty) and social maturity (independence, capacity to form a household and raise children), we should also expect young people to form quasi-committed but impermanent living relationships in the transition period between late teens and the stage of social maturity when two people are ready to establish a household and perhaps raise children. In many cases, these "living together" relationships are later transformed into committed marriages. There is no evidence that marital fidelity is lessened because the marriage covenant was preceded by earlier, impermanent relationships. Most earlier tribal societies allowed such a period of experimentation and yet expected permanent and exclusive bonding from the couple once they marry. The traditional Christian practice has often made both sex and marriage a rude awakening for the woman who marries a man she does not really know on an intimate basis and discovers his bad habits only after marriage.

Moreover, the chastity-at-marriage rule has generally applied in patriarchal societies only to the female. The male was expected to experiment sexually but then not marry sexually available women. This created not only a sexual double standard, but also a sexual class division between "bad girls"—those who are sexually available before marriage—and "good girls,"—chaste women who can safely be married. Much of this division has broken down today, yet it often means simply that males transfer their concepts of sexual availability without responsibility to all women. Women who resist these demands are told they are "square."

We are still far from a genuine ethic of sexual responsibility for both males and females. Young males need puberty and sexual initiation guidance from older males that would promote responsible sexuality. I have not constructed such material in this book because it must come from males. It awaits the formation of the male counterpart of Women-Church, through which human-church—church of women and men beyond patriarchy—can be formed.

Couples who decide to enter a committed relationship that includes a common household, but who are not ready to make a permanent commitment to each other, should reflect in an intentional way on their relationship and work out understandings about sharing work and money. They may decide to enter a short-term covenant relationship that would be renewed on a periodic basis. A housewarming party in which they announce these intentions and are affirmed by friends would signal their intention to enter into this type of relationship.

The following two covenant celebrations envision couples that have developed a mature sexual and personal friendship and are ready to enter a committed, family-building covenant with each other. I assume that such couples intend their covenant to be exclusive and permanent, the basis of creating a new family that will not only have the stability for raising children (if the couple wishes to do so), but also will sustain each partner to the end of their lives. Although such covenants may not be able to sustain these hopes, there seems to me no reason to enter into such family-building covenants unless one intends in good faith to create a faithful and committed relationship that will sustain both partners' lives on a long-term basis, especially since less committed and impermanent relationships are available to those who do not wish to make this kind of commitment.

I include here both a covenant celebration for a heterosexual couple and for a lesbian couple. I intend the concept of family building to apply in a similar way to both types of relationship. Women in lesbian couples may have had earlier heterosexual relations and may be raising children from those relationships, or they may acquire their own children either by adoption or artificial insemination. I therefore assume that child raising may also be included in the lesbian covenant, while the heterosexual covenant may or may not include child raising.

COVENANT CELEBRATION FOR A HETEROSEXUAL COUPLE

This covenanting should be preceded by a careful period of preparation and counseling. The period of preparation should include an investigation of the legal aspects of marriage under the state laws of the area. One should find out whether property brought into the marriage or acquired during the marriage will pass under the husband's name. Also the question of the legal change of the wife's name should be discussed. Since the disappearance of the wife's name into that of her husband is the most conspicuous remnant of the old patriarchal marriage law under which the woman lost her legal identity at marriage, a joint name constructed of both family names or a new family name taken by the couple is preferable. Prenuptial agreements may be drawn up with a lawyer to circumvent these patriarchal aspects of marriage laws.

In addition, the couple should explore in depth their assumptions about male and female roles in marriage and come to a personal covenant agreement about shared household work, shared finances, and shared promotion of paid work and personal development in society. Some summary of these agreements might be included in the marriage ceremony.

The Marriage Rite

The marriage rite may include songs and readings that are chosen by the couple to express their particular understanding of love and relationship. It may include an announcement by a presiding minister of the intention to marry and form a new family, with the affirmation of this intent by each member of the couple. The vows then taken by the couple to each other not only should be egalitarian (that is, not use the word obey for the female), but they need to be explicit about the aspects of mutuality intended by the couple. The following vows adapted from the *Alternative Celebrations Catalogue*[4] are a good example:

The couple faces each other, joins hands and repeats:

> I take you (name) to be my (husband/wife), and
> I promise you these things:
> I will be faithful to you and honest with you.
> I will respect you, trust you, help you, listen to you, and care for you.
> I will share my life with you in plenty and in want.
> I will forgive you as we have been forgiven, and I will try with you to better understand ourselves, the world, and God(ess),
> so that together we may serve God(ess) and others forever.

The minister then announces the marriage to the community present and asks if they will support them in this covenant. The community affirms its intention to do so. The vows can then be followed by a wedding Eucharist or a banquet, or both. Since there is much material available on alternative marriage services, I make no attempt here to spell out this rite in further detail.

COVENANT CELEBRATION FOR A LESBIAN COUPLE

Much less available are covenant services for homosexual couples. The following rite was developed for the covenant celebration of Phyllis Athey and Mary Jo Osterman on August 19, 1982, at Wheadon United Methodist Church in Evanston, Illinois.[5]

Covenant Rite

Gathering Music: "Shooting Star," by Chris Williamson, and "The Road I Took To You," by Meg Christian.

Call to Awareness:

Phyllis: We stand here today in the presence of people from so many parts of our journeys. You are the people who have been family for us. We rejoice that you have come to witness our beginning, our new family.

Mary Jo: We have brought this community of friends and colleagues together to celebrate the beginning of a new part our journey. We are here to make a covenant together.

Community: We rejoice to be part of this celebration. We have loved and valued you separately. We will continue to love and value you in relationship. (The community is now invited to make statements of reflection and celebration.)

Prayer of Confession

in unison:

Oh God of freedom and wholeness, we confess that we have all faltered on our journeys to the New Earth. We have been divided against each other by jealousy and competition. We have been restricted in our relationships by hierarchies of power and limitations of roles. These burdens have caused us to stumble on our journeys, but we have been afraid to give them up. (Silent reflection on the confession.)

Words of Assurance:

God has given us the gifts of freedom and commitment. The Spirit enables us to claim them. We can go forward in joy.

Song of Awareness:

"We Are Gathered Here Together in the Presence of the Spirit," by Dorie Ellzey.

Scripture Reading: Ruth 1:6–18

(Naomi returns from Moab to her own country of Judah, telling her widowed daughters-in-law to return to their own people. But Ruth refuses to be parted from Naomi, saying, "Where you go, I will go, and where you lodge, I will lodge; your people shall be my people, and your God my God; where you die I will die and there will I be buried.")

Interpretation of the Word:
Reflection on the meaning of covenants and families.

Statement of Intentions:

Phyllis: Out of all the people and places of my life, it is you with whom I choose to be in a special covenant. It is you whom I have chosen to rearrange my life around and with. I celebrate the gift of this relationship and the work of giving that gift.

Mary Jo: Of all the people I have known on my journey, it is you with whom I choose to journey on in covenant. With you and your life I choose to weave the strands of my life. I celebrate the gift of this relationship and the work of receiving that gift.

Covenant Vows:

I love you, special woman, and I want to give you the best of who I am and who I am becoming. I choose to live in covenant with you. I know that the journey will not be easy, but I live better when I live with you.

I promise to work, to play, to dream with you and to do my best to make those dreams come true. I promise to share your tears and your laughter and allow you to share mine. I promise to respect the need of both of us to have separate space and to come back to you as I trust you will come back to me. I promise to respect you and to celebrate the ways you are different from me. I promise to seek your forgiveness when we have failed to live up to our covenant.

Exchange of Rings; Claiming a Common Name:

Minister: What is it you have brought to each other to symbolize this covenant?

Phyllis/Mary Jo: I give this ring to you.

Mary Jo: It represents tears turning sideways into laughter,

Phyllis: and a flame burning toward the future.

Phyllis/Mary Jo: It is a gift and a symbol of our love.

Minister: What name do you now claim as your common name?

Phyllis/Mary Jo: We claim the name of Kinheart as the name for ourselves in relationship. This is the name that conveys the kinship we have in our hearts and in our lives.

Song of Covenant:
"Wherever You Go I Will Go," by Weston Priory
Pronouncement of the Covenant:

Minister: Phyllis Kinheart Athey and Mary Jo Kinheart Osterman, you are two people now joined in covenant before God and this community (embrace).

Community Response: We claim this new relationship between you, Phyllis and Mary Jo. We will hold you accountable to the covenant you have made here today. We will support you with our prayers and with the gifts of our community.

Communion Rite

This communion is our gift to the community. It symbolizes connections of the past with the present and the present with the future. We invite the congregation to join in a circle for the rite of connection, the prayer circle, and the communion. It is an open circle to which all are invited.

Mary Jo: This chalice of water holds the tears of the oppressed ones who have gone before us. I draw the sign of the tear on your face.
(Cup is passed from person to person with each marking a sign of a tear on the next person's cheek.)

Phyllis: This basket of raisins is the dried-up dreams of the generations who were not free. It symbolizes the work and the hopes that we have lost.
(Raisins are shared.)

Mary Jo: This basket of fresh cool grapes symbolizes our work, our dreams and our hopes; it is the fruit of the New Earth.

Phyllis: This loaf of bread made with raisins is the new wheat and the old raisins mixed together to feed us for the journey. We claim the past, we move into the future. We offer this bread for communion.

Prayer Circle:

The people are invited to offer prayers of reflection and celebration. The grapes and bread are then passed and shared, to the accompaniment of the Communion Song, "Take and Eat."

Benediction by Minister:

We have claimed past tears and lost dreams. We have entered into a new covenant and tasted its goodness. We now go forward on the journey. Amen.

Sending Forth Song: "Song of the Soul," by Chris Williamson.

All are invited to a reception.

BIRTHING PREPARATION LITURGY

Men and women gather in a circle with the pregnant woman in the center. The father of the coming child holds up a bowl of seeds and says:

From ancient times people have seen a symbolic connection between seeds sown in the earth and the semen sown in the womb. This symbol of seeds links the mystery of fertility in humans with that of all nature. We are all part of one mystery of life, which is sown with seeds full of germinal power to create humans, animals, and plants. These seeds in human and animal males fuse with other seeds created by females and gestate in the mysterious life-giving powers of the womb to bring forth living, moving beings. We share together this mystery of seeds from males and from females."

The bowl of seeds is passed around and shared.
All now lie in the circle touching one another's stomachs. One woman says:

In the beginning was the egg, and the egg teemed with the life of all living things. All living things mingled together in the waters that were within the egg. And the egg expanded until it filled all the space. Its upper curve became the vault of heaven and its lower curve became the earth. And the waters separated into the waters held in the vault of heaven that made the rain, and the waters below that became the rivers and oceans. And the Mother-Spirit moved within the egg, shaping and forming all the living things that grew within the egg; plants emerged bearing many kinds of fruit; and animals of all kinds, fish that swam in the sea, birds that flew in the air, and four-footed animals that frolicked across the face of the earth. Finally there emerged between the vault of heaven and the curve of earth human beings, male and female. They were the most vulnerable of all living creatures. They lacked warm coats of fur to shelter them from the cold, or sharp claws to scratch the bark off trees, or keen instincts to tell them what to do and what to avoid. They were not fleet of foot, or keen of ear like some of the other animals. So the Mother-Spirit took pity on them and gave them the gift of intelligence to make up for all they lacked, and she told them, "Know that you are dependent on all the other beings of the earth. The animals and plants will clothe and feed you. You need them, but they do not need you. Take from them only what you need, taking care always to thank the animals and plants that clothe and feed you. Learn to live in harmony with all other beings that I have made. Through you all living creatures will become conscious, will be reflected through the intelligence of your spirit, and will celebrate themselves in song and story and image. Guard well this treasure of intelligence and use it to protect and celebrate life."

The group rises to a kneeling position. One woman says:

But the humans gradually forgot how to use their gift of intelligence wisely. They began to look on the animals and plants as mere objects to be used and consumed, and they forgot to thank them for their gifts. Instead, they imagined themselves to be the rulers of nature, controlling and using all things as they pleased. And they also began to look on one another as mere objects to be used and thought they should rule over each other. And men forgot the Mother-Spirit and sought to become themselves the eternal Creator and the Lords of creation. And they looked on woman's body as a tool to be enslaved and used, through which they could create life by command, rather than giving and receiving life one from another as a gift from the Mother-Spirit. And all things became violent and hard. Animals became enemies of humans: rivers ran with poisons; the air became fetid with death; and even birth giving became hard and unhappy. But each new child brings to us the promise of restoration of our original goodness and harmony with all living things. Just as the Mother-God of Israel labored for forty years to bring forth a new people in the wilderness, and the Mother-church fled into the wilderness to protect and nurture the Christ-child, so every mother repeats the primal mystery of the Mother-Spirit of the original creation and the Mother-God who nurtures a redemptive people. Every new child is the promised child, the child who comes forth innocent of the history of evil and who catches a glimpse of the original harmony of all living things. Through this new child we too catch a glimpse of the original harmony and turn our feet toward the restoration of love and peace between human and human, humans and animals, humans and plants, humans and the Mother-Spirit who bears us all within her womb.

The pregnant woman squats in the birthing position, while all the others gather round her and uphold her on all sides, chanting:

Let the primal Mother-Spirit empower you. Let her great birthing energy flow through you. Bring forth with victory and joy the promised child.

All rise and join in upraised hands and dance in the circle, singing:

Alleluia, alleluia, a child is born; original blessing is with us; hope be restored to us."

RITUAL OF MOVING FROM AN OLD TO A NEW HOUSE

Household members and friends gather in the old house. After an initial welcome and statement of the purpose of the ritual, the group moves from room to room in the house. In each room various household members recall sad and happy events that took place in this room. Gathering around a table, one says:

We put now a closure to the sad or painful events that took place in this house. These difficult moments are now behind us. They do not need to be forgotten, but they no longer cause us pain. We will not let them control our future. We carry with us the happy memories, drawing strength from the good times that we have had in this house.

A plant is carefully unpotted, taking care to keep the ball of earth around the roots. The ball of earth is put in a porous cloth sack, soaked in water, and then wrapped in plastic. Someone says:

To move from one house to another is like unpotting this plant. Our roots have gone down into the soil of this community and drawn nourishment from the network of friends. Like an uprooted plant, we must extract with care our lives from this place, seeking not to bruise the many roots that support our life, but to draw them up intact and transplant them to another community, another house, and new networks of friends.

The plant is then carried in a journey to the new house. The ritual of dedication of the new house begins with the householders and friends standing outside the house. Someone says:

This our house we transform into a home, a place of peace, security, and love. Let it be a place of joy, of fruitful work, refreshing relaxation, and strengthening ties with those we love.

With a pot of incense and fragrant branches, the group now traces a circle around the house. A pointed stick draws a furrow, and grain is scattered in the furrow as the group circles the house. The group stops at certain points and says together:

The peace and security of Holy Wisdom and good friends surround this house and guard it from all evil.

The group then enters the house. They go from window to window and from door to door, saying:

The peace and security of Holy Wisdom and good friends secure this window (door) and keep all evil from entering here.

As each room is entered, the good possibilities of the activities that will take place in this room are evoked. For example, in the kitchen:

In this kitchen let the walls echo with laughter and good conversation. Let the smell of fragrant dishes arise from the stove. Let the work of this kitchen be shared by all who partake of its good things. Let its work be the expression of creative imagination, our bodies and spirits nourished into health and strength by its produce.

After the invocation of the good spirits of each room, incense is wafted and water, made fragrant with rose petals, is sprinkled throughout the room.

The ritual ends with the group gathering at the table. The plant is carefully taken out of its protective sack and repotted in a new container. Some final reflections are made by the person or persons moving into the house about what it means to put down their roots in this community, among these friends and the activities of this new place. The group joins hands and pledges support in this process of putting down roots in new soil.

MENOPAUSE LITURGY

Women gather in a circle. Women who have not yet reached menopause are given purple candles. Those who no longer menstruate are given yellow candles. The candles are lit, and each woman meditates on her candle while the meditation is read:

In woman is the great birthing and creating energy. This creating energy takes many forms. It is the power of ovaries to create eggs and womb to nurture the seeded egg into another human being. It is the creative energy to bring forth poetry, song, image. It is the creative energy to reflect on all reality, to mirror the world in the mind and bring forth rationale discourse, and to teach others of the secrets of the workings of the world around us. It is the creative energy to create homes, communities, gatherings of people to accomplish tasks and to live together as friends. It is the creative energy to work the clay of the earth, the fibers of plants, and the wool of animals into useful vessels to carry things and many colored clothes to vest our bodies and the walls and floors of our homes. All of these are our many creative mother-energies. Today one among us lets go of one kind of birthing energy, the energy to create other human beings. As she relinquishes this one kind of birthing energy, she takes up all the more fully the other kinds of birthing energies, the energy to create poetry, art, song, vessels, textiles, knowledge, and communities of people who work and live together. As one kind of birthing energy ebbs away and is no more, she enters fully into her many other birthing energies. We pause for a moment of regret for the one birthing energy which is no more. (All turn their candles upside down and pour out a drop of wax, and then turn them right side again.) We rejoice as she enters into her full powers in the many other birthing energies which are hers.

The menopausal woman extinguishes her purple candle and is handed a yellow candle which is lit by one of the other women with a yellow candle. The women with yellow candles say to her:

Welcome to the community of women who no longer ovulate and bleed and who create now with their minds and their spirits.

The woman now has an opportunity to reflect on what this transition moment means in her life. She may speak of pleasures and regrets she had in her years as one who bled and could bear children, and what hopes she sees ahead of her as a creator of culture.

A cup of herbal tea (witch hazel) is raised and is blessed with the words:

206 / LITURGICAL LIFE AND WOMEN-CHURCH

This is the healing tea which our mothers and their mothers before them drank to calm the distresses of the monthly cycle of egg and blood. This healing tea links all women—those who do not yet bleed, those who bleed, and those who no longer bleed—in one community of creators and caretakers of life in its many forms.

The cup of tea is passed and shared among all present.

CRONING LITURGY

In American youth-oriented culture, people lack ways of experiencing positively the transition to old age. Old women past child-bearing and child-raising years particularly are seen as useless. It is not accidental that the persecution of women as witches focused mostly on postmenopausal women who were widows or single and independent of men. The words for old women such as "crone, "hag," "witch," and "old bag" evoke images of women who are ugly, withered, decrepit, useless, repulsive, and evil. The following "croning" liturgy transforms this negative connotation of the old women into a positive one. It connects the word *crone* with *cronus* (time) and the wisdom of long life and experience. To become a "crone" is to become one of the "wise old women" who have gathered up the fruits of their long experience into profound understanding, and who serve as resources of wisdom for younger women. It can be celebrated on the birthday of a woman sometime between sixty and seventy years of age.

This is the time of retirement for employed people. Although retirement is not as traumatic for women as for men, since their identities have not been as tied up with paid employment as men, this transition can also be wrenching for women, as they identify more with paid work today. If a woman has raised children, they are usually gone from the home by this time, and often women are left without husbands as well, through divorce or death. The old woman alone is particularly likely to be in poverty in our culture. Thus to surround and affirm old women as wise ones and resources of wisdom is to transform the hostile attitudes toward both women and old age in our culture. The following croning liturgy was done for Janet Kalven, a longtime member of the Grail, (a Catholic women's religious community) and one of the midwives of feminist theology and Women-Church, on her seventieth birthday.

Gathering Music

The rite starts with some gathering music as people settle down together and come into awareness as a community. This is followed by singing to the tune of "Jacob's ladder":

> We are casting Janet's circle . . . sisters all around.
> Come now, join us, cast the circle . . . sisters all around.
> All together, form a circle . . . sisters all around.

Statement of Theme

This is Janet's circle. Like Janet herself, it is rooted in the earth and blooming. Like Janet herself, it represents a communal on-goingness. Today Janet will be crowned crone. And a crone is —to recover a name—a wise woman, a wise old woman. You must have lived a long time to gain wisdom, and Janet has not wasted a moment of her long life.

Casting the Circle

Circle-Casting Incantation #1

> Stand in faith and make a difference
> Women growing make a difference
> In this world, make a difference
> Women can make a difference
> Janet has made a difference
> > standing firm
> > speaking out
> > striding forth
> Women can become different
> Difference can become women
> Women can make a difference
> Difference, difference, women-difference
> Janet can/has made a difference.[6]

Circle-Casting Incantation #2

Jewish women of the early Jesus movement in Israel, Mary Magdalene, Salome, and the many others, gather round us, claim Janet as one of yourselves. Give her, give us courage and strength for today.

Jewish women of the early Christian missionary movement, Prisca and Junia, and the many coequal colleagues of Paul, gather round us, claim Janet as one of yourselves. Give her, give us inspiration for the new missionary task of today.

We cast this circle with you and around you, Janet, one who affirms the mighty vision of Jesus for justice—justice for the powerless, the sick, the oppressed, the women.

God/Goddess in our midst, claim Janet as one who has always loved and followed you. Help her, help us in the building of your human world, over against the resistance and pull of all oppressive powers and patriarchal structures. Help her, help us in the making whole of your creation.[7]

Circle-Casting Incantation #3

One of the four issues that we are addressing as we form this circle is a closet item which Janet has not flinched about bringing out. This is the concern Janet has about the problems of aging in our ageist society; the concern that people growing old must have more options than are available, that people can bloom into and through old age. Janet has not hesitated in the struggle to get people to listen to the voices of the older persons in our midst.[8]

Circle-Casting Incantation #4

Spirit of air
Spirit of fire
Spirit of water
Spirit of earth
Come join us as we celebrate the bloomings of one of yours.

Janet plants and tends your flowers
    herbs
    and trees.

She rejoices in your fullness.
She defends your resources against the weapon-manufacturers.
She refuses to pay taxes for nuclear weapons
    which threaten to destroy all your life.

Spirit of air, come join us.
Spirit of fire, come join us.
Spirit of water, come join us.
Spirit of earth, come join us.
Fill and renew Janet.
Fill and renew us.[9]

Readings:

From one of the books of Wisdom, such as the book of Sirach 51:12–20, 22. (The text speaks of the rewards of the lifelong pursuit of Wisdom. "I sought Wisdom from my youth and will seek her to the end of my life. She has been my delight. Through her I made progress in my studies, learned to practice virtue and gained eloquence and understanding to praise God.")

Wisdom Sharing:

Some of the passages from the writings of Janet Kalven at different periods of her life were then read. Others shared how they had experienced Janet's wisdom. Horoscope picture and interpretation was then presented. Each person then took a flower from a vase and presented it to Janet, who gathered the flowers into a bouquet. Janet then responded to the presentations by her own reflections.

The croning liturgy ended with singing the last two verses of "Janet's Circle."

THE DYING VIGIL

Along with birth, death is one of the major points in the natural life cycle that has been placed primarily in the hands of doctors and thus made to appear "unnatural." Although one should avail oneself of modern medicine to do all that is reasonable to cure curable illness and prolong conscious and productive life, it is an inappropriate denial of death to expend great amounts of money and medical equipment to prolong a person's life in a comatose state. If possible, when it is clear that a person is dying and yet is still conscious, she should be released from the hospital to die at home amid friends and family. Home nursing help is increasingly available to do the more difficult tasks of the home care of the dying, thus allowing family and friends to surround the dying person on the personal level and support her in their dying.

The room where the person is dying should be kept sweet smelling with fresh flowers. Softly glowing candles might be placed in the room, particularly on each side of the person's bed. Friends and family can take turns sitting with the person even if unconscious, reading or thinking quietly or speaking to the dying person and listening to her. The dying person may want poetry read or music played. The dying person should, above all, be allowed to define how she wants to die and not have others decide things against her wishes.

Rite of Reconciliation and Passage for the Dying

If the dying person wishes it, and while she is still conscious and able to participate, a simple rite of reconciliation and passage might be developed. The rite should have three aspects: reconciliation with family and friends, relinquishment of responsibility for ongoing tasks to those who will remain, and in gathering of the spirit.

Reconciliation:

Here the dying person might be allowed to say things about her life with which she feels dissatisfied, areas where she feels she has failed or has unresolved conflicts. At the end of this confession, the dying person is blessed on the forehead with water, with the words:

Through the power of the Mother-Spirit we are empowered to forgive one another. Our brother Jesus has shown us the way of forgiveness and has gone ahead of us in the passage through death to resurrection. In the name of Christ and in the power of the Spirit you are forgiven all your sins. Let all feelings of failure, guilt, and sadness at things done or left undone pass away from your mind and heart.

Relinquishment of Responsibility:

Here the dying person might mention areas where she feels not yet ready to let go. She may be worried that other people will not do things as she would wish them to be done. Her spirit may be still drawn into and attached to tasks that she feels she has left undone and yet can no longer do. She may want to charge certain members of the family or friends to perform certain tasks. After these reflections, the dying person is invited to relinquish these concerns for ongoing tasks to the community of those who will remain after her. The person is anointed on the forehead, breast, hands, and feet with fragrant oil, with the words:

The reins of responsibility for work and for care for others now slip from your hands. Let go of the lines that attach you to the tasks of daily life. These need no longer be your responsibility or concern. These concerns and tasks now belong to others. They can do them. And they will do them. For well or for ill, it is now their job, and no longer yours. Be now at peace. Allow yourself to let go and be at peace.

The Ingathering of the Spirit:

A basket of fruits and flowers is placed in the dying person's arms with the words:

These fruits and flowers represent the good fruits and blossoms of your life. Think now on all that is happy and productive in your life, your accomplishments, your joys, your times of fullness of life.

The speaker pauses, while the dying one reflects on and perhaps mentions things with which she feels particular satisfaction. Others may also choose to mention things they see as the person's important accomplishments. While raising the basket into the air in offering, these words are said:

All this goodness of doing and being of your life is gathered here together into one, brought together into a single whole and offered up to the Mother-Spirit, the source of all life, who will take it back into herself and make it immortal and everlasting. Your human spirit now rises to the Eternal Spirit and joins with it in everlasting life. Rejoice and be glad. Alleluia, alleluia.

The vigil with the dying continues with the person until death, seeking to help her take into herself as much as possible this passage from self-blame to self-acceptance, from attachment to relinquishment, to the final focusing of the spirit toward transcendent life.

THE FUNERAL

Funerals should be simple and, as much as possible, kept in the hands of family and friends, without ostentatious expense that taxes the resources of the living. (For examples of simple funerals, see the *Alternative Celebrations Catalogue.* [10]) Flowers can be brought from peoples' gardens or as potted plants available from garden shops, which can then be shared after the funeral, rather than using expensive and perishable floral displays.

The funeral may take the form of a banquet, or else a eucharistic meal followed by a community meal. During the assembly, songs, poems, and readings that the dead person particularly liked may be read. In some cases the dying person has suggested things she wants done at the funeral. There should be a sense that the person's spirit is present and celebrating with the community.

The main part of the funeral takes the form of testimonies to the dead person by those who knew her in various roles, such as a spouse, a child, a friend, and a work colleague. Each shares memories of the person, not in a falsely laudatory way, but in a way that can both highlight the best of the person's spirit and also can recall faults and foibles in a humorous and forgiving way.

After the tributes and banquet, there may be a procession to the place of interment. The prayers at the grave should indicate both an acceptance of the mortal aspects of our human being, as well as a trust in the mystery of the transcendence of mortality.

Now the body of (name) returns to the earth, becomes again earth, earth to earth returning, the matter of the body dissolving back into the great source of all life and becoming compost for the nourishment of new living things. Just as leaves fall from trees and decay into the ground so that the new plants may arise in spring, so too our bodies must disintegrate into the earth to become matter for the next generation of living things.

At these words a spring of grain is placed in the grave, along with the body or the urn of ashes.

Yet our perishable bodies contain also the mystery of imperishable life. As Paul says (1 Cor. 15), "What you sow does not come to life unless it dies. And what you sow is not the body which is to be but the bare kernel, perhaps of wheat or some other grain. . . . What is sown is perishable, what is raised is imperishable. It is sown in dishonor. It is raised in glory. It is sown in weakness, it is raised in power. It is sown in a physical body. It is raised in a spiritual body." Unless a seed falls into the earth and dies, it does not rise again. So our human spirits must let go of their perishable form to be transformed into imperishable spirit. This is a great mystery which we do not pretend to understand. But we trust with that faith of little children who put their hand into the hand of a loving parent, knowing they will be led aright. So we trust, even without knowledge, in that great Creator-Spirit from which all life comes, and to which it returns, to raise this human spirit to immortal life. Take back now our sister into your bosom, O Wisdom-Spirit. In faith we entrust her into your arms.

Rather than a permanent grave, some may prefer to scatter ashes into water or into a mound of earth, which will be used to fertilize vegetable and flower plants, to symbolize their relinquishment of their mortal selves back into the earth as the matrix for new generations of life.

10. Encircling Our Transformation: Seasonal Celebrations

The hallowing of planetary rhythms that shape the cycles of the day, the month, and the year have traditionally been an important framework for religious observance. The Hebrew tradition added the nonnatural cycle of the week. Jewish and Christian religious observance continues to be shaped by the weekly cycle, as does global secular culture influenced by the Jewish and Christian traditions. Modern technology has made human life much more oblivious to these fundamental cycles of our environment. Heating and cooling modify our awareness of changes of temperature, and electric light allows us to ignore the setting of the sun, which once determined the human workday. Technological alteration of our awareness of these environmental changes tends to make us oblivious to the deeper ways in which our bodies and psyches are still subtly attuned to these variations. This obliviousness to our personal and cosmic body has increasingly destructive consequences. Perhaps some restoration of religious observance of these cyclic changes can help us to become more aware of the interdependence of our micro- and macrocosm and so more concerned for their health.

THE CYCLE OF THE DAY AND NIGHT

The Hebrews saw one day ending and the next beginning when the sun set, and so they counted the beginning of the day at sunset. Christian culture has tended to think of the day starting at sunrise. But whether one is a "day person" or a "night person," greeting new light and the tasks of the new day, and then withdrawing from daily tasks, preparing for night and rest, is an important rhythm for daily prayer, although one which each person needs to shape according to their own patterns of work and rest, rising and sleeping. The prayer of rising might take the form of the hatha yoga "Salute to the Sun" (see p. 274) or some other bowing and stretching exercise, together with some whispered thought of thanksgiving for the renewal of light and life after darkness and sleep. The night prayer, in turn, might take the form of a meditational posture with deep breathing that relaxes all the parts of the body, unwinds from the activities of the day, and allows care and anxiety to be put aside so that mind and body can rest.

The practice of gathering one's family or household for a common meal once a day (without television and other distractions) is also an important practice that needs to be revived to humanize our increasingly inhuman life patterns. We can offer a prayer of blessing over food to thank God/ess for the plants, animals, and water that sustain our life and remembers all those whose work goes into our nourishment. Some attention to the kind of food we eat, avoiding additives and eating low on the food chain with a concern for making food available for all, can be a new way of "keeping kosher."[1] This may also take the form of avoiding the "foods of oppression"; that is, foods presently being boycotted because of the excessively unethical means of their production, although until there is a significantly new world system of food production and distribution, we cannot be ethically pure in our habits of consumption. We should pursue conscientious food habits, not in order to be righteous, but to be reminded of our links with other people and our need to pursue justice in matters of food.

THE CYCLE OF THE WEEK

If it is not possible to gather one's household or community on a daily basis, at least a weekly community meal can be a way of renewing human relationships around the dinner table. The weekly or Sabbath meal can be a more elaborate ritual of blessing of food and renewal of community. Ideally, those who gather for this meal should not be hurried, but they should feel comfortable spending at least two hours or more talking together over food. For those of Christian tradition, I suggest studying the traditional prayers and practices of the Shabbat meal, which can be adapted to the language and perspective of the group (see the inclusive language prayer book of Congregation Beth El of Sudbury River Valley, Sudbury, Massachusetts).[2]

The Shabbat meal begins by kindling the Shabbat lights (traditionally done by the woman of the household). The Shabbat lights recall the original creation of light by God at the beginning. Light is also the symbol of divinity, both as the creative source of all things, and as the symbol of life and consciousness in each person. It represents the warmth and light that nourish all created things. It is also the light of remembrance and hope that links us to all that has been and is to be.

After kindling the lights, someone blesses the cup of wine that symbolizes the vivifying power of blood and soul that inspirit all creation. Then the bread is blessed, and we reflect not only on the gifts of the earth from which food comes, but also on the work of human hands, which shapes these gifts into forms that are both fit and delightful to eat. The interdependence of human work and divine gift is summed up in the prayer:

Holy One of Blessing, your presence fills creation, bringing forth bread from the earth.

This can also be a time of thanksgiving and remembrance of the work of the week, when each person at the table can share something of their week's experiences. The meal is brought to a fitting closure with a blessing at the end of it.

In a world that increasingly values people by their ability to work continually or else to vacation in an expensive and frenetic way, a renewal of the weekly Sabbath rest is imperative to the salvation of the world. Traditional Jewish wisdom has said that salvation will come only when Israel learns to fully observe the Sabbath.[3] These injunctions take on a new meaning today in a world that only knows how to "do" in a compulsive and functionalist way, but has little sense of the larger design and purpose of doing and has lost the ability to "be." To learn to rest, to celebrate being rather than doing, is essential to recovering the balance of life. One way to begin recovering the balance is to make firm commitments to do no alienating work on one day a week.

Refusing to go to meetings, carry work home, go to the office, shop, or engage in any other workday activities on the Sabbath is the first step for clearing one day for genuine relaxation and renewal of oneself and one's relationships with others. This should not be done in a spirit of legalistic repression, but in a spirit of happy protest against the workaholic lifestyle. The demands to work all the time as the measure of one's worth have grown so endemic that one needs to make little vows and rules for oneself to resist them. The weekly celebration of the Sabbath should be both a way of renewing oneself and creation in its authentic balance and rhythm, and anticipating the ultimate redemption of all things. By doing only restful, life-enhancing, and playful things once a week, one anticipates the redeemed state of things and thus keeps the ultimate goal and meaning of life during the week in its proper focus. The Sabbath is not a time to work or fight for the redemption of the world, but a time to anticipate and celebrate its presence already in our midst.

THE CYCLE OF THE MONTH: MENSTRUAL AND NEW MOON RITUALS

Menstruation has been turned by patriarchal religion into a source and symbol of the marginalization of women from sacred power. Menstruating women were regarded as ritually taboo in Judaism. Remnants of this idea were restored in Eastern Orthodox and Medieval Christianity to suggest that the menstruating woman should refrain from the Eucharist, and that women's generic pollution forbids them to enter the sanctuary or touch holy objects.[4] This taboo lives on in secular myths that menstruating women are weak and irrational, and that their instability prohibits women from exercising responsible roles of power. Rites of menstruation in Women-Church exorcise this negative tradition that defines woman as taboo or cursed because of her monthly menstrual flow.

The exploration of the roots of these negative myths suggests that they originated in male fear of women's menstrual blood. This was due not only to male ignorance, which was mystified by the ability of women to bleed and not die, but also to a dim recognition that this flow of blood was connected with women's life-giving powers to conceive and bear new human beings. Menstruation is the end of one cycle of female potency and the beginning of another. In reclaiming menstruation as a symbol of female potency, women may be tempted to deny any element of weakness or negation involved in menstruation, and to claim instead that they are particularly powerful when they are menstruating. To combat patriarchal myths that women are raving maniacs and invalids during this period, women may wish to claim that they are energized by menstruation. But such a compensation also misses the mark.

Most women are a bit more fatigued when menstruating, and with good reason: their bodies are going through a process of sloughing off the uterine lining that had built up in preparation for conception and gestation. Although most women can carry on quite adequately in demanding tasks during this time, it is appropriate for women to find their own female-defined way of affirming the menstrual cycle. We should not deny that menstruation is the "autumn" within the female body, in which capacity for new life is shed and preparation is made for the birth of new potency.

Rachel Adler, in an article on the theological meaning of pollution taboos,[5] shows that the deep roots of the taboos against both menstruating women and those who have handled corpses lie in the awe and fear of the death side of the life cycle. She believes that women need to appropriate the rite of the *mikvah* (ritual bath) as a way of experiencing their own participation in the great mystery of dying away and regeneration by which the universe continually recreates itself. The waters of the *mikvah* must be living waters or running waters which connect with streams, rivers, and finally the seas of the cosmos. The descent into the *mikvah* (which also became the model for baptismal rites in Judaism, taken over by Christianity) is seen as a descent into the primal sea from which all things emerged in the original creation. Each month women participate in the descent into the void, in which mortal things dissolve and disappear to make way for new mortal things to spring forth, upheld by the immortal matrix of divine life.

Associated with the women's rite of monthly purification is Rosh Hodesh, or the ritual of the new moon.[6] It was traditionally a special women's holiday in which women did no work or only light work, withdrawing particularly from women's work such as spinning and weaving. It was preceded by a day of repentance, which repeated monthly the day of repentance after the New Year celebration Rosh Hashanah and Yom Kippur. The birth of the new moon was a celebration of new beginnings, associated with women's new beginnings of potency after menstruation. It carried a note of redemptive restoration of women to their original and promised equality with men, repairing the injustice done to them in history by repressing them to auxiliary status. In a similar way it was promised that in the day of redemption the moon would shine with equal light to the sun, receiving that light directly from the divine Shekinah (presence of God) and no longer as reflected light from the sun.

We have divided this rite into three sections: a reclaiming of menstruation, the *mikvah* ritual, and then the celebration of the new moon as a promise of women's redemption.

Reclaiming Menstruation

Women gather in a circle with a light green candle and a red candle for each woman. There is also a bowl with an egg for each woman and a ball of red yarn.

These two candles symbolize the mystery of life, its continuous dying and regeneration and the immortal Spirit which upholds this life process. Each month our bodies participate in this mystery, just as the earth participates in it each year as the old leaves fall off the trees and disintegrate into the soil to make rich fertile earth, and, in the spring, the new leaves shoot forth from the branches again. This green candle stands for that power of new life, and these eggs are the eggs that are born in our bodies each month and are implanted in the uterine wall, waiting to receive the sperm and grow into a new child. This red candle stands for the dying egg and the falling away of that place built up for the potential child, and the blood that washes it away into the primal waters, to make way for the new powers of life.

The red yarn is now wound around the wrists of each woman and back and forth between their bodies linking them together in a circle. They say together:

We are the circle of the mothers, the life-bearers. This yarn is the stream of power that unites us with each other, with all women, and with all the powers of life in the universe. This is our power, and yet it is more than our power. It is ours and yet greater than we. We celebrate this power, and hold it in deepest reverence and awe. We are its guardians, and not simply its owners. We seek to use it wisely and well.

The group may then spend some time telling stories of their experiences of their monthly cycles, their physical feelings of it, how it has been interpreted to them in the past, how they are coming to understand it in new ways. A scissor is passed at the end of this discussion and the thread binding each woman to the other is cut. Each winds the yarn around their right wrist.

The Mikvah Ritual

Shedding their clothes, the women now move to a pool of water. Standing together at its edge, someone says:

These are the waters of the primal sea, the waters of life from which all things came in the beginning and into which all things dissolve. Each month the powers of our bodies drain away and are washed back into the primal sea. Each month the powers of new life arise from this primal sea and empower us with the capacity to bring forth new life.

The women enter the pool and stand in a circle with their hands outstretched in front of them. Bending their knees they immerse themselves three times in the pool and rise to an upright position, saying each time the blessing: "Blessed is the dying away and blessed the regeneration." The women then emerge together from the water and clothe themselves in bright robes made of new cloth.

The New Moon Ritual

The women gather in a circle either outside or in a glassed, domed room where the sky is visible. Candles are set up in a circle in the center, around a bowl in which a large candle floats on liquid. Crowns of flowers are placed on each woman's head. The following prayer is said together:

Out of the void the new moon rises, giving promise of a great light to come, which will light up the night sky. Just so, the powers of new life arise from our bodies out of the void of the primal sea.

So too today women are arising from the night of hostility and fear of their life-making powers, reclaiming their holiness, remaking their lives. Never again will these mysteries of life and death and new life be defamed as cursed and evil. By learning to bless our bodies, we learn to bless again all creation and to live in harmony and peace with the earth.

Great Mother-Spirit of the universe, you bring new life to all things. You recreate the world in every instant, and shower the earth with all good things. Every night the stars appear, singing their song of love to you, and every morning the sun bursts forth from its resting place, showing your glory. The grasses dance in your breezes, the trees stretch forth their hands in delight, all things upheld with your ever-renewed energy.

Recreate us and all things anew, O Mother-Spirit. Banish the powers of destruction that crush the spirits of living things and choke the channels of communication of life-giving energy. Make the earth fresh with promise, as on the first day of creation. Make us new again, as on the day of our birth. Surround us with your life-giving energy and make us channels of your life-giving power.

Holding hands, the women may then sing some appropriate song. The celebration concludes with a feast.

Although this total ritual might be celebrated only occasionally, women should find ways to appropriate this understanding of their menstruation by constructing their own version of the ritual. They should find ways to retire from the press of regular activities during this period, taking some hours to withdraw entirely from regular work. In the Women-Church Center, small retreat houses are provided for women to get away for a few hours or days for walks, meditation, and restful pursuits. In this way, women become more alert to the actual experiences of their bodies through the month and learn ways to respond to their body signals and to renew themselves. Saunas and whirlpools help to relax and restore the body. An ordinary bathtub can have something of the same effect by first showering with hot jets all over the body and then immersing oneself in cool water. The mikvah ritual can be done by oneself after relaxing the body in water.

THE YEAR CYCLE: FALL FESTIVALS AND REMEMBRANCES

Many of us in modern society think of fall as the beginning of the year, in the sense of the new school and work year. Judaism traditionally began the new year with a season of repentance, although we have followed the Christian calendar in making the preparation for Easter and Passover the season of repentance. It is a good time for recovenanting celebrations (see p. 122). Fall is also the time when we reap the fruits of the year's planting in harvests and see the foliage of the growing time fall to the earth and decay to make new soil. Thus it is also traditionally a time to remember the dead. The eve of All Saints Day (October 31) was traditionally a time to think of departed friends or relatives. In Hispanic countries it is celebrated by eating sugar skeletons and holding candlelight all-night vigils in cemeteries. The fearful aspects of departed spirits have also been a part of this time, with children's rituals focusing on witches and ghosts and receiving bribes from adults not to do evil tricks. The next day, All Hallows, turned to the positive side of the view of the dead, by remembering the blessed departed that rest in the bosom of God/ess.

We have chosen to make this time a remembrance of the holocaust of women, recalling the hundreds of thousands of women that were killed as "witches" and the millions of others tortured by inquisitors in this patriarchal obsession with the supposed evils of women's potential power. We also recall all the women throughout the generations who have been killed, beaten, raped, deprived of education and opportunities for development, in order to be made servants of the male gender.

Fall:

HALLOWMAS: REMEMBRANCE OF THE HOLOCAUST OF WOMEN

The group should assemble in the evening. On a central table put a small brazier; corn, apples, and flowering branches are around the table. The rite begins by lighting the brazier.

Song:

Sister-Woman-Sister, can you still feel any pain

or have they robbed you of your anger,
while putting thorazine in your vein? Oh . . .

Sister-Woman-Sister, have the walls grown up so high?
That you can't even dream of leaving
And you've forgotten how to fly, Oh . . .

Sister-Woman-Sister, did they take away your child?
and lock her up in some juvenile hall
to grow up weary and wild, Oh . . .

Sister-Woman-Sister, have you found any love inside?
Or do they hold that love against you
As they take away your pride? Oh . . .

—Holly Near[7]

Introit Chorus:

Gone is our history, burned to ashes
Our poetry forgotten as time passes
Return deep memory, root of our dissension
Nurture the tree of present invention.

Gone is our dignity, gone our powers
Once in freedom we blossomed like wild flowers
Life moved among us, like a loving mother
Sharing our wisdom, we cared for one another.

Without our mother, how shall we start living?
Without our mother, how shall we seek beauty?
Without our mother, how shall we die peacefully?
Without our mother, how shall we be reborn?

—Chris Carol[8]

Remembering:

She was carried out of her house in an oak linen chest and taken to the prison in Leonberg. She was then seventy-three years of age. There were forty-nine accusations against her, numerous supplementary charges. She was said to have failed to weep when the Holy Scriptures were read to her. Katherine Kepler replied that she had shed so many tears in her life, she had none left. Her son, Johannes Kepler, answered the Act of Accusation by the Act of Contestation, which was refuted by an Act of Acceptation to which was submitted an Act of Exception and Defense, which was answered by an Act of Deduction and Confutation. Finally in her defense her son submitted an Act of Conclusion, one hundred and twenty-eight pages long. After that her case, by order of the duke, was sent to her son's university, where the faculty found that Katherine should be questioned under torture, but suggested that proceedings stop at the *territio,* questioning under threat of torture. She was led to the place of torture, the executioner was presented to her; all his instruments shown her and their effect on the body described. Great pain and dolor awaited her if she did not confess, she was told. The terror of the place has wrought confessions from many before her, but she said that even if they tore her veins from her body one by one, she had nothing to confess. She fell on her knees then and asked God to give a sign if she was a witch or a monster, and then said that she was willing to die, that God would reveal the truth after her death. In this way, and due to the efforts of her son, and the respect he commanded in the world, Katherine Kepler was released, after fourteen months of imprisonment. She could not return to Leonberg, though, because the populace threatened to lynch her. Six months later she died. It was against this background that Johnannes Kepler wrote his mathematical treatise on the *Harmony of the World.* [9]

Litany of Remembrance:

At each name, grains of incense are thrown into the brazier. Repeat the syllables until the lesson is drummed along the arteries:

> Margaret Jones, midwife, hanged 1648
> Joan Peterson, veterinarian, hanged 1652
> Isobel Insch Taylor, herbalist, burned 1618
> Mother Lakeland, healer, burned 1645
> What have they done to you. . . .

Repeat the syllables until the lesson is pumped thru the heart:

> Nicriven, accused of "lasciviousness," burned 1569
> Barbara Gobel, described by her jailors as "the fairest
>   maid in Wurzburg," burned 1629, age 19
> Frau Peller, raped by Inquisition torturers because her
>   sister refused the witch judge Franz Buirman, 1631
> Maria Walburga Rung, tried at a secular court in Mannheim
>   as a witch, released as "merely a prostitute," accused
>   again by the episcopal court at Eichstadt, tortured
>   into confession, and then burned alive 1723, age 22
> What have they done to me. . . .

Repeat the syllables before the lesson hemorrhages through the brain:

Margaret Barclay, crushed to death with stones 1618
Sister Maria Renata Sanger, subprioress of the
        Premonstratensian Convent of Unter-Zell, accused of being a
        lesbian; the document certifying her torture is inscribed
        with the seal of the Jesuits and the words "AD MAJOREM
        DEI GLORIAM"

To the Greater Glory of God
What have they done to us. . . .

Repeat the syllables before the lesson perforates the uterus:

Anna Rausch, burned 1628, 12 years old
Sybille Lutz, burned 1628, 11 years old
Emerzianne Pichler, tortured and burned together with her
        two children, 1679
Agnes Wobster, drowned while her young son was forced to
        watch her trial by water, 1567
Annabelle Stuart, burned alive 1678, 14 years old
Veronica Zerritsch, compelled to dance in the warm ashes
        of her executed mother, then burned alive herself
        1754, 13 years old
Frau Dumler, boiled to death in hot oil while pregnant,
        1630
What have they done. . . .[10]

Keening Chorus: Weep, O my sisters
                  Weep for the blood of woman shed for you,
                  the blood of the matriarch, the blood of the
                  prophet, the priestess and the witch;
                  Weep for the women slaughtered
                  Weep for the lovers raped
                  Weep for the daughters stolen, the mothers
                  humbled and enslaved
                  Weep for the sisters burned Ad Majorem Dei
                  Gloriam
                  Weep, O my sisters
                  Weep for purification on this most hallowed
                  eve
                  Weep until we rise in blood and flame to re-
                  dress and rebirth.[11]
Turning Chorus: We can rise with the fire of freedom
                  Truth is a fire that burns our chains
                  And we can stop the fires of destruction
                  Healing is a fire running through our veins.[12]

Litany of the Oppressed (recite antiphonally)

They have sinned in their greed
And we have let them rob us of our wealth

They have sinned in their lust
And we have let them hurt and use our flesh

They have sinned in their envy
And we have let them have more than their share

They have sinned in their wrath
And we have let them intimidate and rule

They have sinned in their gluttony
And we have let them take our children's food

They have sinned in their hatred
And we have let them make us hate ourselves

They have sinned in their pride
And we have let them tell us what to do (think, feel)

Holy Maiden, inspire us now and all the days of our
life, Amen.
Holy Mother (repeat as above).
Holy Wisdom, inspire us now.[13]

The flowering branches are passed around and held in the hands of the assembled, while they recite together:

Memorial Offering

We are bringing these flowers in remembrance of all the women who died in all the wars that men have fought.

We remember the nurses who died tending the wounded of both sides.

We remember the women who were raped by soldiers of their own country and by the invaders, and who were then rejected by their fathers and their brothers and their sons.

We remember the women who died or were wounded because they lived in cities where bombs fell out of the sky.

We remember all our sisters, noncombatants, whose lives were ended or foreshortened or crippled because their fathers and brothers went to war against the fathers and brothers of their sisters in another land.

We weep for them. We do not forget them. And as we remember them, we dedicate ourselves to making a new world where we and our daughters can live free; a world where our granddaughters and our sisters' granddaughters and great-granddaughters may look back in wonder at some archaic, almost forgotten time when women died because men went to war.[14]

A procession carries the corn and apples to the center and places them on the table. The flowers also are placed on the altar, while the chorus sings:

Offertorium

All good gifts around us spring from our mother earth
Then thank her now, O thank her now
With song and dance and mirth.[15]

The fruits and flowers are blessed:

Bountiful mother, we offer to you these good gifts of the earth which you have given to us. Blot out the bitter from our earth and restore the sweet.

The assembled turn and bless each other. Holding hands, they sing together:

Hey, sister, come live at the edge of the world
Not living inside, there's no place to hide
But the self that you find will be finally whole,
will be finally one, will be finally yours.

To gather as sisters together we'll learn to be free
Here on the boundary, finding the courage to be (chorus)

Hey, sister, come live on the edge of the world
There is room here to grow, and you'll come to know
who you are, where you've been, and who you might become
and that you might become who you want to be.[16]

The apples are shared among the participants.

THANKSGIVING: CELEBRATING THE HARVEST AND REMEMBERING THE HUNGRY

The Thanksgiving celebration in autumn is traditionally a time to feast and thank God/ess for the abundance of the harvest. Yet at a time when half the world goes to bed hungry, it is not a season for the affluent simply to rejoice. Those who have plenty should think of those who have insufficient and seek ways to share the agricultural goods of the earth. The simulation game, "Hunger and Space Ship," prepared by the American Friends, can be a learning ritual by which people can be made not only to know, but to feel concretely the inequities of the distribution of food today.[17]

The practice of creating Thanksgiving feasts in many churches and community centers so that the hungry and homeless might have their turkey dinner has become widespread, particularly with increasing hunger in the United States. It is important for many affluent people to commit some time to actually going and helping serve such meals for the poor, and not simply contributing some money or food to them. Nevertheless, not all of this day should be spent in concerns for the hungry. There is also an appropriate time for communities of kin and friends to gather to renew their ties and to celebrate the blessings of their harvest of the year's work.

Winter:

Since 1980, December 2 has become for many North American Christians particularly a time to recall the four women who were raped and killed by soldiers in El Salvador because of their solidarity with the liberation struggle in that country. It has also become a time to remember the martyred Archbishop Oscar Romero and the thousands of men and women tortured and killed by government terrorism. I have chosen to include a "Martyrs for Justice" liturgy as our winter remembrance.

LITURGY OF MARTYRS FOR JUSTICE, IN SOLIDARITY WITH EL SALVADOR

Kyrie (From the "Misa campesina Salvadoreña").[18]

Señor, ten piedad. Señor, ten piedad.
De tu pueblo, Señor. Señor, ten piedad.
La sangre de Abel escucha el Señor,
el llanto del pueblo despierta en Moises.
El grito que nace de nuestras entrañas
con mil artimañas lo quieren callar.

Señor, la injusticia nos duele y oprime,
ponte a nuestro lado, somos los humildes.
Las botas y tanques aplastan con saña
a quien da su cara por todo, Señor.

Lord have mercy, Lord have mercy on your people,
Lord have mercy.
The Lord hears the blood of Abel.
The shout of the people awakens a Moses
They wish to silence with a thousand deceits
the cry that is born from our guts.

Lord, injustice injures and oppresses us.
Come to our aid.
We are the humble ones
All those who give their face for others,
Lord, the boots and tanks crush with rage.

Leader: Among us the terrible words of the prophets of Israel continue to ring true.

People: There exist among us those who sell the just for money and the poor for a pair of sandals; those who mount up violence and spoils in their palaces; those who crush the poor; those who make the kingdom of violence to come closer while lying in their ivory beds; those who add on house after house and annex field after field until they occupy all the space there is and are the only ones left in the country.

Leader: These texts of the prophets Amos and Isaiah are not far away voices from many centuries back, they are not just texts that we reverently read in the liturgy.

People: They are everyday realities, whose cruelty and intensity we live daily. We live them when mothers and wives of captured and disappeared persons come to us, when disfigured corpses turn up in clandestine cementeries, when assassination is the lot of those who fight for justice and peace.

—Oscar A. Romero

Song (From the Misa Campesina Salvadoreña):

Nosotros pensamos que era la verdad.
Vino Su Palabra y nos hizo cambiar.

Me dijo mi abuelita, "Si te quierés salvar
los cruces de la vida tenés que soportar."
Pero resignaciones no es lo que quiere Dios.
El quiere tus acciones como obras del amor.

Qué felíz va Don Pancho como nuevo epulón,
creyendo que del mundo tiene la salvación.
Pero Dios dice al pobre: "Te doy bendición,
que el mundo nuevo nace de manos del peón.

"Confórmense y trabajen" nos ha dicho el patrón,
"que sólo en la otra vida tendrán la salvación."
Pero Dios hoy no aguanta a un nuevo Faraón
y manda a todo el pueblo hacer su liberación.

Piensan que el poderoso lo es por trabajador
que todo lo ha ganado con su propio sudor.
Pero Dios hizo al mundo para la comunión:
no quiere al orgulloso in al acaparador.

We thought that was the truth,
Your word came and made us change.

My dear Grandmother says to me,
"If you wish to be saved, you must
endure the sufferings of life."
But resignation is not what God wants,

He wishes our actions as works of love.
How happy is Don Pancho who goes confidently along,
believing that the world provides salvation.
But God says to the poor, I give you my blessing
that the new world will be born from the hands of
the workers.

Conform and labor, says the Patron to us,
only in the life to come will you have salvation.
But God does not stand for another Pharoah
and demands that all the people liberate themselves.
The powerful think they have earned everything by the
work of their own sweat.
But God has made the world for community.
He does not desire the proud or the monopolist.

The four large candles are now lit by representatives of the congregation.

Readings of the Four Women[19]

During the following readings, meditative music can be played. A moment of silence should follow each passage. Leader: Friends, let us listen to the voices of our four sisters.

Reader 1: My fear of death is being challenged constantly as children, lovely young girls, old people are being shot and some cut up with machetes and bodies thrown by the road and people prohibited from burying them. A loving Father must have a new life of unimaginable joy and peace prepared for these precious unknown, uncelebrated martyrs . . . I want to stay on now. I believe now that this is right. At times I miss the comfort of having many friends made over the years in Nicaragua. Here I am starting from scratch but it must be His plan and He is teaching me and there is real peace in spite of the many frustrations and the terror around us and the work, etc. God is very present in His seeming absence.

—Words of Sr. Maura Clarke, Nov. 20, 1980

Reader 2: What does December bring for us here in El Salvador? . . . First of all, it will bring us the Advent season—a time of waiting, a time of hoping, a time of yearning . . . On the first Friday in December we have a Mass for Anointing the Sick. This means that we take our jeep and minibus and go up and down the hillsides picking up the sick and bringing them to the celebration . . . All this goes on as normally as possible. And yet if we look at this little country of El Salvador as a whole, we find that it is all going on in a country that is writhing in pain—a country that daily faces the loss of so many of its people—and yet a country that is waiting, hoping, and yearning for peace. The steadfast faith and courage our leaders have to continue preaching the Word of the Lord even though it may mean "laying down your life" in the very REAL sense is always a point of admiration and a vivid realization that JESUS is HERE with us. Yes, we have a sense of waiting, hoping, and yearning for a complete realization of the Kingdom, and yet we know it will come because we can celebrate Him here right now.

—Words of Sr. Dorothy Kazel, Nov. 1980

> *Reader 3:* When it's late at night, I hear you come through
> the front door.
> "Hey are you guys awake"—you whisper.
> I'm half out of bed when I remember—
> you won't call to me anymore.
> For nine months I carried you under my heart.
> Now you live in my heart forever.
> Sometimes I forget—
> I think of you in Ireland, Virginia, El Salvador.
> I see a blouse you'd like or a pair of jeans.
> I feel a fist in my stomach—
> There's no one to buy them for!
> When Oliver sings, "Jean," I stop, I cry, I cry hard.
> My beautiful baby, my little girl.
> I love you so, I miss you so.
> I have one hope left—Heaven.
> With love, Mom.
> —Words of Patricia Donovan, mother of Jean.

The Peace Corps left today and my heart sank low. The danger is extreme and they were right to leave . . . Now I must assess my own position, because I am not up for suicide. Several times I have decided to leave. I almost could, except for the children, the poor bruised victims of adult lunacy. Who would care for them? Whose heart would be so staunch as to favor the reasonable thing in a sea of their tears and helplessness? Not mine, dear friend, not mine.

—Words of Jean Donovan, Nov. 1980

Reader 4: Phil. 1:21, "For me, Christ is my life." As usual, the Scripture is not only appropriate, but right to the point. Not just that Christ is the Lord of life, in charge of the day and hour— something which has to be thought about in this country of 40 to 50 and sometimes 100 assassinations a day—but that he is the meaning all along the way and in the fullness. I don't know if it is in spite of, or because of the horror, terror, evil, confusion, lawlessness—but I do know that it is right to be here. That may be the only surety as, with Carla, I start a work that is going to put us in contact with some of the hurting, homeless, hungry, and to God knows who else! . . . "Each of you has received some spiritual gift; use it for the good of all; activate the different gifts that God has distributed among us" (1 Pet. 4:10). To activate our gifts, to use them in this situation, to believe that we are gifted in and for El Salvador now, that the answers to the questions will come when they are needed, to walk in faith one day at a time with the Salvadorans along a road filled with obstacles, detours, and sometimes washouts—this seems to be what it means for us to be in El Salvador. And it is good for us to be here.

Words of Sr. Ita Ford, June 1980

Allow a short time of quiet reflection as the music comes to an end, then:

Song: "The Lord Hears the Cry of the Poor," by the St. Louis Jesuits.[20]

Words of Monseñor Romero **in his last Sunday service the day before the assassination:**

We want the government to take seriously the fact that reforms are worth nothing if they are stained with so much blood . . . In the name of God, then, and in the name of this suffering people, whose cries rise up to heaven more tumultuously each day, I beg you, I ask you, I order you in God's name: Stop the repression![21]

Prayer of Intercession

Leader: Let us now bring our intentions before God and pray for the people of El Salvador, of all of Central America, and for those who are oppressed anywhere in our world.

In the name of our four sisters, and our brother Oscar Romero, we pray for the uncelebrated martyrs of El Salvador, the 40,000 innocent and poor who have died at the hand of violence in El Salvador, that they may be at peace now with God.

All; God, hear the prayer of your people.

We pray for the refugees, those among whom our sisters worked, those who have fled persecution, repression, and war to refugee camps in their own country, in Honduras, and in our own nation. May we welcome them, respond to their needs, offer safety and shelter, solidarity and love, until they can return safely to their homes.

All: God, hear the prayer of your people.

We pray for our government officials and legislators, that they may have a change of heart and lead our country out of the ways of war and hostility into the ways of justice and peace.

All: God, hear the prayer of your people.

We pray for ourselves, that the 4 and the 40,000 will not have died in vain, that each of us will work for justice in El Salvador, Central America, and in our world.

All: God, hear the prayer of your people

The congregation is invited to add its own intercessions.

Poem, by Julia Esquivel, Guatemala.[22]

I am no longer afraid of death;
I know well
its dark and cold corridors
leading to life.

I am afraid rather of that life
which does not come out of death
which cramps our hands
and retards our march.

I am afraid of my fear
and even more of the fear of others,
who do not know where they are going,
who continue clinging
to what they consider to be life
which we know to be death!

I live each day to kill death;
I die each day to beget life,
and in this dying unto death,
I die a thousand times and
am reborn another thousand
through that love
from my People,
which nourishes hope!

Canto de Despedida (De la Misa Salvadoreña).

CUANDO EL POBRE CREA EN EL POBRE
YA PODREMOS CANTAR LIBERTAD.
CUANDO EL POBRE CREA EN EL POBRE
CONSTRUIREMOS LA FRATERNIDAD.

Hasta luego, mis hermanos, que la misa terminó;
ya escuchamos lo que Dios nos habló.
Ahora sí ya estamos claros, ya podemos caminar,
la tarea debemos empezar.

Todos nos comprometimos en la mesa del Señor,
a construir en este mundo el amor,
y al luchar por los hermanos se hace la comunidad.
Cristo vive en la solidaridad.

Cuando el pobre busca al pobre y nace la organización
es que empieza nuestra liberación.
Cuando el pobre anuncia al pobre la esperanza que El nos dio
Ya su reino entre nosotros nació.

When the poor believe in the poor,
then we can sing of liberty.
When the poor believe in the poor,
we shall have fraternity.
Until we meet again, my brothers and sisters,
the mass has ended. We heard what God has said to us.
Now that we are clear, we can be on our way.
We must begin the task.
We commit ourselves at the table of the Lord
to construct a world of love, and to struggle
for the community of brothers and sisters.
Christ lives in solidarity.
When the poor seek the poor, and organization
is born, then our liberation begins.
When the poor announces to the poor the hope
He gives, then his reign will be born among us.

CHRISTMAS

Christmas has gathered a multiplicity of observances around it, both as a Christian festival of the birth of the messianic child, and as a holiday season. Every family, region, and nation has its favorites. The favorite Christmas rite observed in our family was one I learned at college in California where the Mexican festival of the Posadas was celebrated. The Posadas represent the search of Mary and Joseph for a place to stay before the birth of Jesus. In contemporary American urban life this festival might be combined with some remembrance of the many homeless people who throng our cities. Traditionally, a procession representing Mary and Joseph goes from house to house asking for a place to stay. Rebuffed at each house, people join the procession and it grows as it progresses through the streets. The following song is sung during this search for a place to stay: [23]

Humble Pilgrims, Jesus, Mary and Joseph,
My soul I give you, my heart also.
O beautiful pilgrim, most blessed Mary,
I offer you my soul to have as a resting place.

Finally, a house is reached which receives the couple, together with the procession that follows them. The outside of the houses might be decorated in the Mexican fashion with "luminarias" (candles in a paper bag with sand at the bottom). The "Holy Queen," "Mother of the Creator" is welcomed in to hallow the house with the song:

Enter Queen most holy, Enter mother of the Creator
to sanctify the house of this poor sinner
Enter holy Joseph to this poor house,
fill all its inhabitants with grace.
Enter contendedly with your spouse.
I give you lodging in my heart.

*A crèche might be set up in he living room around which the company gathers.
This might be a time to reflect both on the meaning of the ancient story of the
Holy Family's search for a place to stay where the messianic child might be born,*

but also the issue of homelessness today, including some information on groups working on homelessness. This time of serious reflection should be brief and followed by a good party, which includes the breaking of a piñata by the children. The closing song goes like this:

Nos despedimos contentos
todos con grande placer
Hasta el año venidero
que nos volvamos a ver
Hasta el año venidero
que nos volvamos a ver.

We depart contented, all with great happiness,
until the coming year when we will meet again.

WINTER SOLSTICE

The observance of Christmas was placed at the time of the traditional festival of the winter solstice because this time, when the daylight reaches its ebb tide and then begins to increase, was seen as the birthday of the sun, and hence a fitting natural correlation to the birthday of the redeeming child who will be the spiritual light of the world. I suggest separating the two ideas and enjoying the profound meaning of the year's turning from darkness to light with all its natural and symbolic associations. The winter solstice is much more dramatic in northern countries where daylight dwindles to a few hours at this time of year.

Bringing in the yule log, lighting special candles, and decorating the house with mistletoe and evergreen (plants that keep their green leaves in winter and thus represent the hope for new life) are all a part of this celebration in northern countries. A family or household outing to cut one's own tree can be followed by a party around its decoration. When the tree is prepared, the lights might be turned out and a candle lit. Each person, in turn, lights a candle from the original candle and, as each person's candle is lit, that person speaks on the meaning for her or him of new light in the midst of darkness. When the circle is completed, the lights of the yule tree are lit and there is a party.

Spring:

ASH WEDNESDAY LITURGY: REPENTENCE FOR THE SINS OF THE CHURCH

Lent is the traditional beginning of the Christian season of repentance and self-examination. For catechumens, this period leads to baptism in the midst of the community during the vigil of Easter on Holy Saturday night. But Christian understandings of repentance have been notably individualistic. Christianity has paid little attention to turning away from collective systemic evils. Still less has the Christian church been able to admit that as a historical institution it is the source and perpetuator of evils. The following liturgy is designed for a public liturgy of repentance for the sins sanctioned in various ways by Christian theology and church institutions among the Christian people. It was written and celebrated in the spring of 1976 at Garrett-Evangelical Theological Seminary in Evanston, Illinois, and was used again several years later at Union Theological Seminary in New York City.

1. Sins of Christian Society Against the Jewish People

Introduction: The Church and the Synagogue are two children of a common origin, both sprung from the prophetic and ethical faith of the Hebrew Scriptures. It is a great sin and tragedy that such terrible enmity rose up between us at our beginnings and that Christians have used their power as the established religion to persecute the Jewish people. Let us think on this collective part of our life together and our own participation in it.

Angel of Judgment (reading from scroll): This is a reading from the Scroll of Destruction.

In A.D. 300 the Council of Elvira promulgates the first anti-Jewish laws. In A.D. 439 the code of Theodosius forbids Jews all public office. Christian mobs violate synagogues and massacre Jews in many cities.

In 1096 the crusades turn into pogroms in the Rhineland. Jews are massacred at Speyer, Worms, Mayence, Cologne, Mainz, Trier, Metz, Rouen, and elsewhere.

In 1215 the Fourth Lateran Council orders Jews to live in a ghetto, wear the Jewish badge and dress, not to appear in public during Christian holidays, to have no Christian servants or hold office in Christian societies.

In 1348 Jews were massacred in France, Spain, Hungary, Germany, and Italy on suspicion of having caused the black plague.

Pogroms continue in the twelfth and thirteenth centuries, culminating in expulsions. In 1182 Jews are expelled from France; in 1290 from England; 1492 from Spain; and in 1497 from Portugal.

In 1478 Jewish converts are subjected to the Laws of Pure Blood in Spanish society forbidding them public office, under the supervision of the Inquisition.

In 1648 the Cossack pogrom against Jews of Poland slaughters 200,000 persons.

In 1881 new pogroms arise in Russia, killing tens of thousands and causing hundreds of thousands to flee for their lives.

From 1943 to 1945 the Great Destruction ran like fire through the congregations of Israel throughout Europe, and six million died.

At each citation a candle is lit. Kaddish music is played fading in and out throughout the readings.

Two prophets now come down from the sanctuary and stand on either side of the congregation.

First Prophet: And it came to pass when Moshe descended from the Mount that a pillar of fire consumed the tribes of Israel that stood at the foot of the Mount. And six million of the children of Israel went up in smoke. And all that remained was a pillar of smoke that ascended to the uppermost heaven and has remained there to this very day. And when Moshe saw that his people had been made into smoke, he cast the tablets down from his hands and broke them at the foot of the Mount and cried out with a great and terrible shout: HAS THE WHOLE WORLD GONE CRAZY!

Second Prophet: And the Lord spoke to Moshe saying, Speak to the children of Israel and tell them to make a yellow star upon their garments throughout their generations, one star over their heart and one on their back of equal size and proportions, and it shall be for you a sign that you may look upon and remember all the commandments of the Lord.

Do not follow your own heart and your own eyes, by which you are seduced, but *remember* all these things and do my commandments and be holy unto your God. For I am the Lord your God who brought you out of the land of Egypt, that I should be your God and you should be my people.

Period of Silent Meditation (kneeling)

2. Sins of Division Among Christians

Introduction: "Look at those Christians, how they love one another" was the boast of the early Christians before the pagan world. But how often throughout Christian history relations between groups of Christians has been that of factionalism, hatred, and contempt, putting asunder the unity of Christ's body. Let us think of this part of our life together and our own participation in it.

Two groups carry placards to the front with Reformation cartoons.

Spokesperson for first group (while adherents wave fists): You are espousing the pestilent errors of John Hus. You are heretical, erroneous, blasphemous, presumptuous, seditious, and offensive to pious ears respectively.

Spokesperson for second group (adherents still waving fists): What whore of Babylon is this? You are called sanctissimus, but are you *Sanctus?* You don't look it, cassock over armor, eyes savage, mouth insolent, forehead brazen, eyebrows arrogant, body poxed by debauchery, reeking with drink, a shambles of a man!

The congregation shouts in chorus: *Right Side:* What fanatics are these which infest Great Britain! This Wesley is a Reynard in a masters of arts gown. This is naught but hypocrisy and nonsense. What a tribe of mock saints! You are schismatic, schismatic, schismatic . . .

Left Side: What kind of Christians are these! They are nothing but devil Christians. Is there true Christian fellowship here? The bulk of parishioners are mere ropes of sand, there is no true faith here, all is faithless, faithless, faithless.

Song (sung by opposite sides of the congregation at the same time):

Right Side: "The Church's One Foundation"
Left Side: "Were You There When They Crucified My Lord?"

Period of Silent Meditation (kneeling)

3. Sins Against Women and Sexual Minorities

Introduction: Women and men were both created equally in the image of God, yet human sinfulness has used the advantages of men to confine women to limited roles and opportunities. Too often religion has been used to sanctify the subjugation of women and the hatred of those with a different sexual orientation. Let us think on this part of our life together and our own involvement in it.

Four persons, one in a toga, one in medieval vestments, one in an academic robe, and one in modern garb seated at the front:

Church Father: We do not permit women to practice the office of teaching in the church; instead they should pray and listen to teachers. For our Teacher and Lord, Jesus himself, sent only us Twelve to instruct the people [Israel] and the heathen, but he never sent women, although women were not lacking: with us was the mother of the Lord and her sisters, and also Mary Magdalene and Mary, the mother of James, and Martha and Mary, the sisters of Lazarus, Salome, and some others. Thus if it would have been suitable for women to proclaim the teachings of Jesus, he would himself have called them from the beginning to undertake with us the instruction of the people. *For if the man is the head of the woman, it is not proper that the rest of the body should rule the head.* [24]

Medieval Canon Lawyer: Women must cover their heads because they are not the image of God. They must do this as a sign of their subjection to authority and because sin came into the world through them. Their heads must be covered in church in order to honor the bishop. In like manner they have no authority to speak because the bishop is the embodiment of Christ. They must thus act before the bishop as before Christ, the judge, since the bishop is the representative of the Lord. Because of original sin they must show themselves submissive.[25]

Puritan Reformer: Now as concerning the Wives Duty, What shall become her? Shall she abuse the gentleness and humanity of her Husband, and at her pleasure turn all things upside down? No surely, for that is far repugnant against God's Commandment; for thus doth St. Peter preach to them, "To Wives, be ye in subjection to obey your own Husbands." To obey is another thing than to controle or command, which yet they may do to their Children and to their Family. But as for their Husbands, them must they obey, and cease from commanding, and perform subjection, for this surely doth nourish Concerd very much, when the Wife is ready at hand at her Husbands commandment, when she will apply herself to his Will, when she endeavoreth her self to seek his contentation, and to do him pleasure, when she will eschew all things that might offend him.

Here you understand that God hath commanded that ye should acknowledge the Authority of the Husband, and refer to him the honor of Obedience.[26]

Twentieth-Century American Fundamentalist: Suppose a woman feels God is leading her definitely opposite to what her husband has commanded. Who should she obey? The Scriptures say a woman must ignore her "feelings" about the will of God, and do what her husband says. She is to obey her husband as if he were God Himself. She can be as certain of God's will, when her husband speaks, as if God had spoken audibly from Heaven![27]

Black Woman, coming from one side:

Well, children, where there is so much racket there must be something out of kilter. I think that 'twixt the negroes of the South and the women at the North, all talking about rights, the white men will be in a fix pretty soon. But what's all this here talking about?

That man over there says that women need to be helped into carriages, and lifted over ditches, and to have the best place everywhere. Nobody ever helps me into carriages, or over mud puddles, or gives me any best place! And ain't I a woman? Look at me! Look at my arm! And ain't I a woman? I could work as much and eat as much as a man—when I could get it—and bear the lash as well! And ain't I a woman? I have born thirteen children, and seen them most all sold off to slavery, and when I cried out with my mother's grief, none but Jesus heard me! And ain't I a woman?

Then they talk about this thing in the head; what's this they call it? (Intellect, someone whispers.) That's it, honey. What's that got to do with women's rights or negro's rights? If my cup won't hold but a pint, and yours holds a quart, wouldn't you be mean not to let me have my little half-measure full?

Then that little man in black there, he says women can't have as much rights as men, 'cause Christ wasn't a woman! Where did your Christ come from? Where did your Christ come from? From God and a woman! Man had nothing to do with Him.

If the first woman God ever made was strong enough to turn the world upside down all alone, these women together ought to be able to turn it back, and get it right side up again! And now they is asking to do it, the men better let them.

Obliged to you for hearing me, and now old Sojourner ain't got nothing more to say.[28]

Period of Silent Meditation (kneeling)

4. Sins Against Racial Minorities

Introduction: Scripture tells us that all human beings are descended from one common ancestry, all children of one God and brothers and sisters to each other. Yet how often we have denied our common humanity in our relations with peoples of other races. Let us think on this part of our life together and our own participation in it.

Two men come down from sanctuary, one in top hat, another in cowboy hat.

First Man: I will say then that I am not, nor ever have been in favor of bringing about in any way the social and political equality of the white and black races, . . . that I am not nor ever have been in favor of making voters or jurors of negroes, nor of qualifying them to hold office, not to intermarry with white people; and I will say in addition to this that there is a physical difference between the white and black races which I believe will forever forbid the two races living together on terms of social and political equality. And inasmuch as they cannot so live, while they do remain together there must be the position of superior and inferior, and I as much as any other man am in favor of having the superior position assigned to the white race.

Abraham Lincoln, 1858[29]

Second Man: I suppose I should be ashamed to say that I take the Western view of the Indian. I don't go so far as to think that

the only good Indians are the dead Indians, but I believe nine
out of every ten are, and I shouldn't inquire too closely into the
case of the tenth. The most vicious cowboy has more moral
principle than the average Indian.

Theodore Roosevelt, 1890[30]

Third Man speaks from sanctuary: Behold, my brothers, the
spring has come, the earth has received the embraces of the sun,
and we shall soon see the results of that love!

Every seed is awakened and so has all animal life. It is through
this mysterious power that we too have our being and we therefore yield to our neighbors, even our animal neighbors, the same
right as ourselves, to inhabit this land.

Yet, hear me, people, we have now to deal with another race
—small and feeble when our fathers first met them but now
great and overbearing. Strangely enough they have a mind to till
the soil, and the love of possession is a disease with them. These
people have made many rules that the rich may break but the
poor may not. They take tithes from the poor and weak to
support the rich who rule. They claim this mother of ours, the
earth, for their own and fence their neighbors away; they deface
her with their buildings and their refuse. That nation is like a
spring freshet that overruns its banks and destroys all who are
in its path.

We cannot dwell side by side. Only seven years ago we made
a treaty by which we were assured that the buffalo country
should be left to us forever. Now they threaten to take that
away from us. My brothers, shall we submit or shall we say to
them: "First kill me before you take possession of my Father-
land. . . . "

Sitting Bull, Sioux Leader,
Powder River Council, 1877[31]

Voice of Martin Luther King: (record) part of "I Have a
Dream" speech.

Song: "Nobody Knows the Trouble I Seen," while
congregation kneels in silent meditation.

5. Sins Against the Poor

Introduction: The Prophet Amos said: "Hear this, you who trample the needy, and bring the poor of the land to an end, who say, . . . When will the Sabbath be over so we may sell grain and deal deceitfully with false balances, that we may buy the poor for silver and the needy for a pair of sandals and sell the refuse of the wheat." And the Evangelist John said: "If anyone has the world's goods and sees his brother or sister in need, yet closes his heart against him, how does God's love abide in him?" And Saint Ambrose, bishop of Milan, said, "Nature has poured forth all things for common use. God has ordered all things to be produced, so that there should be food common to all and that the earth should be the common possession of all. Nature therefore has produced a common right for all, but usurpation has made it a right for a few." Today with nations and classes deeply divided between the few who are rich and the many that are poor, we must think on our responsibility for this unjust usurpation of the world's goods and our own involvement in it.

Reading: Open Letter to North American Christians from Latin American Churchmen

It is very significant that in these days we Latin Americans are following with such intense interest the political process of the people of the United States. The reason is that we are trapped in the same system—with the exception of Cuba—, we all move within one economic, political, military complex, in which one finds committed fabulous interests of financial groups which dominate the life of your country and the creole oligarchies of our Latin American nations. Both groups, more allied today than ever, have held back time after time, the great transformations that our people need and desperately demand.

The scandalous intervention of the United States in the installation and maintenance of military regimes in Guatemala, Nicaragua, Brazil, Paraguay, Bolivia, etc.; the revelation of the activities of the I.T.T. and other North American businesses in Chile;

the resounding case of Watergate; the discoveries around the CIA and other agencies of penetration and espionage in our countries; the shameful Panamanian enclave with its military training centers which our Christian and Latin American consciences cannot tolerate any longer; the brazen domination and colonization practiced by Rockefeller and many others, which has been eliminating one after the other all possibilities of economic independence and authentic development in our rich but excessively bled nations.

Today we Latin Americans are discovering that not a few of our misfortunes, miseries, and frustrations flow from and are perpetuated within a system that produces substantial benefits for your country, but which goes on swallowing us more and more in oppression, in impotence, in death. In a few words: your precious "American Way of Life," the opulence of your magnates, your economic and military dominion, feeds on the blood which gushes "from the open veins of Latin America."

Tyrannical regimes, like Somoza in Nicaragua, Stroessner in Paraguay, Pinochet in Chile, which represent and serve the interests of your large corporations associated with powerful local interests, are intensifying repression and terror to a degree rarely equalled.

Now it is necessary to subject to systematic persecution, to scientifically perfected torture, union leaders, political and student leaders, priests and pastors, intellectuals and artists, journalists and other professionals, all who attempt to denounce the injustice. The prisons of Latin America no longer suffice to hold so many prisoners detained for indeterminate times. The few countries that still enjoy some margin of liberty and security have already stretched their capacity to receive exiles and refugees of all nationalities. Paramilitary and parapolice organizations multiply in a fearful manner; the streets of many towns are sown daily with cadavers. All this is carried out in the name of "Western Christian civilization," on the backs of our people, and with the benediction and the support of your government, of your armed forces, without which our dictators could not maintain themselves in power for much time. Friends and fellow-Christian, it is time that you realize that our continent is becoming one gigantic prison, and in some regions, one vast cemetery. That human rights, the grand guidelines of the Gospel, are becoming a dead letter, without force. And all this in order to maintain a system, a structure of dependency that benefits the mighty privileged person of your land and of our land, at the expense of the poor millions.

For this reason this open letter seeks to be the lamentation and the outcry of those who now have no voice in our America because they are rotting in prisons or concentration camps; or because they languish in incredible conditions of malnutrition and misery.[32]

Each person now writes on a slip of paper ways in which they see themselves personally involved in these sins of Christian people. The papers are collected and burned in a brazier. Ashes are sifted out and cooled and passed in small bowls. Each person anoints the forehead of the person next to them with ashes, saying: "The old world of inhumanity collapses into ashes. Out of the ashes let a new humanity arise like a phoenix within each of us."

A final collective statement of the new humanity and new earth into which we are being called is read together. The kiss of peace is passed. The liturgy ends with a final benediction.

GOOD FRIDAY WALK FOR JUSTICE

A Good Friday march for justice can be organized in the downtown area of any major American city. This one has been done for a number of years by a coalition of justice groups in Chicago. [30]

Opening Statement: We are here today to reenact symbolically the Way of the Cross, commemorating different moments of Christ's passion and death. The various stations represent the continuous suffering of Christ and his people, especially in poor nations, at the hands of repressive governments and institutions. We also recognize the role of the Reagan Administration, local government, and U.S. corporations and banks aggravating this suffering by strengthening and legitimating forces of repression and exploitation around the world and at home. In many ways we, ourselves, are complicit or participate in these injustices.

Responses at Stations

At the beginning and end of each station, the sung refrain will be:

Our God hears the cry of the poor; Blessed be our God.

I. Jesus is condemned to death: International Harvester

—unemployment runs rampant as U.S. corporations abandon workers and their communities for greener pastures.

A series of statements are read cataloging unemployment in the U.S. Response after each statement:

"Christ, who was condemned to death, set the workers free."

Response after final statement: Christ, who was condemned to death, set us free to do those works of justice that will lift the condemnation of death by unemployment that is laid upon your people. Amen.

II. Jesus is Burdened with the Cross: South African Consulate

—whose racist apartheid policy tramples human rights and forces children to say, "No more."

Statements are read describing policies of apartheid in South Africa. The group may then repeat several chants, such as:

1. What do we want?   Freedom!
For whom?   The people of South Africa
When do you want it?   Now!
2. Down with apartheid   Free South Africa!
3. Down with apartheid   Out with the Consulate!

Let us now join hands and pray for strength in the struggle for freedom in South Africa. Let us join hands and pray that we might be used as earthen vessels to pour justice, freedom, and righteousness over South Africa to free our brothers and sisters in South Africa.

End by repeating chant # 3.

III. **Jesus Falls the First Time: South Korean Consulate**

—where U.S. multinational companies profit from systematic governmental repression of innocent people in South Korea, the Philippines, and Asia.

Statements are read describing oppression in South Korea and the Philippines.

An Bayan Ko

In my golden land of the Philippines, fragrant flowers
    filled the morning breeze.
Loving fingers built a paradise, a resting place
    for humankind.
One day foreign ships and strangers came, seeking
    out her wealth and beauty.
Left her people bound in chains, our hearts in misery.

Refrain:

Birds go winging freely through the sky.
Try to catch them and they surely cry.
Take away a people's liberty, sons and daughters live
    to set them free.
Soon one day our trials will be done, night will fade
    and golden morning come.
Now my life and love I give to set my country free.[33]

IV. **Veronica Wipes the Face of Jesus: IBM Plaza**

—whose contribution to the arms race and production of nuclear weapons threatens humanity and robs the poor.

Opening meditation on the costs and dangers of the arms race.

V. **Simon Helps Carry the Cross: El Salvador Consulate**

—thousands of people are being assassinated in Central America as people struggle for the right to determine their own destiny.

Meditational readings on oppression in Central America.

VI. Jesus Falls Again: Theaters

—where sexual abuse and violent oppression of women are portrayed in film.

Opening meditation on sexual and physical abuse of women in theater and film.

Let us call to mind our future:

God, our Creator, you continue to lead us from slavery to freedom, from bondage to liberation, from the present to the future by the example of your son. Let the suffering we have expressed bring about your kingdom and ours within our human history.
All: Amen.

VII. Jesus Meets His Mother: Greyhound Bus Station

—the homeless, those forgotten by social services.

A series of statements are read on homelessness in Chicago. After each statement, all respond:

God, open our hearts to the needs of the homeless.

VIII. Jesus Meets the Weeping Women: Chicago Government

—which shares in Reagan's robbery of the poor and hungry through drastic cuts in survival programs.

All Sing: (To the tune of Kum Ba Yah.)

> Someone's crying, Lord, be with us,
> Someone's crying, Lord, be with us,
> Someone's crying, Lord, be with us,
> O Lord, be with us.

A series of statements are read on cutbacks of programs to the poor in Chicago. After each statement,

Sing: Someone's *crying,* Lord, be with us . . . (once)
Sing: Someone's *groaning,* Lord, be with us . . . (once)
Sing: Someone's *moaning,* Lord, be with us . . . (once)
Sing: Someone's *hurting,* Lord, be with us . . . (once)

IX. Jesus Falls Again: First National Bank

—fails to invest in jobs in Chicago, lends to Chilean and other repressive regimes in South America.

A series of statements are read on investment policies of First National Bank. Response after each statement: Jesus, Liberator, help us to rise up.

Closing Prayer: Prayer for a Laborer, by Victor Jara

Arise and look at the mountains, from which come
    the wind, the sun, and the waters.
You who control the course of the rivers, you who
    planted the flight of your soul.
Arise and look at your hand; to grow, take your brother's
    and sister's hands.
Together we will walk, united in blood, for this is
    the day that could become tomorrow.
Free us from those who dominate us in misery, bring
    us your kingdom of justice and equality.
Let your will finally be done here on earth; give
    us your strength and courage to struggle.
Blow like the wind the flowers by the stream; clean
    with your fire the barrel of my gun.
Arise and look at your hand; to grow, take your brother's
    and sister's hands.
Together we will walk, united in blood, now and at
    the hour of our death.[34]
Amen.

Group repeats chant of solidarity with the people of Latin America

¡ El Pueblo unido jamás será vencido!
The people united will never be defeated!

X. Jesus is Stripped of His Garments: Federal Plaza

—Palestinian rights are violated as people on the West Bank are brutalized by an occupying army.

The leader offers a meditation on the conflicts and hopes of Jews and Palestinians in the Middle East.

People:

We pray for justice and peace for all of your children, O God, who live in the Holy Land and suffer from the endless cycle of violence and occupation. And may peace begin with us who are Americans.

Remember those who are in prison,

As though in prison with them;

And those who are ill-treated,

Since you are also in the body (Heb. 13:3).

Put away violence and oppression,

And execute justice and righteousness;

Cease your evictions of my people (Ezek. 45:9).

Let justice roll down like waters,

And righteousness like an everflowing stream (Amos 5:24).

Amen.

XI. Jesus Is Nailed to the Cross: Immigration Detention Center

—symbol of U.S. oppression of refugees, the undocumented, and those workers defending their rights.

Leader: This nation has been built on the backs of immigrants and refugees: Africans, Italian, Polish, Chinese, Irish. These persons entered this country, passing the Statue of Liberty whose base proclaims the great invitation to the oppressed of the world.

All: "Give me your tired, your poor, your huddled masses yearning to breathe free, the wretched refuse of your teeming shores. Send these, the homeless, tempest tossed to me. I lift my lamp beside the golden door."

Leader: Yes, this country has taken the sweat and tears of immigrants and refugees through the years, used them, and when their services were no longer convenient, turned its back and crucified them, nailing them to the crosses of oppression and injustice.

  —The Immigration and Naturalization Service incarcerates Haitians for years in inhuman camps, refusing to allow them entrance to the U.S.

—U.S. business abuses the cheap labor of Mexicans to harvest fruits and vegetables; then the Immigration and Naturalization Service deports them when harvest is over.

—The Immigration and Naturalization Service deports Salvadoran and Guatemalan refugees who are fleeing crucifixion in their homelands.

—The Immigration and Naturalization Service is an arm of U.S. foreign policy, instead of upholding national and United Nations laws regarding political asylum.

We stand here in front of the Immigration and Naturalization Service building—the place where the unjust policies of the U.S. government are carried out and the lives and futures of immigrants and refugees are decided daily.

On this Good Friday we remember the lives of all immigrants and refugees who have known injustice and crucifixion.

All: Our God, we demand a *stop* to the continuing crucifixion of Jesus represented in the Immigration and Naturalization Service denial of just treatment for refugees and immigrants from Haiti, El Salvador, Guatemala, Mexico, and other countries. Amen.

XII. Jesus Dies on the Cross: Institutional Racism

—racism still flourishes in government and private employment practices, media stereotyping, educational and housing opportunities, and medical services, etc.

Meditations on institutional racism.

XIII. Jesus Is Taken Down from the Cross and Buried: Metropolitan Correctional Center

—symbol of all prisons which our society fills with the poor, blacks, and Latinos.

Scripture Reading: Luke 23:50–56

Song: The Lord Is with Us/Con Nosotros Está

Con nosotros está y no lo conocemos
Con nosotros está, su nombre es el Señor

Su nombre es el Señor y sed soporta
Y está en quien justicia va sediento
Y muchos que lo ven pasan de largo
Aveces ocupados en sus rezos.

Su nombre es el Señor y está desnudo
La ausencia del amor hiela sus guesos.
Y muchos que lo ven pasan de largo
Seguros y al calor de su dinero.

Su nombre es el Señor y está en la carcel
Está en la soledad de cada preso
Y nadie lo visita y hasta dicen:
Tal vez ese no era de los nuestros.

English translation:
With us is he, and we do not recognize him
With us is he, his name is Lord.

His name is Lord and endures thirst
He is in those who thirst for justice.
And many who see him walk on by
Ignoring him while deep in their prayers.

His name is Lord, and he is naked.
The absence of love freezes his bones
And many who see him walk on by
Secure in the warmth of their wealth.

His name is Lord, and he is in prison.
He is in the loneliness of each prisoner
And no one visits him and even say:
This is not one of ours.

XIV. Resurrection:

As we believe Jesus was resurrected, so do we believe in and hope for the resurrection and for a new world to come.

Song: The Last Day

And we will raise them up,
And we will raise them up,
And we will raise them up
On the last day.

These are brothers and sisters, Lord;
They have died that we shall not hunger;
They have believe that we shall not
        thirst;
Now we have come to you.
We know that you will hear us.

The gift that we now ask
Is the strength to stand together
until oppression shall cease;
We will stand together.
We will stand together.

SEDER CELEBRATIONS

The celebration of the Passover or the coming forth of the people of Israel from Egypt is the most beloved of Jewish family liturgies. In recent years there has been a recovery of this liturgy among Christians who have sometimes adapted it to the observance of Holy Thursday, a traditional time to remember the foundation of the Lord's Supper which, in some gospel accounts, was a Passover meal of Jesus with his disciples. There has also been a great development of new types of Passover liturgies in the Jewish liturgical renewal, linking the seder meal with modern hopes for justice and liberation. One of the earliest of these new seder meals was written by Arthur Waskow on the first anniversary of the death of Martin Luther King, Jr. Called the "Freedom Seder," it was celebrated with black Christian leaders in Washington, D.C., in April of 1969.

The Freedom Seder, and other new justice seders,[35] focus on concerns both for justice for the poor and also the redemption of the world from the fear of the final holocaust from nuclear weapons. A seder for the children of Abraham focuses on reconciliation

260 / LITURGICAL LIFE AND WOMEN-CHURCH

between Palestinian and Israelis in the Middle East. The stories of the two peoples mingle together in such a way that each community enters into and identifies, not only with their own story, but with the story of the other community as well. Here the seder takes on a new function of being a liturgy of reconciliation.

There have also been a variety of feminist seders developed in the last two decades. Jewish feminists have written several versions of a woman's haggadah.[36] Another feminist haggadah is directed toward the recovery of early Semitic Goddess traditions.[37] "A Seder for the Sisters of Sarah" adapts the feminist seder to Jewish and Christian feminists together.[38]

EASTER LITURGIES

Diann Neu has developed a book of Women-Church celebrations for the Lenten Season and for Easter, and I recommend these for liturgies for Christian feminists for this season.[39]

YOM HASHO-AH: HOLOCAUST REMEMBRANCE DAY

The slaughter of the six million Jews, as well as many millions of other peoples in Europe, by the Nazi death machine has become the great symbol of the reign of the demonic in modern life. It has taken on a quasi-official status as a new yearly observance among Jews, and many congregations have developed their own liturgies for this day. Yom Hasho-ah is a particularly fitting time for Jews and non-Jews to come together in a common remembrance of this modern infamy and a common dedication to prevent new genocides in our times. The following liturgy has been adapted from several in use in Jewish congregations for joint Jewish-Christian remembrance of the Holocaust.[40]

Opening Meditation

Legend tells us that one day man spoke to God in this wise: "Let us change about. You be man, and I will be God. For only one second." God smiled gently and asked him, "Aren't you afraid?"

"No," the man said, "and you?"

"Yes, I am," God said.

Nevertheless, he granted man's desire. God became man and the man took the place of God and immediately availed himself of his omnipotence. He refused to revert to his previous state. So neither God nor man have been ever again what they seemed to be. Years passed, centuries, perhaps eternities, and suddenly the drama quickened. The past for one and the present for the other were too heavy to be borne. As the liberation of man was bound to the liberation of God, they renewed the ancient dialogue whose echoes come to us in the night, charged with hatred, with remorse, and most of all with infinite yearning. (Period of silence.)

Let us remember the terrible legacy of destruction of those days:

First voice: They took us to the town square where the selection began. Men separately, young women separately, and on one side mothers with children and children alone. The Ukranians searched through our things and took our gold rings and watches. They shot people on sight. There was confusion, shouting, and crying. We stepped over corpses. My mother held me tight by the hand. She was sure we were going to die and began to beg me: "Run, you will get away, you don't look Jewish! Let at least one of us remain to remember us. Listen to your mother's plea, escape and save your life." She gave me a knife and a kerchief, so I would resemble a peasant girl returning from the fields. I understood. Tears choked me and my head began to spin. I suddenly found myself at the end of the line. A Nazi came over and asked, "Who are you?" I said I was Polish. He told me to go home. I walked to the other side of the street to see what would happen to my mother. I saw from a distance people running and a stream of bullets following them.

Second voice: My father's voice drew me from my thoughts
. . . My forehead was bathed with cold sweat. But
I told him I did not believe that they could burn
people in our age, that humanity would never
tolerate it. ". . . Humanity? Humanity is not concerned with us. Today everything is allowed.
Anything is possible, even these crematories . . .
" "Father," I said, "If that is so, I don't want to
wait here. I'm going to run to the electric wire.
That would be better than slow agony in the
flames." He did not answer. He was weeping. His
body was shaking convulsively. Around us everyone was weeping. Someone began to recite Kaddish, the prayer for the dead. I don't know if it has
happened before, in the long history of the Jews,
that people have ever recited the prayer of the
dead for themselves.

Third voice: At this station another girl I saw, about five years
old. She fed her younger brother and he cried, the
little one, he was sick. Into a diluted bit of jam she
dipped tiny crusts of bread, and skillfully she in-
serted them into his mouth . . . This my eyes were
privileged to see! To see this mother, a mother of
five years feeding her child. To hear her soothing
words . . . My own mother, the best in the whole
world, had not invented such a ruse, but this little
one wiped his tears with a smile, injected joy into
his heart, a little girl in Israel.

After silent meditation all recite together:

I believe in the sun even when it is not shining;
I believe in love even when feeling is not;
I believe in God even when he is silent.

> (An inscription on the walls of
> a cellar in Cologne, Germany, where
> Jews hid from Nazis.)

Let the names of these places of infamy and those who died there not be forgotten:

Auschwitz   Response: Never, never again.
Majdanek
Treblinka
Buchenwald
Mauthausen
Belzec
Sobibor
Chelmno
Dachau
Theresienstadt
Warsaw
Vilna
Skarzysko
Bergen-Bergen
Janow
Dors
Neugengamme
Pustkow

Out of many nations and peoples came the slaughtered ones. From out of the Jews. From Poland, 3,271,000; from the U.S.S.R. and the Baltic states, 1,050,000; from Romania, 539,000; from Hungary, 390,000; from Czechoslovakia, 255,000; from Germany, 195,000; from France, 140,000; from Holland, 104,000; from Yugoslavia, 64,000; from Greece, 64,000; from Belgium, 57,000; from Austria, 53,000; from Italy, 20,000; from Bulgaria, Luxembourg, and Norway, 9,000.

Light six candles as these numbers are read.

Also the slaughtered from among the many other nations of Europe: the communists and other political dissidents, the gypsies, the Slavic peoples, the homosexuals, the handicapped, the mentally ill.

Light four candles, completing a circle of ten candles.

Reading: The Resurrection[41]

One day they will assemble in the valley of bones—ashes sifted out of furnaces, vapors from Luneburg, parchments from some fiend's books, cakes of soap, half-formed embryos, screams still heard in nightmares. God will breathe upon them. He will say: Be men.

But they will defy Him: We do not hear you.
      Did you hear us?
There is no resurrection for us. In life it
      was a woundrous thing
For each of us to be himself, to guide his limbs
      to do his will.
But now the many are one. Our blood has flowed
      together,
Our ashes are inseparable, our marrow commingled,
Our voices poured together like water of the
      sea.
We shall not surrender this greater self.
We are the Abrahams, Issacs, Jacobs, Sarahs,
      Leahs, Rachels
Are now forever Israel.

Almighty God, raise up a man who will go peddling through
      the world.
Let him gather us up and go through the world selling us
      as trinkets.
Let the peddler sell us cheaply. Let him hawk his wares
      and say:
Who will buy my souveniers? Little children done in soap,
A rare Germanic parchment of the greatest Jew in Lodz.
Men will buy us and display us and point to us with pride:
A thousand Jews went into this and here is a rare piece
That came all the way from Krakow in a box car.
A great statesman will place a candle at his bedside.
It will burn but never be consumed.
The tallow will drip with the tears we shed
And it will glow with the souls of our children.

They will put us in the bathrooms of the United Nations
Where diplomats will wash and wash their hands
With Polish Jews and German Jews and Russian Jews.
Let the peddler sell the box of soap that once was buried
With Kaddish and Psalms by our brothers.

> Some night the statesman will blow upon the candle
> And it will not go out.
> The soul of little children will flicker and flicker
> But will not expire.
> Some day the citizens of the German town
> Will awake to find their houses reeking
> With all the vapors from all the concentration camps,
> From Hell itself, and the stench will come from the
> Soap box.

Then they will all rise up, statesment, diplomats, citizens
And go hunting for the peddler: You disturb our rest
And our ablutions, you who haunt us with your souvenirs,
You who prick our conscience, death upon you!

> But the peddlers shall never cease from the earth
> As long as children die untimely deaths.
> They will haunt us with their memories.

Renewal of Creation

And God created humanity in God's own image, in the image of God they were created, male and female. God blessed them and said to them, "Be fertile and increase and fill the earth and rule over it."

Renew the image of God in us, O Holy One, convert us to the care and preservation of your earth.

And God said, "Let the waters bring forth swarms of living creatures, and birds that fly above the earth across the expanse of the sky." God said, "Let the earth bring forth every kind of living creature, cattle, creeping things, and wild beasts of every kind."

Teach us to be brothers and sisters to your creation, O God, our Mother and Father.

And God said, "Let the water below the sky be gathered into one area and the dry land appear." And God said, "Let the earth sprout vegetation, seed-bearing plants, fruit trees of every kind on earth that bear fruit with the seed in it."

Save us, O God, from the final flood of fire that threatens to engulf our earth. Return us to the waters of original blessing that bring forth nourishment for humans and animals alike.

God said, "Let there be lights in the expanse of the sky to separate day from night. They shall serve as signs for set times, the days and the years, and they shall serve as lights in the expanse of the sky to shine upon the earth."

In time when darkness threatens to overwhelm us, let the light of your truth shine upon us, O God, separating the reality from illusion, truth from falsehood.

In the beginning God created heaven and earth, the earth being unformed and void with darkness over the surface of the deep and the Spirit of God sweeping the water, God said, "Let there be light," and there was light. God saw how good the light was and God separated the light from the darkness.

Breathe your spirit upon us, O God. Separate what is good from what is evil, and restore us and all your creation to their intended state, so that we can look upon each other and the world and exclaim, "Behold, it is very good."

Happy are those of steadfast faith who can still bless the light of candles shining in the darkness. Rejoice O Earth in those who keep the way,
For there is still light with them within you,
May the lights which we have kindled inspire us to use our powers to heal and not to harm, to help and not to hinder, to bless and not to curse, to serve you, O God of Freedom.

Summer:

EARTH DAY CELEBRATION

Group gather in circle out of doors. A central table holds a bowl of earth, a pitcher of water, a bell, and a Bible. A hole has been dug and a tree is ready for planting.

Opening Song: "Morning Has Broken"[42]

Responsive Reading:

Leader: And God said, "Let the earth bring forth," and it was so, and God saw that it was good. And God said, "Let us make humans in our own image and in our likeness, and let them have dominion over the land," and it was so. And God saw everything that was made and beheld that it was good.[43]

The earth moans and withers; the world languishes and withers; the heavens languish together with the earth.

People: The earth lies polluted under its inhabitants, for they have transgressed the laws, violated the statutes; they have broken the everlasting covenant.

Leader: Therefore a curse devours the earth, and its inhabitants suffer for their guilt. Therefore the inhabitants of the earth are scorched and few are left whole.

The city of chaos is broken down; desolation is left in the city; the gates are battered to ruin; every house is shut up so that none can enter.

People: The foundations of the earth tremble; the earth is utterly broken; the earth is rent asunder; the earth is violently shaken; it staggers like a drunken man. It sways like a hut in a storm. Its transgressions lie heavily upon it. It falls and shall not rise again.[44]

Exorcism of the Spirits of Pollution from Earth, Air, Water, and Society

Song: "Air" (from *Hair*)[45]

Welcome, sulphur dioxide, Hello carbon monoxide,
The air, the air is everywhere.
Breathe deep while you sleep, breathe deep.
Bless you alcohol blood stream,
Save me nicotine lung steam,
Breathe deep while you sleep, breathe deep.

Cataclysmic ectoplasm, Fallout atomic orgasm,
Vapor and fume, at the stone of my tomb,
Beating like sullen perfume,
Eating at the stone of my tomb.

Litany of Saints and Demons: (divide into two groups)

Right:

St. Francis, pray for us.
Rachel Carson, pray for us.

Johnny Appleseed, pray for us.

J. J. Audubon, pray for us.
Anne Morrow Lindbergh,
    pray for us.
Henry David Thoreau, pray for us.

Justice Paul Douglas, pray for us.

Frederick Elder, pray for us.

Teilhard de Chardin, pray for us.

Margaret Mead, pray for us.
Robert Frost, pray for us.
All Indian peoples, pray for us.

All gardners, earth watchers,
    and poets, pray for us.

Left:

From CTA deliver us.
From General Motors deliver us.
From Dow Chemical deliver us.
From Gulf Oil deliver us.

From DDT deliver us.
From Atomic Energy deliver us.

From Strontium 90 deliver us.

From carcinogens deliver us.

From atomic fallout deliver us.

From pesticides deliver us.
From acid rain deliver us.
From the Department of the Interior deliver us.

From greed and apathy deliver us.

Together:	Lord have mercy!
Leader:	Lord have mercy!
People:	Lord have mercy!

Anthem: "New Life, New Creation," by Gregory Norbet[46]

New life, new creation, alive our sense of wonder;
the time has come to be reborn; the kingdom is right here.

Do we know within us the call to change our heart?
If we do, the Spirit is alive in us.

Is our willingness to forgive a sign of openness
to receive the greatest gift of God's great love?

Do we celebrate with joy the Good News ev'ry day?
If we do, the Spirit is alive in us.

The exorcism of earth, air, water, and society is symbolized by a bowl of earth and a pitcher of water, a bell, book (Bible), and candle. The candle is held up during each exorcism, the Bible is mounted on a stand, and a bell is read at the conclusion of each chant (done in plain chant style).

Exorcism of Earth

Depart, deadly spirit of pollution from our earth. We recognize you for what you are . . . an ever-growing threat to all life forms, to all created things. You appear on our landscape in many forms: paper, glass, metals, and plastics. Beer cans, car hulks, nonreturnables, slag, ash, and garbage testify to our wasteful society. Even beyond our vision you lurk and poison our bodies and our world in the form of pesticides and acids rained into our soil.

Now, in repentant hope to return our earth to its healthful state, we call upon you to make way for fair earth; to remove from us all forms of your noxious presence.

Hear our cry and depart, deadly spirit of pollution!
Response: "Out, demons, out!"

Exorcism of Air

Depart, deadly spirit of pollution from our air and skies. We recognize you for what you are . . . an evergrowing threat to all life forms, to all created things. You pour from paper mills and burning waste dumps, from the chimneys of homes and factories and from the exhaust pipes of automobiles and trucks. You fill our air with lethal gases, with carbon monoxide and nitrogen and sulfur oxides. Humans choke and forests die in the assualt on the air we breathe.

Now in repentent hope to restore our air to its healthful state, we call on you to make way for pure air, the life breath of all living things.

Hear our cry and depart, deadly spirit of pollution.

Response: "Out, demons, out!"

Exorcism of Water

Depart, deadly spirit of pollution from our waters that flow upon the earth and under the earth. We recognize you for what you are, an evergrowing threat to all life form, to all created things. You pour your wastes from factories and steel mills, plastic manufacturers and chemical processors. You take the form of phosphates, detergents, raw sewage, insecticides and herbicides that drain from the soil, acid runoff, and oil spills. Our waters absorb the heats and wastes of our industrial life, destroying marine life, killing our fellow creatures, the plants and animals of the rivers and oceans.

Now, in repentant hope to restore our waters to their healthful state, we call upon you to make way for uncontaminated waters and the fresh taste of pure springs.

Hear our cry and depart, deadly spirit of pollution!

Response: "Out, demons, out!"

Exorcism of Society

Depart, deadly spirit of exploitation. We recognize you for what you are . . . an evergrowing threat to all life forms, to all created things. You come to us in deceptive form, in the name of progress, science, and development. You parade in the pomp of modern skyscrapers, ever denser networks of urbanization, technology, and transportation systems. But behind the glittering facade of steel and glass lie the hovels of impoverishment and misery of the great masses of our fellow human beings. In an effort to retain your grip upon the unjust share of the resources of our earth, you threaten all life with nuclear annihilation.

Now, in repentant hope to bring back our societies to that just balance where all may share in the goods of God's creation, we call upon you to relax your greedy and destructive grip upon our peoples and our earth; to make way for that good earth of justice and peace.

Hear our cry and depart, deadly spirit of exploitation!
Response: "Out Demons, out!"

Affirmation of Life

In the beginning the world was rock. Every year the rains came and washed off a little. This made earth. By and by plants grew on the earth, and their leaves fell and made more earth. Then trees grew, and their leaves and needles and cones fell every year and with the other leaves and bark made more earth and covered more of the rock.

If you look closely at the ground or the woods, you will see that the top is leaves and bark and pine needles and cones, and a little below the top these are matted together, and a little below that they are rotting and breaking up into earth. And this is the way the earth grew and how it is growing still.

Northern Miwok Creation Story

Canticle to All Creation, by St. Francis of Assisi

Leader: Be praised, my Lord, with all your created things. Be praised brother Sun, who brings the day and gives us light. He is fair and radiant with shining face and he draws his meaning from on high.

People: BE PRAISED, MY LORD, FOR SISTER MOON AND THE STARS IN THE HEAVENS. YOU HAVE MADE THEM CLEAR AND PRECIOUS AND LOVELY.

Leader: Praised be my Lord for our brother Wind, and for the air and the clouds and calm days and every kind of weather, by which you give your creatures nourishment.

People: PRAISED BE MY LORD FOR OUR SISTER WATER, WHICH IS VERY HELPFUL AND HUMBLE, PRE-CIOUS AND PURE.

Leader: Praised be my Lord for our brother Fire, by which you light up the darkness; he is fair, bright and strong.

People: PRAISED BE MY LORD FOR OUR SISTER, MOTHER EARTH, FOR SHE SUSTAINS AND KEEPS US AND BRINGS FORTH ALL KIND OR FRUITS TOGETHER WITH GRASSES AND BRIGHT FLOWERS.

Leader: Praise be my Lord for our sister, bodily death, from which no living person can flee, praise be my Lord for all your creatures. We give you thanks.

Recessional with Tree

Song: "This Land is Your Land"

Chorus:

This land is your land, This land is my land,
From California to New York island,
From the redwood forests to the Gulf Stream waters,
This land was made for you and me.

I roamed and rambled and I followed my footsteps
To the sparking sands of her diamond deserts,
While all around me a voice was sounding:
This land was made for you and me.

Chorus

Well, the sun came shining and I was strolling,
The wheat field waving, the dust clouds rolling,
The fog was lifting, a voice was chanting,
This land was made for you and me.

Chorus

Tree Planting

Leader: Then I saw a new heaven and a new earth, for the first heaven and the first earth was no more.

People: AND I SAW THE HOLY CITY, THE NEW JERUSA-LEM COMING DOWN FROM HEAVEN FROM GOD.

Leader: And I heard a great voice from the throne saying, Behold the dwelling of God is with you; God will dwell with you and you shall be God's people; and every tear will be wiped from your eyes.

People: THEN I SAW THE RIVER OF THE WATERS OF LIFE BRIGHT AS CRYSTAL AND FLOWING FROM THE THRONE OF THE LAMB, THROUGH THE MIDDLE OF THE CITY.

Leader: And also on either side of the River the Tree of Life, with its many fruits yielding fruit each month and its leaves were for the healing of nations.

People: AND THERE SHALL BE NO MORE ANYTHING ACCURSED, FOR GOD WILL BE WITH YOU AND YOU WITH GOD.[47]

Final Song "America the Beautiful" (holding hands)

O Beautiful for spacious skies, for amber waves of grain,
For purple mountain majesty, above the fruited plain.
America, America, God shed her grace on thee,
And crown thy good with sister (brother) hood
From sea to shining sea.

SUMMER SOLSTICE PARTY[48]

The summer solstice party is an all-night picnic and camp-out around a bonfire representing the sun at the longest day of the year. It is a time of celebration and gratitude for this source of light and warmth that brings all physical life to our planet. In addition to the bonfire, a totem pole is set up on one side of the camp. Each participant will bring a totem representing an important aspect of her identity.

The party begins by the group assembling in a circle. Each person holds up her totem and tells a story about herself represented by the totem. The totems are then arranged around the pole. Then there is a picnic supper. After the supper the group gathers around the fire. Each person should have brought a story to tell, a poem to recite, or a song or dance to teach the others. These are shared into the night, with additional songs, stories, and dances arising spontaneously.

Sleeping bags are arranged around the fire as members of the group grow sleepy. At sun rise, all stand and greet the sun with a chant:

Hail sister sun, brother fire. You gladden our hearts, you warm our bodies, you warm our earth. Plants spring from the warm ground with your rays, birds warble, cocks crow, brooks sparkle, fish leap into the sunlight, insects hum across the soil, all things blossom for the dance at your touch. You are the light bearer, life giver, energy source of our planet. Hail, all hail our Sun.

The group do together the Hatha Yoga Sun Salutation in thirteen body postures (Fig. 1). The party concludes with breakfast.

HIROSHIMA MEMORIAL DAY (AUGUST 6)

The liturgical space is surrounded by a circle of large photos or paintings of the atomic mushroom cloud, the ruined cities of Hiroshima and Nagasaki, and bomb victims. On a central table a brazier with coals and wood is placed, and a bowl of ashes. Below the table are bowls of water and towels.

Introductory Statement

(While lighting the coals):

This fire represents the power of the sun, the power of light and heat, the energy that holds the universe together, the energy that knits together the nucleus of the atom itself, the basis of all matter. For billions of years these great matrices of energy have upheld all existing things, the sun bringing light and warmth to our planet, causing all things to grow, the the energy locked in the nucleus of the atom, holding together the foundation of matter itself. In 1945 this great cosmic energy of the universe of life was unleashed and turned into an instrument of war. What had been the basis of life was turned by humans into an instrument of death, to annihilate two Japanese cities. A new era of human history began at that moment, one in which the symbol of the ultimate annihilation of planet earth now hovers, like a mushroom cloud, above all our heads. We are all marked by the Mark of the Beast on our foreheads and on our hands,

Fig. 1   Hatha Yoga Positions for Salute to the Sun

1. (Breathe in/out)   2. (in)   3. (out)   4. (in)

5.   6. (out)   7. (in)

8.   9. (out)

10. (in)   11. (out)   12. (in)   13. (in/out)

the Beast of Destruction, of technological creativity gone mad, of human evil turned into terminal illness that may destroy us all—humans, animals, plants, the life-giving waters, and oxygen of the planet itself.

An angel of Death dressed in white robes and whitened face daubs everyone's forehead and hand with ashes from a bowl of ashes held by a figure dressed in a mask and garb symbolizing nuclear technology.

In the face of this impending apocalypse, this final holocaust of all creation, we stand as if paralyzed, mesmerized by the presence of all-powerful death, which promises no new future in its wake. The signs of this catastrophe are all around us, and yet our awareness of it remains mostly in our minds, in an occasional flicker of mental consciousness which we push out of our mind as quickly as it comes into our mind. Our occasional awareness of this great danger generates depression, but not grief; apathy, but not resistance. We are becoming more and more voyeurs of our own downfall; passive bystanders in the face of the annihilation of our world. How can we begin to awake from this stupor, this numbing of our hearts that is the inward expression of our bondage to the power of death?[49]

Let us hear the accounts of the survivors of the first atomic destruction of a city, the city of Hiroshima on August 6, 1945": (A drum roll follows each reading.)

First Reader: A blinding . . . flash cut sharply across the sky . . . I threw myself onto the ground . . . in a reflex movement. At the same moment as the flash, the skin over my body felt a burning heat . . . [Then there was] a blank in time . . . dead silence . . . probably a few seconds . . . and then a . . . huge "boom" . . . like the rumbling of distant thunder. At the same time a violent rush of air pressed down my entire body . . . Again there were some moments of blankness . . . then a complicated series of shattering noises . . . I raised my head, facing the center of Hiroshima to the west . . . [There I saw] an enor-

mous mass of clouds . . . [which] spread and climbed rapidly
. . . into the sky. Then its summit broke open and hung over
horizontally. It took on the shape of . . . a monstrous mushroom with the lower part of its stem—it would be more accu-
rate to call it the tail of a tornado. Beneath it more and more
boiling clouds erupted and unfolded sideways . . . The shape
. . . the color . . . the light . . . were continuously shifting and
changing . . .

Second Reader: I kept screaming "Mother!" very loudly, and
then I saw my mother staggering toward me . . . I think she
pulled the debris away from my body, and then there was a
hole I could crawl out through . . . We were also able to dig
out my baby brother, and my grandmother carried him away
. . . But my mother was very weak and began to collapse and
fall on her side. So I helped her up and tried to drag her along.
But the road was cluttered with pieces of destroyed houses,
and I couldn't move her at all . . . The fire was all around us,
so I thought I had to hurry . . . I was suffocating from the
smoke, and I thought if we stayed like this, then both of us
would be killed. I thought if I could reach the wider road, I
could get some help, so I left my mother there and went off
. . . I found a neighbor . . . and told him my mother was lying
in there and asked him to please fetch her . . . He went back
for her . . . while I held his child . . . but after a while he
returned and said that he could not get into that place any
more . . . I was later told by a neighbor that my mother had
been found dead, face down in a water tank . . . very close to
the spot where I left her . . . If I had been a little older or
stronger I could have rescued her . . . Even now I still hear my
mother's voice calling me to help her . . .

Third Reader: Everything I saw made a deep impression—a
park nearby covered with dead bodies waiting to be cremated
. . . very badly injured people evacuated in my direction . . . The
most impressive thing I saw was some girls, very young girls,
not only with their clothes torn off, but with their skin peeled

off as well . . . My immediate thought was that this was like the
hell I had always read about . . . I had never seen anything which
resembled it before, but I thought that should there be a hell,
this was it—the Buddhist hell, where we were taught that people who could not attain salvation always went . . . And I
imagined that all of these people I was seeing were in the hell
I had read about.

Fourth Reader: The appearance of people was . . . well, they all
had skin blackened by burns . . . They had no hair because their
hair was burned, and at a glance you couldn't tell whether you
were looking at them from in front or in back . . . They held their
arms bent [forward] like this [he proceeded to demonstrate their
position] . . . and their skin—not only on their hands, but on
their faces and bodies too—hung down . . . If there had been
only one or two such people . . . perhaps I would not have had
such a strong impression. But wherever I walked I met these
people . . . Many of them died along the road—I can still picture
them in my mind—like walking ghosts . . . They didn't look like
people of this world . . . They had a special way of walking—
very slowly . . . I myself was one of them.[50]

*The group kneels down together, and holding on to each other, moan softly, while
the Angel of Death reads the apocalypse, the drum rolling softly and building
to a cresendo at the end of the reading:*

AND BEHOLD
I saw an Angel
      (all his cells were electronic eyes)
and I heard a supersonic voice
saying: Open up thy typewriter and type
      and I beheld a silver projectile in flight
        which went from Europe to America in twenty minutes
and the name of the projectile was the H-Bomb
      (and hell flew with it)
      and I saw a kind of flying saucer fall from heaven
And the seismographs platted a shock like an earthquake

and all the artificial planets fell to earth
     and the President of the National Radiation Council
     the Director of the Atomic Energy Commission
     the Secretary of Defense
       were all deep in their sheltering caves
and the first Angel set off the warning siren
     and from the heavens rained Strontium 90
       Caesium 137
       Carbon 14
and the second Angel set off the warning siren
and all eardrums for 300 miles were shattered
by the sound of the explosion
all retinas which saw the flash of the explosion
were seared throughout those same 300 miles
       the heat at ground zero was like that of the sun
and steel and iron and glass and concrete were burnt up
       and sucked into the skies to fall as radioactive rain
and there was loosed a hurricane wind the force of Hurricane
     Flora
and three million cars and trucks flew up into the skies
and crashed into buildings bursting
     like Molotov cocktails
and the third Angel set off the warning siren
and I beheld a mushroom cloud above New York
     and a mushroom cloud above Moscow
   and a mushroom cloud above London
     and a mushroom cloud above Peking
(and Hiroshima's fate was envied)
And all the stores and all the museums and all the libraries
and all the beauties of the earth
     were turned to vapor
and went to form part of the cloud of radioactive dust
which hung above the planet poisoning it
the radioactive rain gave leukemia unto some
     lung cancer unto others
   and unto others cancer of the bone
     or cancer of the ovaries

children were born with cataracts
and the genes of man suffered unto the twenty-second generation
        And this was known as the 45-Minute War . . .
    Seven Angels came
bearing cups of smoke in their hands
        (smoke like a mushroom cloud)
and first I saw the great cup raised over Hiroshima
        (like a cone of venomous ice cream)
    engendering one vast malignant ulcer
and the cup was poured into the sea
    making the whole sea radioactive
        so that all the fishes died
and the third Angel poured forth a neutronic cup
and it was given unto him to sear men with a fire like solar
        fire
and the forth Angel poured his cup which was of Cobalt
and it was given unto Babylon to drain the chalice of the grapes
        of wrath
And the loud voice cried:
        Smite her with twice the megatons with which she smote!
And the Angel who controlled the firing of this bomb
        pushed down the firing key
And they said unto me: Thou hast as yet not seen the Typus Bomb
        nor yet Q fever
I continued watching the vision in the night
and in my vision I beheld as on TV
emerging from the masses
    a Machine
    fearful and terrible beyond all measure
and like a bear or an eagle or a lion with the wings of an aircraft
many propellers numerous antennae eyes of radar
its brain a computer programmed to give the Number of the Beast
roaring through hosts of microphones
        and it gave orders unto men
and all men went in fear of the Machine
Likewise I saw the aircraft in my vision
aircraft faster than sound bearing 50-megaton bombs
and no man guided them but the Machine alone
and they flew toward every city of the earth

each one precisely on target
And the Angel said: Canst thou not see where Columbus Circle
    was?
    Or the place where the United Nations Building stood?
And where Columbus Circle was
    I saw a hole which could contain a 50-story building
and where the United Nations Building stood
I saw only a great grey cliff covered with moss and duck shit
with wave-swept rocks beyond it and sea gulls crying
And in the heavens I beheld a mighty light
    like a million-megaton explosion
and I heard a voice saying unto me: Switch on thy radio
and I did switch it on and heard: BABYLON IS FALLEN
    BABYLON THE GREAT IS
        FALLEN[51]

There is now a long pause while this message is reflected upon. Then in antiphonal chorus:

First Group: Can Babylon the Great fall without taking us all with it, all humans, plants, animals, air, water, life itself?

Second Group: Must not Babylon fall, its systems of destruction dismantled, its power transformed from machines of death to instruments of life in order to save all humans, plants, animals, air, water, life itself from destruction?

Both Together: How do we begin? We must cleanse our minds and hearts of the Mark of the Beast, free ourselves of the stupor and apathy that holds us bondage, cease to be voyeurs at the funeral of our world. We must become outraged; we must say "No. This violence stops here, now, with us."

Bowls of water are passed to the assembled group, and each turns to the person next to them, cleansing the mark of ashes from their forehead and hand with the words: "Be cleansed of the Mark of the Beast, take courage to defend life on earth." Final Reading, all together:

Two paths lie before us. One leads to death, the other to life. If we choose the first path—if we numbly refuse to acknowledge the nearness of extinction, all the while increasing our preparations to bring it about—then we are in effect become the allies of death, and in everything we do our attachment to life will weaken: our vision, blinded to the abyss that has opened at out feet, will dim and grow confused; our will, discouraged by the thought of trying to build on such a precarious foundation anything that is meant to last, will slacken; and we will sink into stupefaction, as though we were gradually weaning ourselves from life in preparation for the end. On the other hand, if we reject our doom, and bend our efforts toward survival—if we arouse ourselves to the peril and act to forestall it, making ourselves the allies of life—then the anesthetic fog will lift: our vision, no longer straining not to see the obvious, will sharpen; our will, finding secure ground to build on, will be restored; and we will take full and clear possession of life again. One day—and it is hard to believe that it will not be soon—we will make our choice. Either we will sink into the final coma and end it all, or, as I trust and believe, we will awaken to the truth of our peril, a truth as great as life itself, and, like a person who has swallowed a lethal poison but shakes off his stupor at the last moment and vomits the poison up, we will break through the layers of our denials, put aside our fainthearted excuses, and rise up to cleanse the earth of nuclear weapons.[52]

Notes

INTRODUCTION

1. Starhawk, *The Spiral Dance: A Rebirth of the Ancient Religion of the Great Goddess* (New York: Harper & Row, 1979).
2. Rachel Adler and Lynn Gottlieb are among the Jewish feminists involved in liturgical development. See *On Being a Jewish Feminist: A Reader* (New York: Schocken, 1983).
3. Among the various repressive measures directed at Catholic feminists by the Vatican have been orders directing the removal of women pastoral counselors in Catholic seminaries, a series of orders removing nuns from their religious orders when they refuse to leave appointed or elected office (these offices being based in social welfare services), the attack on the twenty-four nuns who signed the New York Times ad calling for pluralism in abortion (October 1984), the rejection of inclusive language as an issue to be discussed, and the rejection of women's participation in even minor liturgical functions such as altar servers. Madonna Kolbenschlag of the Woodstock Center at Georgetown University in Washington, D.C., is presently preparing a documentary source book on the repression from the Vatican experienced by the Sisters of Mercy of the Union, whose president, Sister Theresa Kane, spoke out to Pope John Paul II on women's ordination during his visit to the United States in 1982.
4. The term for the *ecclesia* of women has gone through some changes in the development of this movement, primarily in the United States and among Roman Catholic women. The term first used by the conference developed by the Women of the Church Coalition in November 1983, was *Woman Church* (see Chap. 4). Later, some thinkers in the movement began to use *Women Church*, reasoning that it was important to talk about the plurality of communities of women and that "woman" was too easily read as a generic term, dominated in practice by white, middle-class women. Other critics felt that the juxtaposition of two nouns was ungrammatical. The question of capitalization or not was also a question. On the basis of these discussions, on May 5, 1985, a meeting of representatives of the Women of the Church Coalition voted to adopt the term *women-church* when speaking of the idea and reality of the *ecclesia* of women throughout history, and *Women-Church* when speaking about the particular historical movement and organization today.

CHAPTER 1:

1. The fact that Jesus viewed his ministry as one of prophetic renewal of Israel, and not the founding of a new religion, has long been recognized by New

Testament scholars. For an earlier discussion, see Morton Scott Enslin, *Christian Beginnings*, Parts 1 and 2 (New York: Harper & Row, 1938), p. 166.

2. See Rosemary Ruether, "Church and Family in Scripture," *New Blackfriars* (Jan. 1984), pp. 4–14.

3. *An Inclusive Language Lectionary: Readings for Year A* (Philadelphia: Westminster Press, 1983), appendix.

4. George Williams, two chapters on the development of the ministry in the pre- and post-Nicene periods, in H. R. Niebuhr and D. D. Williams, *The Ministry in Historical Perspective* (New York: Harper, 1956), pp. 27–81.

5. The concept of apostolic succession of bishops in major sees from founding apostles of those sees was developed by second-century Christian thinkers, such as Clement of Rome, Tertullian, and Irenaeus of Lyons, primarily to combat Gnosticism. It originally referred to the faithful carrying down of apostolic teachings by bishops from the founding apostle, thus assuring continuity between the faith taught by the bishops and the original faith of the apostles. Bishop lists are often vague and unhistorical in the earliest or first-century names cited, intending to cover up the fact that Gnostic Christianity often was the first in a region to evangelize. See Walter Bauer, *Orthodoxy and Heresy in Earliest Christianity* (Philadelphia: Fortress Press, 1971).

6. The struggle between Cyprian of Carthage and the confessors about the power to forgive the lapsed is reflected particularly in Cyprian's letter, *On the Lapsed*, A.D. 251. *Library of Christian Classics*, vol. 5, pp. 113–46.

7. See Jeffrey Burton Russell, *A History of Medieval Christianity: Prophecy and Order* (New York: Thomas Y. Crowell, 1968), pp. 138–44.

8. E. W. McDonnell, *Beguine and Beghard in Medieval Culture* (New Brunswick, N.J.: Rutgers University Press, 1954).

9. The classical study of the familial order of creation in relation to the Puritan understanding of salvation is Edmund S. Morgan, *The Puritan Family: Religion and Domestic Relations in Seventeenth Century New England* (New York: Harper & Row, 1944).

10. See Rosemary Keller, "New England Women: Ideology and Experience in First-Generation Puritanism," in *Women and Religion in America: The Colonial and Revolutionary War Periods*, ed. Rosemary Keller and Rosemary Ruether (San Francisco: Harper & Row, 1983), pp. 132–92.

11. Christopher Hill, *Puritanism and Revolution: The English Revolution of the Seventeenth Century* (New York: Schocken, 1958), pp. 75–87.

12. Rosemary Ruether and Catherine Prelinger, "Women in Sectarian and Utopian Groups," in Ruether and Keller, *Women and Religion*, pp. 260–62, 278–85.

13. Gerald R. Cragg, *Puritanism in the Age of the Great Persecution* (Cambridge University Press), 1957, p. 47 and *passim*. Also see Hugh Barbour, *The Quakers in Puritan England* (New Haven: Yale University Press), 1964, pp. 53–54, 63, 66, 207–8.

14. Ruether and Prelinger, "Women in Sectarian Groups," 283–88. See also Mabel Brailsford, *Quaker Women, 1650–1690* (London: Duckworth and Company, 1915), pp. 268–89.

15. Frederick A. Norwood, *The Story of American Methodism* (Nashville: Abingdon, 1974), pp. 90–98.

16. See, for example, Amanda Berry Smith, *An Autobiography: The Story of the Lord's Dealings with Mrs. Amanda Smith The Colored Evangelist Containing an Account of Her*

Life Work of Faith, and Her Travels in America, England, Ireland, Scotland, India, and Africa, as an Independent Missionary (Chicago: Meyer and Brother, 1893).

17. Dorothy C. Bass, "In Christian Firmness and Christian Meekness: Feminism and Pacifism in Antebellum America," in *Immaculate and Powerful: The Female in Sacred Image and Social Reality,* ed. Constance Buchanan (Boston: Beacon Press, 1985).

18. Thus the English socialist Robert Owen founded a Society of Rational Religionists, and the French socialist Saint-Simon published as his final book a volume called *The New Christianity* (1825).

19. Rosemary Ruether, "Women in Utopian Movements", in *Women and Religion in America; The Nineteenth Century,* ed. Rosemary Ruether and Rosemary Keller, (San Francisco: Harper & Row, 1981), pp. 47–52, 63–64.

CHAPTER 2

1. Josephine M. Ford, *Which Way For Catholic Pentecostals?* (New York: Harper & Row, 1976).

2. See, for example, the document entitled "A Summary of Goals, Policies, and Understandings for the Charismatic Renewal in the Diocese of Colorado Springs," worked out by the Bishop of Colorado Springs and the diocesan liason to the Charismatic Renewal and passed out to all charismatic prayer groups in that diocese (1984).

3. Gustavo Gutierrez, *The Power of the Poor in History* (New York: Orbis Books, 1983), pp. 44, 50, 52.

4. Final document of CELAM III, secs. 96–97, 156, 239, 261–63, 373, 629, 641–43, 648–49, in *Puebla and Beyond,* ed. John Eagleson and Philip Scharper (New York: Orbis Books, 1979).

5. Gabriela Videla, *Sergio Mendez Arceo: Un Senor Obispo* (Cuernavaca, Mexico: Correo del Sur, 1982), pp. 115–32.

6. Kate Pravera, *The Primacy of Orthopraxis: Theological Method in the Nicaraguan Church of the Poor* (Ph.D. diss., Northwestern University, 1984).

7. Fernando Cardenal, "Why I Was Forced to Leave the Jesuit Order," *National Catholic Reporter* (Jan. 11, 1985), p. 1.

8. Philip Berryman, *The Religious Roots of Rebellion: Christians in the Central American Revolution* (New York: Orbis Books, 1984).

9. "The Netherlands: Manifesto of a Movement," *Christianity and Crisis* (Sept. 21, 1981), pp. 246–150.

10. Edward J. Grace, "The Christian Grassroots Community of St. Paul's Outside the Walls in Rome: A Case Study," *National Institute for Campus Ministry Journal,* 5, no. 3 (1980), pp. 7–34; also "Italy: Disobedience As Witness," *Christianity and Crisis* (Sept. 21, 1981), pp. 242–46.

11. The NTC News, from the Italian Ecumenical News Agency, Via Firenze, 38, Rome, is the networking newsletter for the European basic Christian community movement. It is edited by Edward J. Grace. For the ecclesiology of basic Christian communities, see Sergio Torres, *The Challenge of Basic Christian Communities* (New York: Orbis Books, 1981), and Leonardo Boff, *Church, Charism and Power: A Radical Ecclesiology* (New York: Crossroad, 1985).

12. Stephen Rose, *Jesus and Jim Jones* (New York: Pilgrim Press, 1979).

13. For example, Starhawk, *The Spiral Dance: A Rebirth of the Ancient Religion of the Great Goddess* (San Francisco: Harper & Row, 1979), pp. 2–5.

14. This seems to be the view taken by Mary Daly in *Pure Lust: Elemental Feminist Philosophy* (Boston: Beacon Press, 1984).

CHAPTER 3

1. Mary Magdalene, contrary to popular assumption, is never referred to as a prostitute or former prostitute in the New Testament. This assumption grew out of a false reading into New Testament texts. The woman who anointed Jesus is nowhere identified as Mary Magdalene, and the original version of the story has nothing to do with a woman who is a sinner. Also, the stories of the woman taken in adultery and the reference to Mary Magdalene as having been cured of "seven devils" is incorrectly read. The first story does not refer to mary Magdalene, and the second story where she is named does not refer to sin, but to some kind of convulsive disease. The apocryphal Gnostic Gospels also make no reference to Mary Magdalene as a sinner, and since they claim her as an apostolic authority for women, if such a tradition were known to them, they would have made some reference to it to refute it. It is likely that the tradition of Mary Magdalene as a sinner was developed in orthodox Christianity primarily to displace the apostolic authority claimed for women through her name. See Rosemary Ruether, *Womanguides: Readings Toward a Feminist Theology* (Boston: Beacon Press, 1985), pp. 177–78.

2. Elisabeth Schüssler Fiorenza, "Word, Spirit, and Power: Women in Early Christian Communities," in *Women of Spirit: Female Leadership in the Jewish and Christian Traditions,* ed. R. Ruether and E. McLaughlin (New York: Simon and Schuster, 1979), pp. 40–41.

3. Numb. 26:59 and 1 Chron. 5:29; see Leonard Swidler, *Biblical Affirmations of Women* (Philadelphia: Westminster, 1979), p. 85.

4. Exod. 15:20–21; Mic. 6:3–4.

5. Exod. 19:14–15.

6. Phyllis Bird, "Images of Women in the Old Testament," in *Religion and Sexism: Images of Women in the Jewish and Christian Traditions,* ed. R. Ruether (New York: Simon and Schuster, 1974), pp. 48–57.

7. For Jesus' view of the kingdom of God, see Albert Nolan, *Jesus Before Christianity* (Cape Town, South Africa: David Philip, 1979), pp. 43–90.

8. Fiorenza, "Word, Spirit, and Power," pp. 32–44.

9. On the discipleship of equals in the early Jesus movement, see Elisabeth Schüssler Fiorenza, *In Memory of Her: A Feminist Theological Reconstruction of Christian Origins* (New York: Crossroads, 1983), pp. 140–50.

10. Swidler, *Biblical Affirmations,* pp. 164–96.

11. Swidler, *Biblical Affirmations,* pp. 198–205; also Winsome Munro, "Women Disciples in Mark," *Catholic Biblical Quarterly* 44 (1982), pp. 225ff.

12. Elaine Pagels, *The Gnostic Gospels* (New York: Random House, 1979), pp. 48–69.

13. The Gospel of Mary, in *The Nag Hammadi Library in English,* ed. John Robinson, et al. (New York: Harper & Row, 1977), pp. 471–74.

14. Walter Bauer, *Orthodoxy and Heresy in Earliest Christianity* (Philadelphia: Fortress Press, 1971).

15. Rosemary Ruether, *Sexism and God-talk: Toward a Feminist Theology* (Boston: Beacon Press, 1983), pp. 141–42.

16. Dennis MacDonald, *The Legend and the Apostle: The Battle for Paul in Story and Canon* (Philadelphia: Westminster, 1983).

17. Fiorenza, *In Memory of Her*, pp. 251–69.

18. This statement is based on remarks in a lecture given at the Waldensian Seminary in Rome, in March 1980, by the president of the Italian Waldensian Church, Giorgio Bouchard. Bouchard stated that the Waldensian Church had had women preachers in the medieval period, but these were repressed when the Waldensian Church was "reformed" to enter into communion with the Reformed Church in Switzerland in the sixteenth century. Ordination to women had been restored in the Waldensian Church only in the second half of the twentieth century.

19. See Keith Thomas, "Women and the Civil War Sects," *Past and Present* 13 (1958). Also Joyce Irwin, *Women in Radical Protestantism, 1525–1675* (New York: Edwin Mellen Press, 1979), pp. 200–36.

20. Earl Kent Brown, "Women of the Word: Selected Leadership Roles of Women in Mr. Wesley's Methodism," in *Women in New Worlds: Historical Perspectives on the Wesleyan Tradition*, ed. Rosemary S. Keller and Hilah F. Thomas, pp. 69–87.

21. Letha Scanzoni and Susan Setta, "Women in the Evangelical Tradition," in *Women and Religion in America: The Twentieth Century, 1900–1968*, ed. R. Ruether and R. Keller, forthcoming, (San Francisco: Harper & Row, 1986).

22. Olympe de Gouges, "The Declaration of the Rights of Woman and Citizen," in *Woman as Revolutionary*, ed. Frederick C. Giffin (New York: New American Library, 1973), pp. 46–49.

23. Rosemary Keller, "Women, Civil Religion, and the American Revolution," in *Women and Religion in America: The Colonial and Revolutionary War Periods* (San Francisco: Harper & Row, 1983), pp. 375–76; also *Feminism: The Essential Historical Writings*, ed. Miriam Schneir (New York: Random House, 1972), pp. 2–4, from the *Adams Family Correspondence* (Cambridge, Mass: Harvard University Press, 1963, 1973).

24. See correspondence of John Adams with James Sullivan, May 26, 1776, *The Work of John Adams*, ed. Charles Francis Adams (Boston, 1856), 9: 375–78.

25. Barbara Taylor, *Eve and the New Jerusalem: Socialism and Feminism in the Nineteenth Century* (New York: Pantheon, 1983).

26. V. I. Lenin's conservativism, paternalism, and aversion to any discussion of the "woman's problem" as an issue in itself, apart from the "proletarian revolution," is well illustrated in the memoirs of her conversation with him by the feminist Clara Zetkin, *The Emancipation of Women*, from the writings of V. I. Lenin, ed. Nazezhda K. Krupskaya (New York: International Publishers, 1934), pp. 97–123.

27. Hilda Scott, *Does Socialism Liberate Women? Experiences from Eastern Europe* (Boston: Beacon Press, 1974), pp. 191–208.

28. Robert Staples, "The Myth of Black Matriarchy," *The Black Scholar* (Jan.–Feb. 1970), pp. 8–16; also "Black Muslims and Negro Family Relationships," in *The Black Family: Essays and Studies*, ed. Robert Staples (Belmont, Calif.: Wadsworth, 1971), pp. 376–87.

29. Calvin Hernton, *Sex and Racism in America* (Garden City, N.J.: Doubleday,

1965), expressed the perspective of the black male on the interconnection of race and gender.

30. See Gerda Lerner, *The Female Experience: An American Documentary* (Indianapolis: Bobbs-Merrill, 1977), pp. 323–24.

31. Ambivalences toward women's emancipation in Third World revolutions are summarized in Shiela Rowbotham, *Women, Resistance, and Revolution: A History of Women and Revolution in the Modern World* (New York: Random House, 1972), pp. 170–247.

32. Amba (Mercy) Oduyoye, "Reflections from a Third World Woman's Perspective: Women's Experience and Liberation Theology," *Irruption of the Third World Challenge to Theology: Papers of the Fifth International Conference of the Ecumenical Association of Third World Theologians, August 17–29, 1981, New Delhi, India,* ed. Virginia Fabella and Sergio Torres (New York: Orbis Books, 1983).

CHAPTER 4

1. One finds such fantasies in older feminist separatist utopias, such as Charlotte Perkins Gilman's *Herland,* (1923; reprint, New York: Pantenon, 1979), and more recent separatist utopias, such as Sally M. Gearhart's *Wanderground: Stories of the Hill Women* (Watertown, Mass.: Persephone Press, 1979).

2. See preliminary report of study of Catholic women in seminaries in the *National Catholic Reporter* (Oct. 21, 1983), p. 13. A larger study is presently in progress under a grant from the Lilly Foundation, which shows large numbers of Catholic women in major nondenominational seminaries such as Harvard Divinity School, Yale Divinity School, the Union Theological Seminary, Chicago Divinity School, and the Graduate Theological Union in Berkeley since the early 1970s but very little follow-up information on what these women are doing with their degrees. Some seem to have become Protestants in order to become ordained, but the exact percentage is unknown.

3. The major speeches from the Woman Church conference were published in *Probe,* the magazine of the National Assembly of Women Religious, 1307 S. Wabash, Chicago, Ill. 60605, in the spring of 1984.

CHAPTER 5

1. Eph. 5:23–32 compares the lordship of the husband over the wife to that of Christ over the Church, but it does not make an analogy between Christ-bridegroom and church-bride, and clergy-laity. Early Christian spokesmen for the monarchical episcopacy, such as Clement of Rome (c. A.D. 96) and Ignatius of Antioch (d. 110), compared the bishop to God the Father and to Christ, but they also did not use the bridegroom-bride analogy.

2. In the ancient Near East the image of the king as divine shepherd vied with the image of the king as gardener, tending the tree of life with the waters of life. This rivalry was represented in Mesopotamian culture by the myth of Dumuzi, the Shepherd, and Enkidu, the Gardener, who both sue for the hand of Inanna, the Queen of Heaven. The Israelites and other Semitic peoples with a nomadic shepherding tradition favored the shepherd image for God

and the king. This is also reflected in the biblical story of the favoring of Abel, the shepherd, over Cain, the farmer. See John Gray, *Near Eastern Mythology* (London: Hamlyn House, 1969), p. 15.

3. For example, John Saward, *Christ and his Bride* (London: Church Literature Association, 1977).

4. For example, Augustine's treatises *On Grace and Original Sin and On Marriage and Concupiscence* in *Nicene and Post-Nicene Fathers,* Donaldson and Roberts, eds. vol. 5 (New York: Christian Literature Co., 1887), pp. 217–308.

5. Apostolic succession was used by second-century Christian writers such as Tertullian and Irenaeus to guarantee the succession of right teaching. Bishops in the second century also came to be seen as the guarantors of the unity of the church at the eucharistic liturgy, but the two ideas became linked only gradually. By the late fourth century the Christian episcopacy was seen primarily as priestly, with an indelible ordination that assures a tactile descent of the power of the Holy Spirit going back to the apostles. See H. Richard Niebuhr and Daniel Day Williams, *The Ministry in Historical Perspective* (San Francisco: Harper & Row, 1956), pp. 75–76.

6. James 5:16.

7. The question of a second repentence for those who fell into serious sin after baptism was hotly debated in second-century Christianity. Rigorists would reject any second repentence, particularly for those who fell into sexual immorality or who recanted their faith under persecution. The apocalypse of the *Shepherd of Hermas* (mid-second century) would allow only one repentence after baptism. Gradually the church developed a penitential system in which reduction to the catechumenate status was imposed on serious sinners who would stand in a penitential posture at the back of the liturgy and would be readmitted to communion only after a set number of years. This penitential status and its termination were both public events.

8. On this conflict between Cyprian and the martyrs, see Hans Lietzmann, *The Founding of the Church Universal* (New York, Meridian, 1961), p. 230.

9. *Oxford Dictionary of the Christian Church,* s.v. "Penance."

10. Samuel Laeuchli, *Power and Sexuality: The Emergence of Canon Law at the Synod of Elvira* (Philadelphia: Temple University Press, 1972).

11. Ibid.

12. Rosemary Ruether, "Virginal Feminism in the Fathers of the Church," in *Religion and Sexism: Images of Women in the Jewish and Christian Traditions,* ed. R. Ruether (New York: Simon and Schuster, 1974), p. 169.

13. Susan Wemple, *Women in Frankish Society: Marriage and the Cloister: 500–900* (University of Pennsylvania Press, 1983).

14. See Clara Maria Henning, "Canon Law and the Battle of the Sexes," in *Religion and Sexism,* pp. 281–84.

15. The Waldensians in the twelfth century and the Hussites and Lollards in the fifteenth century represent such populist medieval preaching movements.

16. The Missouri Synod of the Lutheran Church (U.S.A.) experienced a schism in 1974 closely related to the conflict between advocates of historical-critical method located at Concordia Seminary and the fundamentalism of the popular culture of the church.

17. Popularly based Bible study with a liberation theology method and context is typical in Latin American basic Christian communities. See Kate Pravera,

The Primacy of Orthopraxis: Theological Method in the Nicaraguan Church of the Poor (Ph.D. diss., Northwestern University, 1984).

18. See particularly chap. 3 of *The Constitution on the Church* of the Second Vatican Council, ed. E. H. Peters (Glen Rock, N.J.: Paulist Press, 1965).

19. Stories of the arbitrary granting and removal of sharing in decision making between priests and people could be multiplied endlessly in Roman Catholicism after Vatican II. One notable example was Good Shepherd parish in Arlington, Virginia, where a democratically minded priest was replaced by an autocrat who cancelled the previous policies of consultation with the council of the laity and for a while even locked the lay leaders out of the church. The lay leaders appealed to the bishop and finally even to the pope, but to no avail.

20. See Rosemary Ruether, "Crisis in Los Angeles," *Continuum* 5 (Spring 1967), pp. 652–62 on the conflict between a young priest, William DuBay, and Cardinal McIntyre over DuBay's proposed "priest's union."

21. See for example, H. Brankhorst and B. Alfrink, "The Dutch Pastoral Council," in *The Tablet*, 224 (Jan. 17, 1970), pp. 69–71. Most of these efforts had been undermined by the time the Vatican concluded its campaign against Dutch collegiality in the particular synod of the Vatican and the Dutch bishops in 1980. See John Paul II, "Letter to the Bishops of the Netherlands One Year after the Conclusion of their Particular Synod," *Origins* 10 (Feb. 26, 1981), pp. 577–78.

22. See Peter Hebblewaite, "Ratzinger's Answers Manipulate Truth," *National Catholic Reporter* 20 (Oct. 12, 1984), pp. 5.

23. Matthew Fox, *Original Blessing: A Primer in Creation Spirituality* (Santa Fe, New Mex.: Bear and Co., 1983).

CHAPTER 6

1. "Poems about Anath and Baal," in *Religions of the Ancient Near East: Sumero-Akkadian Religious Texts and Ugaritic Epics*, ed. Isaac Mendelsohn (New York: The Liberal Arts Press, 1955), pp. 224–61.

2. A. S. Herbert, *Worship in Ancient Israel* (London: Lutterworth Press, 1959), pp. 43–44.

3. Giovanni Miegge, *The Virgin Mary: The Roman Catholic Marian Doctrine* (London: Lutterworth Press, 1955), p. 77, n.2 and pp. 84–85.

4. Arthur Waskow, *These Holy Sparks: The Rebirth of the Jewish People* (San Francisco: Harper & Row, 1983).

5. Rachel Adler, "Can Jewish Women Recovenant" (unpublished).

6. Starhawk, for example, is strongly committed to the peace movement and to ethical commitment in WICCA, but she strongly rejects any concept of historical sin or evil. This is partly based on the Christian distortion of its own doctrine of "original sin" as teaching the fallenness or "evil" of nature, rather than fallenness as alienation from nature or creation.

7. *The Shalom Seders: Three Haggadahs,* compiled by the New Jewish Agenda (New York: Adama Books, 1984).

CHAPTER 7

1. Adam D. Finnerty, *No More Plastic Jesus: Global Justice and Christian Lifestyle* (Maryknoll, N.Y.: Orbis Books, 1977), app. A and B.
2. See an account of the first Anabaptist "rebaptism" in the "Reminiscences of George Blaurock," in *Spiritual and Anabaptist Writers*, ed. George H. Williams (Philadelphia: Westminster Press, 1957), pp. 43–44.
3. See particularly Augustine's treatise on *Nature and Grace*, in *Nicene and Post-Nicene Fathers*, ed. Donaldson and Roberts, vol. 5 (New York: Christian Literature Co., 1887), pp. 121–51.
4. Early Christianity closely associated baptism with the biblical symbolism of entering the good land flowing with milk and honey. See the Epistle of Barnabas 6:11–14.
5. Andrea Dworkin, *Right-Wing Women* (New York: Coward, McCann, 1983).
6. Gregory Dix, *The Shape of the Liturgy* (Westminster: Dacre Press, 1945).
7. Ruether, *Womenguides: Readings Toward a Feminist Theology* (Boston: Beacon Press, 1985). See also Letty Russell, *Feminist Interpretation of the Bible* (Philadelphia: Westminster Press, 1985).
8. Tertullian, *On the Dress of Women* 1,1, in *Ante-Nicene Fathers*, vol. 4, ed. James Donaldson and Alexander Roberts (New York: Scribners, 1899), p. 14.
9. Augustine, *On the Trinity* 7, 7, 10; in *Later Works*, ed. John Burnaby (Philadelphia: Westminster Press, 1955).
10. Thomas Aquinas, *Summa Theologica* pt. 1, q. 92, art. 1; ed. Anton Pegis (New York: Random House, 1945).
11. *Malleus Maleficarum*, pt. 2, sec. 6; trans. Montague Summers (London: J. Rodker, 1928).
12. Martin Luther, Lectures on Genesis, Gen. 2:18, in *Luther's Works* vol. 1, ed. Jaroslav Pelikan (St. Louis: Concordia Publishing House, 1958), p. 115.
13. Karl Barth, *Church Dogmatics*, vol. 3, sec. 4 (Edinburgh: Clark, 1975), pp. 158–72.
14. *Declaration on the Question of the Admission of Women to the Ministerial Priesthood*, sec. 27. Vatican City, October 15, 1976.
15. Micah 6:3–4.
16. Judges 4:4–5:31.
17. 2 Kings 22:11–20.
18. Pesahim 62b; Tosefta Kelim Baba Mezia 1:6 (Talmud).
19. John 20:1–18.
20. Romans 16:1–2.
21. Romans 16:3–4.
22. "Acts of Paul and Thecla" in *Ante-Nicene Fathers*, vol. 7, ed. Alexander Roberts and James Donaldson (New York: Scribner's, 1885–1897), p. 487ff.
23. *A New Eusebius*, ed. James Stevenson (London: SPCK Press, 1957), p. 113.
24. Rosemary Ruether, "Mothers of the Church: Ascetic Women in the Late Patristic Age", in *Women of Spirit: Female Leadership in the Jewish and Christian Traditions*, ed. R. Ruether and E. McLaughlin (New York: Simon and Schuster, 1979), pp. 75–88.
25. Julian of Norwich, *Revelations of Divine Love*, trans. John Walsh (New York: Harper & Row, 1961).

26. Catherine of Siena, *The Dialogue,* trans. Suzanne Noffke (New York: Paulist Press, 1980).

27. *A Woman of Genius: The Intellectual Autobiography of Sor Juana Inés de la Cruz,* trans. Margaret Sayers Pedan (Salisbury, Conn.: Lime Rock Press, 1982).

28. Isabel Ross, *Margaret Fell. Mother of Quakerism* (London: Longmans, Green, and Co., 1949).

29. Luther Lee, "Women's Right of Preach the Gospel" in *Five Sermons and a Tract,* ed. Donald Dayton (Chicago, Ill.: Helrad House, 1975), pp. 77–100.

30. Live Gilbert, *Narrative of Sojourner Truth* (Boston: n.p., 1875).

31. Amanda Berry Smith, *An Autobiography* (Chicago, Ill.: Meyer and Brothers, 1893).

32. Rosemary Keller, "Patterns of Lay Women's Leadership in Twentieth Century Protestantism," in *Women and Religion in America, 1900–1968,* ed. R. Ruether and R. Keller, (San Francisco: Harper & Row, 1986), pp. 270–72.

33. *On Being a Jewish Feminist,* ed. Susannah Heschel (New York: Schocken, 1983), p. xv.

34. Norene Carter, "Entering the Sanctuary: The Struggle for Priesthood in Contemporary Episcopalian and Roman Catholic Experience," ed. R. Ruether and E. McLaughlin, *Women of Spirit: Female Leadership in the Jewish and Christian Traditions,* pp. 356–72.

35. *Authority, Community and Conflict,* ed. Madonna Kolbenschlag (New York: Sheed and Ward, 1986), addresses the conflicts between the Sisters of Mercy, headed by Sr. Teresa Kane, and the Vatican.

36. The design for the women-church center was done by Rosemary Ruether and rendered in architectural drawing by Mary Whittaker.

CHAPTER 8

1. Rachel Fruchter, Naomi Fatt, Pamela Booth, and Diana Leidel of the Health-Right Collective, New York City, "The Woman's Health Movement: Where Are We Now?" in *Seizing our Bodies: The Politics of Women's Health* (New York: Random House, 1977), pp. 271–78.

2. An example of feminist recovery of traditions of women's psychic and spiritual healing is Diane Mariechild, *Mother Wit: A Feminist Guide to Psychic Development* (Trumansburg, New York: The Crossing Press, 1981).

3. Del Martin, *Battered Wives* (San Francisco, Calif.: Glide Publications, 1976), pp. 1–5.

4. Florence Hayes is a chaplain at McGill University in Montreal, Canada.

5. Kate Pravera received her Ph.D. degree from the Joint Program in Religious and Theological Studies at Northwestern University in Evanston, Illinois, and is presently teaching at Loyola University in Chicago. The order of the naming ceremony is drawn in part from Carol Christ's *Diving Deep and Surfacing* (Boston: Beacon Press, 1980). For Christ, the process of women's spiritual quest moves through four phases: an experience of nothingness, a mystical awakening, insight, and new naming.

6. Carol Christ, *Diving Deep,* p. 7.

7. Mary Daly, *Beyond God the Father: Toward a Philosophy of Women's Liberation* (Boston: Beacon Press, 1973), p. 2.

8. Ibid., p. 8.

9. Gioconda Belli, unpublished poems.

10. Rosemary Ruether, summarized from "Virginal Feminism in the Fathers of the Church," in *Religion and Sexism: Images of Women in the Jewish and Christian Traditions,* ed. Rosemary Ruether (New York: Simon and Schuster, 1974), pp. 156–59.

11. Carol Christ, *Diving Deep,* p. 17.

12. Gioconda Belli, unpublished poems.

13. Carol Christ, *Diving Deep,* pp. 18–19.

14. This liturgy on affirmation of lesbian identity was written by the Reverend Rebecca Parker of Seattle, Washington, and the Reverend Joanne Brown, professor of Church History at Pacific Lutheran College in Tacoma, Washington.

15. Tune: "Hymn to Joy," arranged from Ludwig van Beethoven, by Edward Hodges. Words: adapted by Rebecca Parker from the *Poems of Henry Van Dyke* (New York: Charles Scribner's Sons, 1939).

16. Ecclus. 1:2–6, Jerusalem Bible.

17. Adapted from Wisd. 7:17–21, Jerusalem Bible.

18. Adapted from Wisd. 7:22–24, Jerusalem Bible.

19. Adapted from Wisd. 7:27a,28–8:1, Jerusalem Bible.

20. Tune: "Slane," traditional Irish Melody. Words: ancient Irish, from Psalm 119, translated by Mary E. Bryne, versified by Eleanor H. Hull; adapted by Ruth Duck in *Everflowing Streams* (New York: Pilgrim Press, 1981).

21. Adapted from Ps. 139, Jerusalem Bible.

22. Wolf Leslau, *Falasha Anthology,* trans. from Ethiopic sources, New Haven: Yale University Press, 1963.

23. Radclyffe Hall, *Well of Loneliness,* New York: Avon, 1981, p. 448.

24. From Ps. 72.

25. Tune: "Nun Danket", Johann Cruger, 1648. Words: Martin Rinckart, c. 1636, trans. Catherine Winkworth, 1858; adapted by Rebecca Parker, 1985.

CHAPTER 9

1. This prayer is adapted from the traditional Prayer for Dew, recited on the morning of the first day of Passover.

2. Carter Heyward, *Our Passion for Justice* (New York: Pilgrim Press, 1984), p. 49.

3. The Coming of Age Ritual was developed by Adele Arlett, a doctoral student in theology at Marquette University, Milwaukee, Wisconsin. It represents the sort of liturgy she would have liked to have done when she left home.

4. "Alternative Weddings," in *The Alternative Celebrations Catalogue* ed. Milo Shannon-Thornberry, (New York: Pilgrim Press, 1982), pp. 25–34.

5. Phyllis Athey and Mary Jo Ostermann are founders of Kinheart, a center on sexuality and homophobia housed at Wheaton United Methodist Church in Evanston, Illinois. They are presently preparing a book on covenant celebrations.

6. Statement written by April McConeghey, a Grailville staff member.

7. Statement by Dr. Mary Buckley, professor of theology at St. John's College, Jamaica, New York, and a longtime Grail member.

8. Statement by Frances Grotty and Helen Davis of the Grail Women's Task Force.

9. Statement by Jude Meyer, former member of the Grailville Staff, Loveland, Ohio.
10. Shannon-Thornberry, *Alternative Celebrations Catalogue*, pp. 35–39.

CHAPTER 10

1. Arthur Waskow, *The Bush Is Burning: Radical Judaism Faces the Pharaohs of the Modern Superstate* (New York: Macmillan, 1971), p. 171.
2. Prayerbook, Congregation Beth El of the Sudbury River Valley (Sudbury, Massachusetts, 1980).
3. Waskow, *Bush Is Burning*, pp. 35–46.
4. Susan Wemple, *Women in Frankish Society: Marriage and the Cloister, 500–900* (Philadelphia: University of Pennsylvania Press, 1983); also G. P. Fedotov, *The Russian Religious Mind* (New York: Harper and Brothers, 1946), pp. 189–94.
5. Rachel Adler, "Tumah and Taharah: Ends and Beginnings," in *The Jewish Woman: New Perspectives*, ed. Elizabeth Koltun (New York: Schocken, 1976), pp. 63–71.
6. Arlene Agus, "This Month is for You: Observing Rosh Hodesh as a Woman's Holiday," in Koltun, pp. 84–93.
7. "Sister-Woman-Sister," by Holly Near, copyright by Hereford Music. The final stanza has new words by an unknown author.
8. "Remembering" and the "Litany of the Oppressed" that follow are by Chris Carol. The liturgy for the Holocaust of women was adapted from the *Hallowmas Liturgy*, developed by Chris Carol, copyright, 1984 (unpublished).
9. Susan Griffin, *Woman and Nature: The Roaring Inside Her* (New York: Harper & Row, 1978), pp. 145–46.
10. Robin Morgan, from Chris Carol. *Hollowmas Liturgy*.
11. Michele Maxwell Jones, from Chris Carol, *Hallowmas Liturgy*.
12. Starhawk, from Chris Carol, *Hallowmas Liturgy*.
13. Chris Carol, *Hallowmas Liturgy*.
14. Words adapted by Chris Carol from a poem by Kate Nonesuch. Hallowmas Liturgy.
15. "Wir Pflügen" (traditional German harvest hymn), composed by Johann A. P. Schulz (1747–1800) and lyrics by Matthias Claudius (1740–1815). English translation by Jane M. Campbell (1817–1878). Adapted by Chris Carol.
16. "Hey Sister, Come Live at the Edge of the World," music and words by Carole Etzler, copyright, 1975. See *Sing a Womansong*, produced by the Ecumenical Women's Centers, 1653 W. School Street, Chicago, Ill. 60657, no. 17.
17. *Hunger and Spaceship Earth: A Simulation Game*, prepared by Jerald Ciekot and Miriam-Therese, O.P., for the American Friends Service Committee, available from the New York Metropolitan Office of the AFSC, 15 Rutherford Place, New York, N.Y. 10003.
18. "Misa Salvadoreña," from *Canciones de mi Pueblo*, ed. Leonel Navas, Lopez and Alfonso Alvarado Lugo, Nicaragua, C. A., no date or publisher, pp. 20, 21, 24.
19. The readings of the martyred women were taken from *Central American Reflections: A Handbook for Religious Witness*, prepared by the Religious Task Force on Central America, 1747 Connecticut Avenue, NW, Washington, D.C.

20. North American Liturgy Resources. 2110 W. Peoria Ave., Phoenix, Arizona 85029 c. 1974.

21. James Brochman, *The Word Remains: A Life of Oscar Romero.* (Maryknoll, N.Y.; Orbis Books, 1982.

22. Julia Esquivel, *Threatened with Resurrection* (Elgin, Ill.: Brethren Press, 1982), pp. 65–66.

23. This version of the traditional Posadas songs was prepared for and used at Browning Hall at Scripps College, Claremont, California in the 1950's. Its source is unknown.

24. *Apostolic Constitutions*, Bk. III, 6, in *Ante-Nicene Fathers*, vol. 7, p. 427.

25. From Gratian, *Corpus*, vol. 1, cols. 1255ff., ed. Friedberg, see Ida Raming, *The Exclusion of Women from the Priesthood: Divine Law or Sex Discrimination?* (Metuchen, N.J.: The Scarecrow Press, 1976), p. 38.

26. From "A Homily on the State of Matrimony," in *Homilies Appointed to be Read in Churches* (London, 1562), p. 541. Excerpted by Rosemary Keller, "Ideology and Experience in First-Generation Puritanism," in *Women and Religion in America: The Colonial and Revolutionary Periods*, vol. 2, ed. Rosemary Ruether and Rosemary Keller (San Francisco: Harper & Row, 1983), p. 151.

27. Elizabeth Rice Handford, *Me? Obey Him?* (Murfreesboro, Tenn.: Sword of the Lord Publishers, 1972), quoted in Letha Scanzoni, "The Great Chain of Being and the Chain of Command," in *Women's Spirit Bonding*, ed. Janet Kalven and Mary Buckley (New York: Pilgrim Press, 1984), p. 49.

28. Sojourner Truth, speech at the First National Woman's Rights Convention, Worcester, Massachusetts, 1850, taken from *Feminism: Essential Historical Writings*, ed. Miriam Schneir (New York: Random House, 1972), pp. 94–95.

29. From a speech at Charleston, Illinois, September 18, 1858, *The Collected Works of Abraham Lincoln*, ed. Roy P. Basler (New Brunswick, 1953), vol. 3, pp. 145–46.

30. Theodore Roosevelt, *The Winning of the West* (New York, 1889–1896), vol. 1, pp. 334–35.

31. From T. C. McLuhan, *Touch the Earth: A Self-Portrait of Indian Existence* (New York: Promontory Press 1971), p. 90.
      The letter was written in September of 1976 and was initially signed by Dr. Sergio Arce, Moderator of the Presbyterian Church of Cuba and Rector of the Evangelical Theological Seminary in Matanzas; Dr. Plutarco Bonilla, Rector of the Latin American Biblical Seminary, Costa Rica; Dr. Augusto Cotto, Rector of the Baptist Seminary of Mexico; Rev. Socundino Morales, Superintendent, Methodist Church of Panama; Rev. Tapani Ojasti, Executive Secretary, Latin American Association of Theological Schools; Rt. Rev. Antonio Ramos, Bishop, Episcopal Church of Costa Rica; Rev. Saul Trinidad, Director, Extension Program of the Costa Rican Methodist Church. A number of other Latin American Protestant leaders also signed the letter.

32. This liturgy was prepared by the Eighth Day Center for Justice in Chicago.

33. A popular Filipino song, words by revolutionary Filipino poet. José Corazon de Jesus, in the 1930's. It is well known to Filipinos and is transmitted here through an oral source.

34. Words of Victor Jara poem taken from unpublished tape, translation by Frank Klein, Casa Chile, Chicago, Illinois (unpublished)

35. *The Shalom Sedars: Three Haggadahs.* The New Jewish Agenda. New York: Adama Books, 1984.
36. Ester Broner and Naomi Nimrod, *The Stolen Legacy: A Women's Haggadah* c. Ester Broner, 1976.
37. ReBecca Beguin, Beth Dingman, Barbara Hirchfeld, Claudia McKay and Amelia Sereen, *Spring Festival For Women: A Feminist Haggadah.* Lebanon, New Hampshire: New Victoria Publishers, 1984.
38. Ronnie Levin and Diann Neu, *A Sedar for the Sisters of Sarah.* Silver Spring: Women's Alliance for Theology, Ethics and Ritual, 1985.
39. Diann Neu, *Women Church Celebrations: Feminist Liturgies for the Lenten Season.* Silver Spring: Women's Alliance for Theology, Ethics and Ritual, 1985.
40. This Yom Hasho-ah liturgy was compiled from several models in use at the Emmanuel Temple, 5959 N. Sheridan Road, Chicago, Ill.
41. David Polish, "The Resurrection," from the *High Holy Day Prayer Book* (New York: Jewish Reconstructionist Foundation, n.d.).
42. "Morning Has Broken," Gaelic Melody; words, Eleanor Farjeon (1881–1965); harmony, David Evans (1874–1965) (Oxford University, 1927).
43. Gen. 1:24, 26, 31.
44. Isa. 24:4–6, 10, 12, 18b–20.
45. "Air" from the musical comedy *Hair,* words by James Rado and Gerome Ragni and music by Galt MacDermot, copyright, 1966, United Artists Music Company.
46. Gregory Norbet, O.S.B., "New Life, New Creation," from *Listen: Songs of Presence,* The Monks of Weston Priory (Weston, Vt.: The Benedictine Foundation, 1973).
47. Rev. 21:1–4; 22:1,2,3.
48. This liturgy was recounted to me orally by Nancy Ore, M.Div., Garrett-Evangelical Theological Seminary, 1985, from one done by a women's group in Appleton, Wisconsin, in the summer of 1984.
49. Adapted from Johann Baptiste Metz, *The Emergent Church: The Future of Christianity in a Post-Bourgeois World* (New York: Crossroad, 1981), p. 9.
50. These accounts of Hiroshima survivors were taken from Robert Jay Lifton, *Death in Life: Survivors of Hiroshima* (New York: Random House, 1967), pp. 19, 40, 29, 27.
51. Ernesto Cardenal, *Apocalypse and Other Poems,* trans. Robert Pring-Mill (New York: New Directions Publishers, 1977), pp. 33–35.
52. Jonathan Schell, *The Fate of the Earth* (New York: Avon, 1982), p. 231.

Bibliography of Feminist Liturgies

PAGAN

Budapest, Z. *The Holy Book of Women's Mysteries, Pt. 1.* Los Angeles: Susan B. Anthony Coven, no. 1, 1979.

—————. *The Holy Book of Women's Mysteries, Pt. 2.* Los Angeles: Susan B. Anthony Coven, no. 1, 1980.

Carol, Chris. *Rainbow Women: Songs to Celebrate Life on Earth.* Portland: Chris Carol, 1983.

—————. *Silver Wheel: Songs of WomenSpirit for Seasons and Circles.* Portland: Chris Carol, 1980.

Spring Festival for Women: A Feminist Haggadah. Rebecca Beguin, et. al. Lebanon, N. H.: New Victoria Publishers, 1984.

Mariechild, Diane. *Motherwit: A Feminist Guide to Psychic Development; Exercises for Healing, Growth, and Spiritual Awareness.* Trumanberg, New York: Crossings Press, 1981.

Starhawk. *The Spiral Dance: A Rebirth of the Ancient Religion of the Great Goddess.* New York: Harper & Row, 1979.

JEWISH

Broner, Ester, and Naomi Nimrod. *The Stolen Legacy: A Women's Haggadah.* Ester Broner, 1976

Heschel, Susannah. *On Being a Jewish Feminist: A Reader.* New York: Schocken, 1983.

Kadima Haggadah. Seattle, Washington: Kadima, n.d.

Koltun, Elizabeth. *The Jewish Woman: New Perspectives.* New York: Schocken, 1976.

Prayerbook, Congregation Beth El of Sudbury River Valley, Sudbury, Mass., 1980.

The Shalom Seders: Three Haggadahs. The New Jewish Agenda. New York: Adama Books, 1984.

Waskow, Arthur. *These Holy Sparks: The Rebirth of the Jewish People.* San Francisco: Harper & Row, 1983.

————. *Seasons of our Joy: A Handbook of Jewish Festivals.* New York: Bantam, 1982.

CHRISTIAN AND ECUMENICAL

Alternative Rituals Committee, Board of Discipleship, United Methodist Church. *Ritual in a New Day: An Invitation.* Nashville, Tenn.: Abingdon, 1976.

Central American Reflections: A Handbook for Religious Witness. Religious Task Force on Central America, 1747 Connecticut Avenue, N.W., Washington, D.C. 20009.

Clark, Linda, Marion Ronan, and Eleanor Walker. *Image Breaking, Image Making: A Handbook for Creative Worship with Women of Christian Tradition.* New York: Pilgrim Press, 1981.

Giekot, Jerald, and Miriam-Therese. *Hunger on Spaceship Earth: A Simulation Game.* New York: American Friends Service Committee, n.d.

The Inclusive Language Lectionary: Readings for Year A, prepared by the National Council of Churches in Christ in the U.S.A. New York: Pilgrim Press, 1981

————. *Readings for Year B.* New York: Pilgrim Press, 1984.

————. *Readings for Year C.* New York: Pilgrim Press, 1986.

International Grail Center. Vogelenzang, Netherlands: International Grail, 1985.*Women Celebrating Death and New Life: A Women's Holy Week and Easter Celebration.*

Kalven, Janet, and Mary Buckley. *Women's Spirit Bonding.* New York: Pilgrim Press, 1984.

Levin, Ronnie, and Diann Neu. *A Seder for the Sisters of Sarah.* Silver Spring, Md.: Women's Alliance for Theology, Ethics, and Ritual, 1985.

Women Church Celebrations: Feminist Liturgies for the Lenten Season. Neu, Diann ed. Silver Spring, Maryland: Women's Alliance for Theology, Ethics, and Ritual, 1985.

Neufer-Emswiler, Sharon and Tom, eds. *Sisters and Brothers, Sing.* Normal, Ill.: Wesley Foundation, 1971.

Shannon-Thornberry, Milo. *The Alternative Celebrations Catalogue.* New York: Pilgrim Press, 1982.

Silvestro, Marsie.e. *Circling Free* Somerville, Mass.: Moonsong Productions, 1985 (album or tape).

Sing a Women's Song. Chicago: Ecumenical Women's Center, 1975.

Swidler, Arlene. *Sister Celebrations.* Philadelphia: Fortress Press, 1974.

Woman-Soul Flowing: Words for Personal and Communal Reflection. Chicago: The Ecumenical Women's Center, 1978.

Index